FASCINATION WITH BALLS:

THE LIFE AND ESCAPADES OF JOHN LEARA

To Marge + Chuck

John Leara

Dorci Leara

D1738495

BY JOHN AND DORCI LEARA

DEDICATION

To our children (Bethany, Matthew, Briana) and our grandchildren
(Nicholas, Isabella, Jackson, Sydni and Alexa), may you remember me
with affection and humor.

To the many athletes whom I coached, those with whom I played, and
the amateurs and professionals I've watched—inspiration works
both ways.

CONTENTS

PREFACE

Why did I write this book? My wife, Dorci, long encouraged me to put in writing stories from my childhood and my teaching and coaching careers for our children and grandchildren who could be enriched by my life's story. She especially wanted me to write about coaching football in Sells, Arizona, an experience she thinks would make a great TV movie, one of those "based on a true story." The plot, in brief, goes like this—"Anglo coach takes a football team of Indian boys, 'pushovers' according to one Phoenix newspaper, to a record-breaking season."

But I couldn't write just about what happened in Sells. Too many other young athletes were a part of my life. I wanted to draft a total picture, not only of coaching but also of my love for sports. From there, I expanded the story to include other life events which might interest people outside my family. Just an ordinary person myself, I hope my tale might appeal to other ordinary people.

The book's title reflects my life's passion.* As a coach and moderately successful participant in sports, I have always been ready to throw, kick or hit a ball. I also like to create new ways to enjoy a game or invent some sort of physical challenge, whether solitary or in competition with others.

This book unfolds in a fairly chronological manner with a bit of back and forth. I couldn't write my story without "connecting the dots" of all my life's events. Thus, for example, after I tell you about my adolescent football dream of a glorious touchdown run, I recall a similar, real life run in a college game with a typical "John Leara twist" to it.

*I attempt to list all the physical and sport-like activities in which I've participated. The list appears in the appendix, #9.

ACKNOWLEDGEMENTS

We want to thank those friends and family who read various drafts of this memoir which has taken too many years to finally put in book form. Their suggestions were most appreciated. To Rose Boyd a special thanks for her encouragement and repeated question, "How's the book coming?" Dennis Kurre, another thanks for your proofreading skills from all those FBI reports you handled. And Pam Brink, your commentary helped clarify passages. With Rose and Pam in mind, we hoped to make the sporting events understandable and interesting to non-sporting readers. And finally, to Briana and her husband, Rich, who handled the formatting and computer aspects so as to take the book to print.

INTRODUCTION

Toss someone a ball, let's say a golf ball. Does the person pluck it out of the air or fumble it? When you throw a baseball, does the receiver awkwardly reach for it? Does he look like he's batting at flies? When you throw a football, what happens? There are some wide receivers in the NFL who can catch a football with one hand. This ability, or lack of it, is usually an indication of how much a person enjoys sports and playing games.

Tory Holt of the St. Louis Rams was interviewed around the turn of the century. He described catching hundreds of footballs flung by a machine. Thus, when required to catch a ball during a game, Holt could gracefully snag the ball on his way out of bounds. The ball seemed drawn to his hands where it stuck—glue was NOT the reason. For most people, slathering their hands with glue still would not enable them to catch a football.

I love to follow the day to day, mundane details about players, their lives and their sports teams. Contrary to people who get caught up in the excitement of a World Series competition, buy tickets to the game and memorabilia, I am intrigued by the journeyman who has been struggling for years to succeed, to win a match or be drafted by a successful team. There are so many stories about the people who earn a living playing with balls.

My fascination with balls leads to the exclusion of other activities. During our retirement, my wife has tried to expand my interests by proposing volunteer work or hobbies to supplement my current passion for golf. She has bribed me with promises of sexual favors. It hasn't worked. Not that her offer doesn't appeal to me. It's just that I have no interest in her suggestions to tour museums or go sightseeing. I remember one time trudging through the Daniel Boone Home in rural Missouri, boredom fatiguing me like a hundred pound weight.

The balls I have played with link my past and present, have been sources of humor and sorrow, ecstasy and pain, success and failure. My fascination has demanded persistence and been a foundation upon which I could formulate principles for living, for raising a family and enjoying life. This fascination is the link I use to hold the story of my life together.

CHAPTER 1

TESTICLES, JUMPING TRAINS AND YEARNING

On a hot summer's day in 1946, I stood on the roof of our garage preparing to jump. My imagination had conjured Superman. Umbrella in hand, I had hauled my six-year-old frame up the side of our garage. Opening the umbrella, I foresaw myself drifting through the air on a trial run. Later, I would master more heroic flights, maybe jump off a towering cliff. Anticipation and adrenaline pumped through my mind and body. I jumped. As my feet hit ground, my vision exploded with the white-hot pain that shot through my testicles. For the next seven days, "Superman" lay motionless in bed. His testicles were so swollen, he couldn't walk.

Like most families in the 1940's and early 1950's, mine did not own a TV. As an active youngster, I frequently used my imagination to entertain myself. And, entertainment for me meant physical activity, exertion and daring, skills and coordination, and playing with balls. For most of my early life, from birth to age 31, "home" was somewhere in the St. Louis area. The exception was the eight years my family lived on the East Coast, from 1941 to 1949. In addition to my "Superman" experiment off the garage roof, at age six I was jumping trains.

Our house in Southbridge, Massachusetts, stood close to railroad tracks at a point where trains stopped. Occasionally, on summer days, my friends and I hid down the tracks at a predetermined spot. When the train reached us, the flagman on the caboose had disappeared, yet the train still lumbered at a sluggish pace. We would then emerge from the bushes and run alongside the slow-moving train. Grabbing the ladder, we hopped into the open boxcars.

The challenge itself inspired us. Our imaginations and desire for adventure tempted us to such dangers. The massive size of the train itself lured us. The power and sound of the engine was too much for a six-year-old to resist. So there we were, fearlessly jumping onto this awesome Behemoth. Once inside the boxcar, we felt our thumping hearts and reveled in the success of our conquest thus far. We rode for a half-mile. Adrenaline coursed through our small frames, for we knew the challenge wasn't yet finished. We still had to exit.

The train crossed a bridge which stood down the line a short way. Our leave had to be taken before then. We positioned our young bodies at the edge of the boxcar. With a bit of apprehension, no fanfare, and little thought, we'd heave ourselves up and out of the opening. Our senses acute and minds focused, we silently screamed. Hitting the ground, our bodies automatically assumed the standard, rolling movement: "feet—bent knees—side of thighs—side of body—back!" We rose unhurt, "hooping" and screaming, exhilarated with our success and the knowledge that, in another week, we'd repeat our daring deed.

Believe it or not, I learned a life-long skill from my days of exiting moving trains: how to fall without injury. I credit my "jumping off trains" to my success as a college running back. I never once hurt myself when I hit the turf on the gridiron. My subconscious knew the mantra: "feet—bent knees—side of thighs—side of body—back!" When I fell on the football field, I controlled and executed a roll with precision, especially when compared to the immediacy of my train-exits when I was six.

The railroad offered unlimited amusements. Walking the tracks was one. We could cross the bridge and come back without fear of an oncoming train as they could be heard far off. I liked to put various objects on the rails. "What will this look like after the train smashes it?" I thought. Large nails became miniature swords; pennies came out flat and shiny in amoeba shapes. Anything made of metal went on the rails. I'd put my ears to the track, concentrating to hear or feel an approaching train.

(Oh, how I long for the acuity of my six-year-old ears. Ironically, because of a condition labeled *tinnitus*, my seventy-four-year-old ears hear the sound of an approaching train without my bending to any railroad tracks. And, if not the sound of a train, my ears ring with the hum of an eighteen wheeler moving along an interstate highway.)

Just as the proximity of the train in Southbridge lured me to it, so, too, did a small wooded area. Therein lay more fodder for my six-year-old imagination and active body. A long rope hung from one tree. All the neighborhood kids swung on it—no jumping here. I would swing out over a depression and back, gripping the rope, kicking myself out to swing again. I climbed many of the trees, finding pliant limbs to propel me, going from branch to branch and tree to tree, sometimes thirty feet off the ground. I envisioned a young "Tarzan" of comic book fame and flexed my burgeoning biceps.

During the summers of 1945, '46 and '47 following WWII, throwing "hand grenades" with a friend was exciting fun. The grenades were actually egg-size rocks that we'd aim at each other. We wanted to emulate soldiers fighting. We thought nothing of its dangers. We never really hit each other with our "grenades," unless a rock bounced off the ground and hit a leg, but that was not for lack of trying. For the most part we just didn't have very good aim with the "target" adeptly dodging the "bombs."

My imagination instigated other summer-time diversions. My friend Bobbie Russo tagged along when I ventured onto the main streets in Southbridge. I had armed myself with a four-foot branch torn from a tree. I timed our excursion for the work hours when the sidewalks were filled with businessmen wearing Fedoras. We'd join the parade of men; I was scouting out a victim. Casually walking behind him, we waited until we were in just the right position. With the stick and as much finesse as a seven-year-old could muster, I'd jab at the back rim of the man's hat, flipping it off his head. Then we'd run like hell.

Usually, the men were satisfied with a retaliatory yell and maybe a shaking fist waved in our direction. But one day my accuracy failed me. Missing the rim of the hat, I poked the man right behind his ear drawing blood. Predictably, he cussed, turned and came after us. "You God-damn kids! What the hell are you doing? Wait 'til I get my hands on you!" His threats pierced the morning air.

"Oh yikes!" we thought. "He's gonna kill us!"

If previously we had scurried away, that day we set a blistering pace, that is, as blistering as seven-year-old legs can go fearing for their lives. However, lucky for us, the forty-year-old businessman had little stamina and quickly gave up the chase.

In 1949 my family moved back to St. Louis. My dad bought half of a two-family flat on Wyoming Street. For a city kid the stoop in front of home held abundant possibilities. There, my true and consuming passion could be fulfilled: playing with balls. Not the kind injured during my Superman escapade. I'm talking rubber balls, baseballs, volleyballs, footballs, and basketballs. My fascination knew no bounds. Balls motivated me—throwing, catching, kicking or hitting them. I could play alone or with friends for too many hours to count.

The front of our two-story, two-family home became my own, personal, step ball court. I sometimes played step ball all day, burning a lot of calories and absorbing more than my "Recommended Daily Allowance" of vitamin D. My rubber ball hit the face of each step as I worked my way up through the second flight. I'd catch the ball on the fly or on one hop. Mental commentary ran through my head. "Way to move!" "Great speed!" I'd think, getting more excited. I constantly challenged myself. "Back up, John... Okay, back up some more... Throw the ball harder!"

In step ball a player awards himself point values for each throw and catch. Normally, I assigned only ten points for a simple bounce against the step with a catch on one hop. A miss meant starting over at the bottom. A ball that hit the point of the step could ricochet anywhere! Catching that ball on a fly was almost as gratifying as hitting a home run in baseball. "Wow, John! That's worth 100 points!" For hitting the point of the very top step and catching the ball, I'd score 500 points. This was a ten-year-old's orgasmic event.

About nine blocks from home lay the school playground at Rose Fanning Elementary. In the summer time I'd head there. Sometimes my buddy Nelson came by and we'd walk together. When my mom saw him, she'd say, "E's a goot boy; e's a goot boy," in her Romanian accent.

During some summers my mother stayed home and during others she worked at a factory. When she was home, she had no way of knowing how or where I was. Our house had no phone. Typically, I'd leave home at eight in the morning. Some days I'd go home to have lunch with Mom; some days I didn't return until 5:30. Her attitude was typical of parents in that era: They didn't worry about where their children were.

I liked hanging around with Nelson because he was the opposite of me—his quiet, withdrawn personality contrasted my outgoing, social nature. My antics entertained him; he thought I was crazy. I enjoyed spending time with him because he was non-judgmental. My personality, even at that age, could turn off other kids who found my abrupt, honest remarks unusual.

Nelson was a really nice fellow; however, he was nervous. That is, I made him nervous; but he would just smile at me. I never got us in any trouble, but created sports competitions and instigated adventures. He was vulnerable and needed a friend. I saw him as kindhearted, without façade. That drew me to him. I now suspect his disquietude may have resulted from family problems because when Nelson was in high school, his step-brother shot his dad.

Some days, my friends would already be at Rose Fanning, deciding on the game of the day. My buddy George favored softball. In one game, he hit seven consecutive foul balls down the third baseline trying for a double. If we had a football, Dick and I loved to practice our moves, trying to tackle and elude each other. And if Bob was there, he'd challenge me to the 50-yard dash where either one of us could win by just a step.

Whether we had four players or thirteen, we adjusted our game for that day. We could play softball for hours—or some form of it like Indian ball or rotation. Whatever game we played, I was one of the strong players.

In rotation, we all wanted to be hitters; but, after drawing straws to determine the first four batters, everyone else dispersed into the field positions. A guy could be a batter all day if he hit home runs or made it around the bases. I was frequently in the batter's box because I smacked line drives or caught fly balls. We all felt pressure to be good hitters. The guy in the field had to advance through outs. He had to work his way through each position. A player might start in right field. Then he'd move to center field, left field, third base, short stop, second base, first, then pitcher and then catcher. Imagine how long that could take. So finally, the guy's at home plate, bat in hand. But, he hits into an out or a fielder makes a sensational play on his fly ball and, guess what—he's right back out in the field chasing balls. It could be very frustrating and motivated all of us to improve our skills.

For the weak hitter or weak glove, rotation was not much fun. A boy might find himself playing defense for most of the game. Fellows stood in the outfield in the hot sun, shifting their weight from left foot to right to left, standing on the hot asphalt. Some of the weak players created distractions or found ways to entertain themselves. A guy could miss a play while engrossed in dislodging deeply buried boogers. The same was true for scratching places that brought gratifying relief.

In the field, anyone who caught a line drive or fly ball immediately exchanged places with the batter. The desire to catch a high, fly ball was spirited. Five guys might yell, "I got it!" or "No, it's mine!" while bumping and shoving each other. Self-motivation was the name of the game.

We always played fair; otherwise, a game wouldn't last long. If a guy claimed not to be out when he was—hell, we'd just walk away from him and the game. Being desperate for entertainment forced us to get along or we wouldn't have any fun. A bully or cheater didn't get far. I never considered myself a bully; however, I did "strong-arm" my cousin one time.

* * *

When school was in session, Rose Fanning allowed students who lived nearby to go home for lunch. Even when my mom worked and the house was empty, I would go home to eat. One day, I just didn't want to go alone. I grabbed Nick, my distant cousin, twisting his arm behind his shoulder. "Come on, you're going home with me," I told him. This was abnormal behavior for me; but on that day, a wild hair consumed me. I wanted company during lunchtime. Nick went with me.

The school secretary kept track of the students during lunch period. When Nick didn't show up in the cafeteria, she phoned his home. His mother became alarmed and rushed to the school. She, the principal, and my teacher stood waiting for us as we returned from my house. To this day I remember the looks they gave me, like I was crazy. Maybe they were right. The expressions on their faces alone straightened me out. I never bullied anyone again.

* * *

In the summer if there were only four of us in the schoolyard, Indian ball was the game of choice. We'd set up side boundaries with rock markers about thirty feet apart, about seventy feet from the batter's box. One player would pitch to his teammate. The batter tried to hit the ball between the boundaries. One opposing player took an infield position in front of the boundary markers; the other, in the outfield behind the markers.

Each team got three outs before switching positions. A hitter was out if the ball was caught on a fly, was hit out of bounds, or the infielder fielded it cleanly. There was no running involved. Four hits in one inning equaled one run, as did a fly ball over the outfielder's head. Occasionally we'd play this game with five to seven players. If we had an odd number, one player became the permanent pitcher.

Some days, touch football was our game of choice. The Rose Fanning School playground was asphalt; therefore, we mostly passed. We had no options. Running on that asphalt until someone touched a guy wasn't any fun. We'd pass for five yards or make long, deep passes—the most dangerous. Two players would be running side by side to catch the ball. If their legs tangled, it was over. They'd have abrasions everywhere. Luckily, legs weren't tangled too often; and I don't remember heads hitting the ground—no concussions. We were lucky. Those were the "good ole days," but I wouldn't want my grandchildren to do such things today.

Sometimes we'd play tackle football in the grass by the school. There were basketball courts, too. We'd play HORSE rather than a game of basketball. Or, we just "horsed" around. A summer's day lasted a long time.

Conspicuously absent at the playground was adult supervision. Whereas today one can see parents or grandparents watching children play, in 1952 their presence was non-existent. We were totally unsupervised during the summer. No parents. No coaches. No organized sports filling fields at schools or city ball parks. There were few threats from perverts, kidnappers and gang members. (My only exposure to guns occurred when I was sixteen. A guy I knew proudly showed off a handgun that belonged to his father. He seemed to think having the gun was "cool." Unimpressed by his behavior, I never associated with him after that.)

The only adult we ever saw was the summer custodian, a man short and slight of build. He worked his ass off all over the school. We called him Mr. Arbeanie.

One of his duties on really hot days included opening some pipes into a small, concrete pool in the schoolyard shortly after midday. From those pipes came regular drinking water. The pool measured about twenty by thirty feet with the water reaching a depth of about three feet. St. Louis summer days frequently passed 95 degrees. Add Midwest humidity. That pool was the most refreshing of treats, especially after playing ball games for several hours. No chlorine, no lifeguards, no rules. From whatever activity we were involved, we'd run to the water, pull off our shoes and shirts and jump in. As a kid I had no impression of the water getting dirty, but imagine all those kids jumping in after playing ball! Around 4 o'clock Mr. Arbeanie appeared and told us, "Time to get out. I have to drain the pool before I go home."

* * *

In addition to enjoying ball games, other physical activity and having an active imagination in my youth, I have distinct memories of yearning. The clarity of these yearnings is probably due to the way they consumed me. I yearned long and hard. From the age of six, I yearned for a bicycle. A few of my friends had bikes, as did kids I didn't know. I'd seen bicycles in the Schwinn store, all shiny, freshly painted—new bikes lacking dents and scratches. Inside the store I'd run my hand along the slick, cool, icy-smooth fenders and relish the smell of new tires.

The desire to have my own bike did not stem from envy. Nor, as the youngest of three siblings, did I possess the expectation of eventually inheriting a hand-me-down bicycle. My sister and brother didn't have bikes. Owning a bicycle wasn't a family or ethnic tradition among Romanian families. Yearning for a bicycle stemmed from my desire for more excitement, another means of physical adventure and daring. The freedom in its ride, the chance to manipulate its movement, to jump, to skid, to race.

Finally, when I was eleven, I got it—my first bike. Someone gave one to my dad who gave it to me. It was old, scratched and dented. But it was mine! Now I could join my friends racing across the playground asphalt. We were great daredevils on two wheels aiming for the loose sand in the schoolyard. I'd slam on my brakes and skid some forty feet, screeching with delight and elation.

Children today have missed out on "yearning." People who grew up right after WWII knew all about it. In that era youngsters waited a long time for some particular toy or activity. Frequently the desired toy or activity never materialized. But, that waiting and yearning made the thing much more precious and valued. I had fewer things than many other children I knew and a lot less than kids today, but I never felt deprived or poor. My imagination and the fascination I had with balls and physical activity filled my life. I didn't need a lot of things.

I also yearned for my very own football—a new football, a good football. By the time I turned twelve, a passion for playing football stirred in my bones. Someone always had a football when we wanted to play, but I yearned for my own, new ball. To carry it around, to smell the leather, to feel it in my hands, to toss it up, and clutch it to my chest as if I were running with it. I imagined that with it, I'd throw perfect spirals. I dreamed of kicking the ball sixty yards. My football would become an extension of myself and my dreams.

Fortunately, about a year before I entered high school, I acquired my own new ball, purchased from money I earned on my newspaper route. Soon I was punting for hours every day against the side of the school building. At this age in the back of my mind, I hoped some cute girl would come by and admire my kicking prowess. Unbeknownst to me, the girls were looking for a cool hair-do, a handsome face and a slick personality. They had no interest in some skinny schlep kicking a pigskin.

I punted in the Rose Fanning schoolyard. I'd stand just inside the fence. I have no idea how many yards away the building stood; but when I first started punting, the ball barely touched the building. The more I punted, the farther the ball would go, eventually hitting the building and working its way higher and higher up the side. Lucky for me the windows were covered with metal screens so that I never broke any. Two hours could quickly pass as I kicked away.

Eventually, one day the ball flew so high that it landed on the school roof. The next day I had to ask Mr. Arbeanie to retrieve it. After the third retrieval, he suggested I change my boundaries. I went outside the fence. I now punted from the street in front of the school, since the fence separated the sidewalk from the schoolyard. Rose Fanning was in a quiet neighborhood; thus, cars or complaints about my being in the street weren't an issue. I could spend half a day kicking the football and my leg never tired.

My fascination with football grew ever stronger during my adolescence, fed by various sources. At thirteen I'd frequent the corner drug store to read magazine articles about college football players. Since I couldn't afford to buy a magazine, I had to read in the store. I knew how to watch for the clerk and slyly return the magazine to the rack, walk around and then return to pick up reading where I'd left off.

By age fourteen when I entered high school, our family had a television. Every Thursday night I ritually watched college football highlights sponsored by Phillips 66. Those highlights fascinated me. I was definitely hooked on the game. With intensity I studied every angle, every movement, every detail of every part of offensive and defensive backs. I had no interest in the linemen. And, although I loved kicking the ball, I knew instinctively that I had the moves to be a running back or a receiver. I knew I could run and maneuver. I created scenarios of how my future football success would play itself out. One imagined dream appeared over and over again in my nocturnal reveries:

"I get the ball on my own 25-yard line. A 210-pound lineman stands waiting to flatten me. A quick juke fakes him out. Noticing on-coming pursuers through my peripheral vision, I cut against the grain and find some open space. After picking up momentum and yardage, I see one person remaining between me and the goal line, a defensive back. With no maneuvering room left and other defenders bearing down, I put my head down and just run over the opposing back. Touchdown! I hear the roar of fans as I hand the ball to the referee and humbly join the huddle to hear the play for the extra point."

* * *

As one of life's ironies, many years later, that imagined scenario that had played like a rerun in my dreams became a reality…almost. In a real college football game at Southeast Missouri State, I intercepted a ball in our own end zone. As though I was acting out the vision of that dream from my youth, still vivid in my mind's eye, I felt compelled to run with the ball. The instincts that had simmered in my veins since age thirteen were boiling on that college gridiron that day. In a split second I thought, "Here's an opportunity sent by Providence. I will fulfill that dream." Through my head flashed the vision of a glorious, 107-yard run, a touchdown scored to the deafening cheers of the fans, the roaring sound that had echoed as my dream concluded.

When finally tackled, I had actually run over sixty yards. Sixty yards was not the 107-yards for a touchdown of my fantasy, but a respectable distance nonetheless. However, with all my "glorious" zigging and zagging, all my swift maneuvers around opponents, dodging them and reversing direction, I had only traveled forward 27-yards! Now, for those of you who don't know football, if I had just caught the ball and knelt down in the end zone, without running at all, our team would have had the ball on the twenty yard line. Instead, my sixty yard run resulted in a gain of only an additional seven yards.

Ken Plassmeyer, the tackle running interference in front of me in that game, huffed and puffed as he approached me. In protecting me, he had probably run more than sixty yards while throwing one block after another. Walking to the huddle he yelled, "John, what the hell were you doing! You ran left; you ran right. You wore my ass out while I was blocking for you! And you gained a whopping seven yards!" My best ever speed of 10.95 (10.95 seconds for a 100-yard dash) wasn't going to set any records nor allow me a "glory run" for 107-yards! Hell, half our linemen could outrun me.

* * *

Although I had really enjoyed my childhood spent entirely in urban environments, once I became a parent, I thought our children would be better off raised away from the city. In the 70's I experienced a sort of back-to-nature phase. I had visions of "Little House on the Prairie." This was the era of the oil embargo and I regularly read <u>Mother Earth News</u>.

In 1975, we moved to fifty acres about three miles outside of the small Missouri town of Wentzville. We built a home that incorporated passive solar heat, and I spent hours cutting logs for our wood-burning stove. Neighbors lived on parcels of at least three acres. Our three children had to rely on each other for playmates. Our first two, Beth and Matt, at twenty months apart, became good companions. I think they adapted to the country life. Our third child, Briana, however, came seven years later. She didn't have a built-in playmate at home and rural life never appealed to her.

Our children were most always supervised though not as rigorously as today's generation. During the 70's and 80's, the world seemed much different from the one I had known as a child. Society had changed and would continue to do so. I thought living in the country was a safer environment, albeit somewhat boring when I compared it to my childhood city-escapades. I sometimes wonder if my three offspring enjoyed their youth in the country as much as I did mine growing up in the city.

Although neither Beth nor Matt settled in Missouri, Briana was the one most anxious to leave. She had complained throughout her childhood and teen years of there being little to do in our small town. She currently lives in New York City. I see a bit of irony in this—with her now living in a city environment which I so enjoyed as a child and yet didn't want for her in her youth.

CHAPTER 2

HIGH SCHOOL FOOTBALL

Graduating from Rose Fanning Elementary School in 1954, I went on to Roosevelt High School that fall. I lived four blocks from the school near Grand and Wyoming, close enough for me to walk. All of my friends from grade school would be attending Roosevelt. I saw high school as the beginning of my sports career. Although I was anxious to focus on playing football, other sports attracted me. I would run track, swim, and play baseball while maintaining my passion for football.

For three seasons, I ran track. My claim to fame came from placing fifth in hurdles my freshman year in the city championship. Track afforded me the chance to remain physically fit for football. By my junior year I could high jump my height, 5' 9". But with other students jumping 6'2", I decided to try baseball my senior year. I played outfield and had a strong bat. However, since other players had been with the team longer than I, mostly I sat on the bench. I tried swimming my sophomore year but I was a natural "sinker." Some people are naturally buoyant, like my wife who can float indefinitely. Swimming required inordinate exertion on my part; so after one season, I moved on.

I went out for football my first year. I made the team—a sort of junior varsity comprised of freshmen and sophomores. I was a running back and a punter, the latter resulting from having honed my skill at Rose Fanning.

However, running the ball became my first love and fulfilled my ever expanding appetite for the game.

The coach concentrated on teaching essentials: blocking, running plays. I had already mastered the fundamentals through my own practice and the osmosis of TV games. "I'll make a great run this season—just like the highlights on TV," I told myself. My dream lacked the reality of other players trying to tackle me. However, early on, confronted by that reality, I decided to hit opponents harder than they would hit me. I intended that they would feel shaken after tackling or trying to tackle John Leara. I loved running the ball; playing running back was a dream come true. With ball in hand, I looked for daylight to scoot through the opening. I dodged oncoming runners, excited to imitate what I'd seen ball carriers in the NFL and college do. When no openings materialized, my resolve to punish oncoming players kicked in, and, with head down and total abandon, I ran into the tacklers. Unfortunately for me, we played only a few scheduled games, and most of my first season consisted of practicing basics and scrimmaging.

Once I began playing football, most of my friends from elementary school faded away. I hung out with other football players. Exceptions were Jim Duban and Jim Meyers whom I knew from Rose Fanning. Our friendship continued in high school. I liked Duban because he was so smart. I could always learn something from him, but he was a "regular guy." And he made me laugh. His personality vaulted him to president of student council his senior year at Roosevelt. He was also voted prom king and shared the spotlight with my steady girl who was the queen. Meyers was a lot of fun. He worked, saved money and, in his junior year bought a car.

Late in that first football season, while I was carrying the ball in a game, I juked (a quick move to fake-out the opponent) one too many times. Sharp pain hit my lumbar area. Walking became difficult because a disabling pain would strike. A few days later my mom took me to the doctor. He couldn't bring me any relief, telling me just to rest. He discovered I had six lumbar vertebrae, not five, a phenomenon not uncommon. The pain lasted for months. It shocked and worried me. I had never been injured like this before in any of my past antics, with the exception of suffering for a couple of weeks after jumping off the garage roof at age six.

The trouble with my back, coupled with the fact that my older brother,

Angelo, was deployed in Korea, lead to my decision not to play football for the sophomore season. Angelo, four years older than I, had successfully played football in high school but academically had struggled. He decided to drop out of school; and, before his senior year, joined the Army. He had always supported my interest in sports but wasn't around, now, to give me suggestions and watch me play like he had my freshman year.

My sophomore year, I sort of "dropped off the map" at Roosevelt. I had begun high school with a bang playing football and, in the spring, running track. School lost its attraction that second year. I attended classes but did not hang out with other students. My dad owned a dry cleaner, and I frequently went there after school to help out.

I also got a job at a movie theater to earn some money. My back hurt because as an usher I stood against the theater's rear wall for hours on the lookout for troublemakers. It felt horrible. Lurking in my mind was a fear that I might not play football again.

With money I had saved, I bought a motorcycle, a German Zundapp. Ten minutes from home at the Mississippi River, I rode in the hills. I knew a fellow from high school with a bike, and we joined other riders there. The motorcycle satisfied my desire for physical activity and excitement. It was my only outlet from the grind that my life had become, between school and work at both the theater and my dad's cleaners. It brought some escape from my anxiety over my back.

In the summer of 1956, Angelo sent a letter saying he was coming home. He wrote that he was looking forward to seeing me play football again. This was the spark I needed to jolt me out of my lethargy and fear. My back injury had sent me into a funk, and the news from Angelo returned me to my football-driven mode. I sold the cycle to my sister Olga's husband; and since I had skipped a full season, I scrambled to join the varsity team.

I showed up for tryouts in August with my permission slip signed by Dad and Mom. The head coach, George Hasser, knew the name "Leara" because of Angelo who had been a successful quarterback. However, since I had not participated the previous year, he relegated me to the line, fourth string guard. That's where guys go when the coach knows nothing about them—or when they join late in the summer. These guys, in trying to block and tackle the first and second string players, often got beat up. Fourth string guard! "Man, I've got a long way to go!" The equipment to choose from had already been picked over. What remained didn't fit; it was old, stiff and cracked; shoes were worn. "Yuck!" I thought. "Oh well, I'll just have to earn a position at running back where I know I belong."

During practice I hit guys as hard as I could, with malice, and usually knocked them on their asses. I found opportunities to display my talent, and Coach saw I had good hands. In scrimmage, I begged Coach to let me play right halfback. He acquiesced and let me run the ball. As I carried it, I remembered some of Angelo's tips. I broke for the sideline and found myself in the open. Coach was impressed with my skills. In my mind, I felt fortunate that my back pain had disappeared. It didn't return during my last two years in high school, a mystery never to be solved.

Angelo arrived home shortly before the first game of the season. From fourth string guard at the first practice, by the end of the first game, I became the only junior in the backfield. Although I didn't start, I was second string halfback behind a senior. At age sixteen weighing 155, when I wasn't carrying the ball, I was sometimes hitting opponents who were nineteen and weighed about 190 pounds. Their age and size did not diminish my passion for hard-hitting. When I had the ball, I ran behind Bob Piles, a powerful senior tackle. He opened holes, knocking opponents right and left, and gave me a path to run through. His success grabbed the attention of the University of Missouri which offered him a scholarship. The Roosevelt team finished 4-2 that year in the public high school league, which tied us for first place.

* * *

After no contact for forty years, Bob Piles and I found each other again. Ironically, in the 1990's when I was living in Wentzville, Missouri, he resided in the neighboring community of Lake St. Louis. Initially, he invited me to join a poker group comprised of other Roosevelt High School alums, the guys who had been seniors with Bob, and some TWA pilots Bob knew from his career. Our friendship grew when Dorci, my wife, and Margaret, Bob's wife, became friends.

Bob and Margaret have a cabin on the Kenai River in Alaska where they spend two to three months during each summer. Their main activity is fishing, and at the end of the season, they would return to Missouri with boxes and coolers filled with salmon and halibut. After inviting us to visit there several times, Dorci and I finally accepted in the summer of 1997. We looked forward to the experience, having never been to Alaska.

Of course we returned home not only with many pounds of fish but colorful stories to match. I had little experience fishing, and Bob and Margaret had to lead me along, step by step. We would get out on the river early in the morning to catch King Salmon. One morning I hooked a large fish. I was having trouble getting it in. Bob, Margaret and Dorci kept telling me, "Pull it up! Pull up." Instead of raising the rod slightly and reeling in some line while lowering the rod, then raising the rod again and reeling in line, I kept trying to lift the rod higher and higher into the air without reeling in much of the line. I was standing on my tip toes as I maneuvered myself around the edge of the boat trying to do as they yelled, "Pull it up!" Dorci thought I was going to fall into the river, I looked so precarious. The three of them were laughing so hard at my antics that they gave up trying to tell me what to do. Finally, something snapped and the fish escaped. When I brought in the line, we discovered that the fish had broken the lure, a lure we had just purchased the day before. For many days thereafter, hell, for years thereafter, the three of them would laugh at the memory of my attempt to "pull up" the fish.

Another time I managed to catch a King that weighed about twenty pounds. This time I reeled in the line and worked the fish into the net Bob held. When Bob saw it, he told me to throw it back. "King Salmon grow much larger, John. You don't want anything less than 25 pounds." As it turns out, I would not catch another fish. In general, that summer was not a good one for catching the Kings. Bob, Margaret and Dorci caught Kings, but they weren't as large as expected.

Then there was the morning we each had our lines out on the four corners of the boat. Not much was happening so Bob was reading the newspaper. Margaret and I were talking. Dorci was observing a fish jumping alongside the boat. Up and down it went, keeping up with us. Finally Dorci asked, "Hey, Bob, is it usual for a fish to be sort of following us and jumping out of the water?" Bob and Margaret, observing the fish, immediately knew what was happening. The fish was hooked on one of the lines from the other side of the boat. We had another laughable story about the fish that kept trying to get our attention.

Dorci tried fly fishing for Red Salmon. She successfully caught a few. She and I drove to Homer where I went out on a boat to catch halibut.

What an experience that was! Halibut don't put up a fight; instead, after I hooked one, it felt like I was reeling in a 4 x 8 piece of plywood.

The Piles shared their fish with us and made sure we went home with about forty pounds. We packed a couple cardboard boxes with the fillets that had been vacuum sealed and frozen, wrapping them with multiple layers of newspaper. The boxes were checked onto the plane with our luggage. What a treat for us through that next winter.

* * *

During my junior year in high school, I began dating Kay. We "went steady" until I left for college. We double dated with several of my football buddies and their girlfriends. Mike O'Reilly, who married his high school sweetheart, Kathy; Al Ellis; Nick Katsaras; Jim Meyers; and Jim Duban completed my social circle. I remember one date when my dad let me take the van used by the dry cleaners. While I drove and Kay sat in front, Mike and Kathy sat on the floor in the back of the van. There were no seats. Jim Meyers liked to joke around. With a big smile on his face, he'd call me "Little Lexi," having heard my mom call my dad "Lexi," the Romanian equivalent of Alex.

Coach Hasser left Roosevelt after my junior year. He took a job as principal at a different city school. The players were disappointed. He had been a father figure. I had had him in geometry and he made learning fun. On the field he always explained things and would talk about what was right and what was wrong. His reputation in the classroom and on the field endeared him to students. My brother so admired Coach Hasser that in the early '70's when Hasser was in his late 60's, Angelo invited him to his home for dinner. That evening Coach told me, "John, you were always too uncompromising." How perceptive of him after coaching me for only one year. He had made an accurate evaluation. He saw right through me, knew what made me tick—a trait typical of successful teachers and coaches.

A new head football coach was hired for the 1957 season. I had hoped and dreamed of culminating my high school football record with long touchdown runs. While I wanted to focus on the glory of the game, the new coach focused on rough practices, armed with masochistic ideas. "Boys," he said, "you're in for some toughening-up drills!" Where did he get the idea that we needed toughening? We had had a good season the previous year and were not softies.

This new coach would place two blocking bags about seven feet apart as side markers. Then he divided the players into two groups. "Alright, boys, half of you go over there, fifteen feet north of these bags. The rest of you line up fifteen feet south. Now, you two at the front, Leara and Mackey, run at each other. Make contact between the two bags. I don't want to see any tackling. That's not what this is about. I want to see hits, hits, hits. I want to see who's a chicken and who's a football player."

In another drill, the whole team dressed in full pads. We lay face down on the field right next to each other, arms along the body's sides, elbow to elbow. The coach told a player at one end to roll over the top of the line of bodies. When the "roller" got to the other end, he took his place on the ground like everyone else. Meanwhile, another boy had started rolling. There could be as many as seven boys rolling on top of us, one after the other, while we lay on the ground.

The punks made this drill dangerous. With the coach looking on, smirking and chuckling, his way of encouraging them, the punks used their elbows and knees to inflict pain. The coach laughed with approval at their antics. Our backs, ribs, kidneys and spleens were vulnerable. One punk in particular seemed much like the coach in his perversion. The kid wasn't much of a football player but seemed to enjoy this drill. He actually lunged with his body to become airborne and landed with his knees on my back. What did the coach think he was achieving? These drills were not developing skills. They didn't hone any techniques. I often wondered just what kind of philosophy guided this coach. Memories of his approach helped me to form a more nurturing approach when I became a coach years later.

Despite the masochistic drills, the football team was pretty good that year, even though only two starters were seniors, me at halfback and another guy at lineman. In the second game, I took a bad hit on my right shoulder. Without Bob Piles in front of me, things weren't the same. I played and practiced the rest of the season with a separated shoulder, another aspect of the inept coaches. They should have given my shoulder time to heal. Instead, I participated in contact drills Tuesdays, Wednesdays and Thursdays each week. Then I played in each game on Saturdays. Mostly, I hit with my left side and tried as best I could to protect my right side. This was to foreshadow a leg injury in college. I suffered a deep muscle bruise

"Cool, man!"

Roosevelt High School homecoming court, 1958
(Kay in center is Queen; John is first male on right)

John Leara (#41) confronts three giants

KXOK (the Sports Voice of St. Louis) honors six best running backs
in prep football 1958 (John Leara second from left)

and played with one good leg for six games in my college senior year.

Coaches do make mistakes. The memory of this injury and the coaches' attitude made an impression on me. It helped me not only to formulate my philosophy when I coached but also to be mindful of things my son faced with his coaches.

In my sixties I had two surgeries on the shoulder injured in high school. The first in 2003 was precipitated by a battle I had with a refrigerator. Why do sixty-year-olds think they retain the muscle power of their twenties? The second in 2008 mended a new tear and involved extensive cutting on the AC joint which hadn't been successfully repaired during the first surgery. It still keeps me awake at night. Hell, what doesn't keep me up at night—pain in my neck and kidney and right shoulder, thoughts of cancer, dreams of golf shots, stomach aches, dizziness, deviated septum in my nose, ringing ears, *ad infinitum*.

That senior season, I also broke my left pinkie. I sort of ignored that injury. I wore a splint and taped the pinkie to the next finger. It was minor compared to the shoulder injury. But, injuries or not, I just kept playing. I was still a punter, and had the added responsibility of the kickoffs, extra points and field goals. In one game, a friend told me my punt went seventy yards.

I received positive publicity at the end of my senior season. Radio station KXOK honored the six best running backs from St. Louis schools. The players and their fathers were invited to dinner at a fancy restaurant. My dad actually attended—even though he had not been able to attend any of those high school games. I know he enjoyed it; pride shone on his face.

But my dad was suffering, physically. Any pleasure from that evening was tempered by the pain and discomfort he endured. The family knew he had heart problems. However, in retrospect, I don't think he died of heart problems. The pain in his abdomen stretched out over several years. I suspect he had cancer. He lived long enough to see me graduate from high school and begin college, the first of his children to do so.

Although I had played my last season in high school with injuries, in the end, I still performed well enough to impress college scouts. Two state schools offered me full scholarships to attend and play football. I would have to choose between Kirksville (Northeast Missouri State Teachers' College) and Cape Girardeau (Southeast Missouri State University).

To some people, high school is the heyday of their life. It's not so much school as a social network. They attain the pinnacle of their life's success before graduation. I feel a bit sorry for them, if they find no other means for achievement and happiness in life. For others, high school is the prelude to college or career. Or, it's just a necessity before joining the work force.

For me, high school was merely a means to an end. I knew playing football then would open doors to collegiate ball. Then, collegiate football would open the doors to a professional career. I thought my talents were impressive. My abilities on the gridiron at Roosevelt High School had earned me two offers to play ball at state schools. My confidence and foresight assured me I had a future in the National Football League. If you had told me I was wearing "rose-colored glasses," I would have scoffed at you—that is, had I known what you meant.

CHAPTER 3

HANDS ON – FOOTBALLS, HOT PANS AND GIRLS

After football season my senior year, two state colleges offered me full scholarships: Northeast Missouri State in Kirksville, Missouri, (now Truman University); and Southeast Missouri State in Cape Girardeau. I accepted the offer from Cape Girardeau. In August I'd be headed for college, the first member of our family to go beyond high school.

The summer after graduation from Roosevelt, I found a union job at Taystee Bread Bakery. I had no money and was not about to ask for money from home since my father struggled in the dry cleaning business. Luckily, this job paid well; but it was brutal. The normal temperature in the bakery for June, July and August hovered at 130 degrees. Conveyor belts moved hot pans all around the place. Although a novice, I was stationed right where trouble occurred. After the baked bread was dumped, four loaves to a pan, the empty pans ran up a conveyor belt to the second floor. To me! The hot, empty pans had to be taken off the belt and stacked on unstable dollies which moved easily on their wheels.

My hand-eye coordination, agility and balance were of little help to me on my first day at the bakery. Although I wore gloves to protect my hands from the heat, my forearms kept getting burned on the large pans. I'd jerk a little each time my arm touched a pan. Then the inevitable happened: I jerked my arm and knocked over a stack of pans. Instead of just writing off the fallen pans and taking care of the ones marching up the conveyer belt, I tried to straighten out the mess on the floor. Meanwhile, more hot pans kept arriving on the belt, one after another after another. They piled up and spilled onto the floor. "Bang... bang... bang," they fell, resounding that shrill noise only a metal pan can make as it hits another pan. "Shit, shit, shit," I kept thinking. "What the hell am I doing?" Anyone who has seen the I Love Lucy episode when she and Ethel wrapped candy while the conveyor belt sped by them can imagine what happened with me and the hot pans. At least Lucy could stuff the extra candy in her mouth or her dress.

Eventually someone took pity on me and stopped the belt. The boss didn't fire me. I don't think many folks were lining up at the door for this job. He willingly gave me a second chance to stack hot pans.

After several weeks and hoping to share my misery, I recommended my brother, Angelo, for a job there. He needed extra cash and I told him it was good money. He lasted only one evening and never came back, asking me, "How can you do this?"

"It builds character," I said.

"Building character in Hell won't get you anywhere," he replied.

Unfortunately for me, my financial fate tied me to Taystee Bakery for the next summer also. My dad would die in November of my freshman year. To earn good pay for ten weeks in the summer, I'd return to 130-degrees among hot pans. Twenty-one years later between teaching jobs in 1981, I worked as a union laborer on a commercial construction site. I found myself pacing my work according to the conveyor belt in the bakery. The other workers implored me to slow down and monitor myself because I moved too quickly. I made them look bad. That laborer's job was much easier than the one at the bakery in 1958.

* * *

When mid-August arrived, I left St. Louis for school. "Cape Girardeau here I come," I thought, "the first step of my football career." I was extremely brash. Actually, "stupid" best describes me. Flashing through my head ran the thoughts, "I was offered not one but two scholarships. Two! I'm going places! After college, I'm headed for the NFL." Imagine such naiveté! My big dreams didn't take into account the reality of my

163-pound frame, 5' 10 ½" height, and lack of break-away speed.

Life during my freshman year consisted of class work and football. Someone had advised me to "study, study, study" when I wasn't playing football. Studying had been foreign to me. In high school from 1954 to 1958, my motto had been, "just get by on natural ability." Although that tactic brought accolades in sports, it hadn't produced stellar academic achievements. My grades weren't bad, mostly "B's" and "C's," my best subjects being English and mathematics. My primary focus in high school had been given entirely to sports, particularly football.

I wanted to be successful in college since I was the first and only member of my family to attend. During that first year, although I concentrated mainly on football, I took to heart that advice about studying. When not on the football field, I hit the books. I knew my high school approach would not work for college. The results were pretty good at the end of that year: a 2.7 grade-point average. Not bad for a slow reader, since reading seemed to be what every teacher assigned.

I didn't mind reading; but, usually exhausted from football practice, I would fall asleep trying to do my assignments. I could fall asleep anywhere. If I just rested my head on my hands, I'd be out. Sometimes it felt like sleeping pills were coursing through my system. Staying awake while reading became a real challenge for me.

Full scholarships in 1958 required recipients to work. My job was sweeping the field house which took a couple hours each week. The job became part of my routine freshman year, between classes, study, and practice. Late in my junior year when I lived in an apartment and had no routine, I failed to sweep the field house and lost an entire month's check from my scholarship. Boy, did that hurt! I didn't eat much that month.

For my first year at Cape, I lived in a dormitory where my scholarship included room and board. When not at practice or in class or working, I was in the dorm—day and night. The award also paid tuition; however, it didn't provide spending money. That came from home. My home had none to send. There was little entertainment available outside the residence hall to anyone without money. Students sometimes became very creative when trying to find "fun."

It's fair to say I had been a junkie all my life—a junkie looking to be challenged by the thrill of physical activity. Hanging from limbs of trees 20-feet above the ground in my youth made my adrenaline pump. In the dormitory I found another way to tempt fate with dangerous heights. The architecture of my dorm included a ledge that circumscribed the building on my floor. Now, didn't the architect imagine that students would see a twelve-inch ledge as an opportunity for shenanigans? That ledge enticed me, called me to crawl out my window and shuffle along it to create havoc. Now, you might think I was on the first or second floor. No, I stood outside the fourth floor, looking down thinking, "If I fall, I'm dead." Yet, even the expectation of death did not deter me from my mission. "I'm going to walk around the perimeter and scare the hell out of the students in their rooms." As I approached each window, if I spied someone in the room, I paused and screamed as loud as I could. The scream was replaced by laughter as I continued my adventure around the building. Obviously, I didn't fall to my demise. Rather, with my inherent agility, I experienced another natural rush stemming from my foolish desire for adventure.

When studying in the dorm became unbearable that first year, I would visit "Fat Mac" Ed McWilliams who roomed right next door. He was two years older, a junior, a powerfully built guard on the football team. His nickname resulted from his short, stocky build—5' 10" and 205-pounds. He bench pressed 420-pounds yet moved very quickly. (At the end of my junior year when I weighed 165-pounds, the most I bench pressed was 230-pounds.) Mac was one of the reasons the 1958 and 1959 football teams were so good. He was a fireplug in the middle of the line. On defense, opponents couldn't move him. He'd hit the guard or center, knock him flat and go after the ball carrier.

Although tough on the football field, Fat Mac had a professorial-philosophical air about him. He'd sit with a pipe in his mouth, his feet propped up, talking about a wide range of subjects. His wisdom and advice opened a whole new horizon to me. I was all ears, a sponge absorbing ideas about the world and politics. He became my personal "Discovery Channel." His parents came to all the home games and were involved in the Brentwood community, a suburb of St. Louis. The only thing I remember my parents ever doing besides working and attending church was taking us to Rockford Beach on the Big River. Their life revolved around work, church and home. To me, Mac's family seemed to be ideal, American middle-class.

He knew I needed refining. My naiveté off the football field was exceeded only by my adrenaline rushes on the field. Fat Mac had repeatedly told me, "John, you don't know anything. I'm going to give you an education." When we ate dinner in the cafeteria, he'd give me etiquette lessons. "John, you need to ask. You should say, 'Please pass the gravy' instead of reaching for it." If Mac only knew that at my house we all ate from the same salad bowl, sticking our forks in for each bite. I loved this guy; he became my mentor. He was a nice guy, belonged to no cliques, had no facade. With Fat Mac there was no ego involved.

One weekend while traveling to an away game, I had Fat Mac in mind when the bus stopped at a restaurant for our dinner. "I want to demonstrate my cultural progress," I thought. Reading the menu, I saw an item I had never eaten before and decided to order it. I imagined, "I can impress Fat Mac." When my turn came to give the waitress my selection, I ordered an entree and then said,

"….and I'd like the 'ess-ka-lop' potatoes."

"The what?" asked the waitress.

"The 'ess-ka-lop' potatoes," I confidently returned, pointing to the item on the menu.

"Oh, you mean **escalloped** potatoes," she said.

Of course, the whole team was listening to this repartee. They had been intrigued by my request thinking, "What is Leara ordering?" Then they all went nuts. They roared with laughter and repeated my order, "John wants 'ess-ka-lops.'" And later, "John, how are those 'ess-ka-lops'?"

* * *

The football team practiced in full pads mornings and afternoons a couple times a week for as many as five hours with heavy hitting. Those two-a-days were hell. Average temperatures were above 90 with typical Missouri/Mississippi Valley humidity. I vividly remember the luxury of standing in the showers for twenty minutes washing the sweat, blood and grime off my body. My aching muscles welcomed the comfort of the water's soothing, healing power.

Practice found me on the "scout team." Each week, one of the coaches scouted our next opponents by attending their football game. Then, at practice during the week before we'd meet that opponent, he had the "scout team," composed mainly of freshman and a few sophomores, run the opponent's plays. As a freshman, I was assigned the role of the running back on the scout team.

In the mid 1950's, I used to watch all the college football games that were on TV. I wanted to absorb every conceivable, natural move that a running back displayed. My mind kept thinking "osmosis," the term I had learned in high school biology. I believed that through osmosis I could learn football moves. "Watch the moves on TV. I can learn via the mesmerizing screen. The agility and talent to maneuver will seep into me." A cocky confidence filled my head. "I'll move just like the players on TV. An NFL scout will see me and offer me a contract." My future seemed assured. College was merely the interim period, the stage on which I would be discovered.

Not only didn't I have the height and weight for a professional career, I lacked speed. Most of the linemen could outrun me in the 100-yard dash. If and when I broke into the open, any one of seven players from the opposing team could catch me from behind. Very frustrating!

But, maneuver I could, faster than the other players. For the first five steps, I moved like a water bug, able to dart here or there for some good, short gains. That "osmosis" theory wasn't all hogwash. Today, coaches actually use much the same technique. It's called "visualization." Coaches encourage and train their players to "see" themselves doing this or that, whatever the sport is. Athletes, in visualizing movements or techniques, are actually able to achieve greater success. My "osmosis" approach preceded its time.

During my first college football season, elements out of my control caused me much pain and unrest. One of these was the line coach's attitude towards the backs. The line coach had recently come from Notre Dame. To him, a freshman running back was of little importance, just an immature peon. He used to bark at us, making references to "the chicken-shit backs." Another element was the success and talent of the experienced players. The Southeast Missouri State (SEMO) football team had the number one defense in the Missouri Intercollegiate Athletic Association. Having to run plays against this number one defense during practice basically meant, "I was the nail; they were the hammer." In addition to these two factors was one I could control but didn't: the attitude with which I entered the college football scene, my know-it-all, "I'm gonna be an NFL star" posture.

The middle linebacker, the player who would be coming after ME on the scout team, was Ken Iman. My freshman year, Iman was a junior weighing 215-pounds. After he graduated from college, he played fourteen years in the National Football League for the Green Bay Packers and Los Angeles Rams. My roommate that first year, Dean Matthews, a junior who played fullback, had described the talents of Ken Iman and portrayed him as the heart of the team. Dean had graduated from Roosevelt High School two years earlier and served as my mentor. He told me how Iman excelled in playing both offense and defense.

I personally discovered Iman's prowess. During scout team scrimmages, the shit hit the fan. Iman became my nemesis. My determination to outrun him came to naught, for, try as I might, he usually tackled me. He'd sometimes say, "You're not going any farther," or "Give it up, freshman." With my "in-your- face cocky attitude," I'd pop right up just to show him that his strength and speed couldn't keep me down.

Ken Iman enjoyed crunching my brash, naïve assertiveness to the ground. That's where the pain came in. With every carry that number one defense smothered me. My teammates came in the form of other, young, freshman linemen. While I ran with the ball, they tried blocking in front of me to open holes. We recent high school graduates were facing intercollegiate champions. Against this outstanding defense and the relentless Mr. Iman, my only protection came from other scrawny newcomers.

I became a target for not only Ken Iman on the defensive team, but also my offensive lineman. Even other backs disliked me. I wore my confidence like my football shirt and pads. I was headed for the NFL. It would take me several years before I realized that my attitude was a major irritant. I later concluded that I deserved all the wrath and pounding heaped upon me.

Occasionally, in the locker room a certain senior lineman would threaten to tear me apart. Standing there without the benefit of pads and helmet and lacking Kung Fu skills, I pretty much just shut up. On the field, however, it was a different story. When a 210-pound lineman threatened me during practice, I just resented him. I saw him as a temporary obstacle. With protective equipment on, I felt indestructible. I knew that in due time I'd have a ball in my hand, running plays, maneuvering around him. Even when tackled, I looked forward to another opportunity to carry the ball under better circumstances. On the field I was like the guy you see in movies who keeps getting up only to be knocked down again. My attitude and behavior said, "So you knocked me down this time; what does that prove? I'll just be up and running again."

One varsity practice in particular my freshman year remains in my memory, not because of any great performance on my part but because of the biting-cold November temperature. Coach had set up the squads for a scrimmage. As usual the freshmen were pieces of meat for the varsity players to knock around. For about twenty minutes I had been standing around—well not really standing. I was jumping up and down, flailing my arms into my body, trying everything I could think of to keep my balls from freezing, as well as the rest of my body. I'm sure any body heat that I generated quickly pumped right out from my helmet.

Finally, coach yelled, "Leara, get ready. You're going in."

"Okay, coach," I yelled. His words had interrupted the image of my toes having to be amputated from frostbite. "Run some sprints," I thought. I dashed about 20-yards. I stretched. I sprinted another 20-yards. I stretched. Relishing every opportunity I had to strut my stuff against the varsity players, I threw myself into the sprints. "Warm up, warm up!" I thought. "You're going out on the field!"

The slightest bit of heat slowly began creeping into my appendages, but I was also tiring. Consumed by the expectation of success, my emotions devoured any common sense I might have possessed. In the middle of my fifteenth sprint, my focus was interrupted by coach yelling, "Leara, are you ready yet?"

"Coach," I said, laboring to catch my breath and feeling enervated, "I'm really winded. I need to catch my breath; I ran too many sprints."

The varsity team had a strong winning season that year. The team was MIAA champion not only in 1958 but also in 1959. I longed to play an important part in one varsity game that first year. Mostly, though, I sat on the bench.

The last game of the season was at home. The game had been decided fairly early in our favor. SEMO's first string had dominated throughout. With just a few minutes left, I went in as a sub for the offensive back. After a couple plays, the quarterback called for a screen pass left to me. That meant I'd actually be carrying the ball! Our offense would attempt to fool the defense into thinking a long throw would be made.

When the ball was hiked, the quarterback dropped back preparing to pass. The right halfback and I, the left halfback, dropped back to block for him. Meanwhile, our receivers were running down field, as though preparing to catch the ball. After throwing my block, I slid out to the left at the last second. The quarterback's short pass, a perfect spiral, came my way.

As soon as I had the pigskin cradled in my hands, I broke straight down the left sideline, gaining about eight yards. Then I made a sharp cut to the right, heading against the grain, meaning, directly into the oncoming pursuit. (My brother, Angelo, had always encouraged me to cut against the grain.) By doing that, I hoped to throw the oncoming players off-balance in their momentum. Had I continued to run down the sideline with my lack of speed, I knew my gain would be minimal. But, with my ability to veer and cut, I had a better chance to out-maneuver my opponents.

Catching them off balance by my cut right, I ran through the on-coming defense. Ahead lay open field. I gained another 30-yards before being tackled. If only I'd had some speed, I could have run for a 50-yard touchdown. The clock ran out and the game ended.

When we watched the film the following Monday, my enthusiasm was evident. The film showed Dean Matthews and me as we danced together in celebration at the end of my run. We looked really corny. But, hey, I was just a freshman.

* * *

The sophomore football season proved quite exciting. My name appeared in the newspaper early on because I caught many passes in the first few games. The quarterback, Gary Nichols, a senior, had a great arm. His intelligence and talent made for pinpoint accuracy. His passes hit me directly "on the numbers" (the numbers on my shirt front) when I turned around as per his instructions in the huddle. Also, our first team, which had Iman, Mac and other seasoned linemen, playing both offense and defense, usually put us ahead on the scoreboard. They wore down the other team by the time I entered the game, adrenaline pumping through me.

Sophomore season was a lot of fun for me. After four games I was the leading receiver on the team. The seniors on that 1959 squad were great leaders; and I had begun to tone down my brash attitude, sensing that there were many people who didn't like that about me. Mac and Iman had great skills and threw their hearts into the game.

Yes, I, too, put my heart in the game; but I began to see that the approach I took made a difference. Football, after all, is a team sport. My self-centered attitude still lingered but was now tempered by my slowly evolving maturity.

I believe the linemen were the key to our team's huge success. We beat Kirksville 36-0 when they had an All-American running back. He had been scoring touchdowns from everywhere on the field in previous games; but we shut him down, thanks to our tremendous defense. In June, Iman, Mac, Nichols, and about seven other seniors would graduate. I can remember thinking, "What's to become of the team next year with these seniors gone?"

By the time the football season ended, I had become savvy enough to know that I was missing out on a lot by living in the dorm. I wanted to start having some fun. You know, drinking on weekends, chasing beautiful girls. Living in an apartment would enable me to do this. I also needed a source for spending money.

If I left the dorm, my scholarship would give me $100 a month to pay my expenses for room and board. Now, basic economics tells you that in 1960 $100 isn't much to cover rent, utilities and food. Add to that "fun." But what did I know? As I said before, the adjective "stupid" fit me like the proverbial glove. My thinking that $100 paved the way to a better life proved to be a big mistake.

Ken Plassmeyer and I had met our freshman year on the football team. He was two years older, having worked before starting college. Ken had come from the same neighborhood as I in St. Louis but had attended St. Mary's Catholic High School. During the two weeks of football practice before school started, we walked back and forth together for meals and practice and lived in the same dorm. Later, when classes began, we were again in the same dormitory for our freshman year. Ken served as a good example to me, had good study habits.

For the second semester of our sophomore year, Ken and I decided to move off campus together. Bad eating habits became the norm for me because I began spending money on drinking. While living in the dorm, I had had all the food I wanted. Now, having to choose between fun and healthy food… well, what kind of choice is that for a college student? The result of my decision: I never weighed more than 165 pounds for the rest of my college years. When I graduated in June 1962, I looked like a refugee—much too skinny.

* * *

After graduation, Ken Iman was not drafted, as often happens to many talented collegiate players. Instead, the Green Bay Packers in Wisconsin invited him to camp as a free agent. There, Coach Lombardi saw him make a crucial hit and said, "Keep that guy!" His professional football career began at that moment. Although he grew up in St. Louis, Ken chose to make Cape Girardeau his home. Cape gladly adopted him. With his instant success in professional football on kick-off coverage and other special teams, I held him in the highest esteem, equal to my regard for Stan "the Man" Musial of the St. Louis Cardinals. I avidly followed Iman's career.

After I graduated in 1962 and worked for a year in sales, I returned to summer school at Cape to earn my teaching credentials. That summer I saw Ken for the first time in two years and was reminded of his competitive fire, the very fire that had made the football team so successful in 1959.

During our football years in college, players had been encouraged to take up handball as part of their training. Several of us really enjoyed the competition and adopted it as a leisure sport. That summer, the handball court beckoned Iman and me. I struck up a game with Ken and John Whittenborn, who played for the Philadelphia Eagles in the NFL. Whittenborn was two years older than Ken and had also played football at SEMO.

On the handball court, we played cutthroat, a game of rotation where one player serves to score points against the other two. When the server misses, one of the players rotates into service to play against the other two.

We weren't playing just to have fun. How could we? Our college football days weren't that far behind us and we harbored some pent-up animosity. It was former running back (me) verses NFL lineman (Iman). Also, I had been competing in handball tournaments in St. Louis during the previous two years. I always played to win, not just for fun. My fascination with balls stemmed from and was bolstered by the competitive spirit of any game or challenge.

As the match heated up, my puny 165-pounds were holding up fairly well against these two monster-men who weighed maybe 240 and 260-pounds. I wanted to be on my good behavior because I really respected these guys for their achievements in the NFL.

At one point in the game, I successfully made a really tough dig.

Ken asked if I had struck the ball before the second bounce. I blithely referred to a known cheater saying I wasn't like him. Ken became ignited, misunderstanding my answer, thinking I had denigrated him. Within seconds all 240-pounds (he had gained twenty-five pounds to my five) were coming my way menacingly. My osmosis kicked in, and I ducked just in time to miss his forearm by inches. Before anything else happened, I clarified my comment, making sure he understood my intention. Had I said what Ken thought he heard, I think I'd be writing my fond memories from a wheel chair.

* * *

In the fall of 1960, my junior year, the football season fell short of everyone's expectations. We had lost many key players from the '59 squad. Most of the first string players were juniors—our center, both guards and both tackles. In fact, juniors comprised virtually the entire offense except for three seniors. I became first string halfback. I'd be running with the ball. The other halfback was a senior, Gene McLanahan, small of stature but a gifted runner with good speed.

With fond memories of my punting in high school, I was hoping to assume that position since the previous punter had graduated. I approached the coach regarding this possibility. Nothing ever came of my request. When I became a coach years later, I recalled the coach's attitude towards his players that year, and resolved to be more communicative and develop an open relationship with my players. In retrospect I reflect on the lack of interaction between the coaches and players my junior year.

Our team definitely did not measure up to those of the previous two years. Something didn't seem right. The burning desire to win seemed to be missing. Maybe inspiration had graduated with last year's seniors. At practice the coaches degraded a couple of players for their attitudes—unfortunately, to no avail. The best athletes seemed to lack "fire in the belly."

The motivation that propels college football players varies; and that year, it worked against us. The fifty-some players on our team, almost all of whom were on scholarships, comprised a mix of backgrounds and situations. Some were just trying to stay healthy and not get hurt so as to maintain their scholarships. Some, who were already married, seemed to approach the game like a job. These guys played with care and had little fun. Luckily for the team there were still some guys who played with abandon, who were in the game mode.

With Iman, Nichols and the rest of the seniors gone, the leadership wasn't the same. I realized I was one of the few who still had "fire in the belly." Even with that fire and having earned the starting running back spot, I would never be able to bust the game wide open. Although I put forth as much effort as ever, I now realized my limitations. I could run hills until nauseous, but I would never be able to increase my speed. And for a running back, speed is all important. Being in the best shape ever, I still could not run any faster, no matter what I did.

Sleeping the night before a game became a struggle for me. Sleep was elusive well into the night, sometimes as late as three in the morning. I'd conjure up one play after another, planning moves to break free for long runs. In the early AM hours, visions of the previous week's game appeared. I'd remember successful plays and replay them over and over. Sleep deprivation seemed to dominate my college years in general; but especially during football season, it affected my performance on the field.

The endless meetings didn't help either. Instead of allowing us to sleep in, coach would require the team to meet early in the morning for breakfast. Many times I felt listless at game time because of the lack of sleep. I'd always wonder how many more yards I could have gained with a good night's rest.

That year I concerned myself too much with not making mistakes, especially on defense where I was responsible for breaking up passes and making tackles. The coaches, too, that year, seemed to be focused on programming the defensive backs "not to fail" rather than to "think for yourself." This is called "preventive defense." More often than not, it doesn't work. Offensively, running the ball just takes a relentless desire to gain yards. I still had that relentlessness. But on defense, if I made a mistake, especially in the backfield, I might give up a touchdown to the other team.

That's exactly what happened against Kirksville—a 50-yard touchdown. In fact, that was the only score of the entire game which we lost 6-0. I think we were out-coached in that game. The opposing coach and quarterback seemed to manipulate us for over half the game.

The Kirksville quarterback kept throwing 6 to 10-yard passes on a down and out pattern. A Kirksville end would run about 8-yards down field, turn and catch the ball by the sideline where he was then forced out of bounds by our linebacker. I was playing defensive back to cover any receiver who might get by the linebacker on our right side of the field. Our linebackers were unable to break up the passes before completion. All they were able to do was tackle the end after he caught the ball. I became really frustrated maintaining my position with no action coming my way.

When the Kirksville coach called for the long touchdown pass, it worked to perfection. The Kirksville end on the right side of their line made a beeline down field. His speed and slight angling toward our safety drew both our safety and left defensive back's attention as they moved to cover him. However, a second Kirksville receiver had positioned himself on the right side. With our safety and corner back focused on the end and me paying attention to receivers on the other side of the field who were running a bit deeper on that play, that second receiver, after hesitating for a second, ran down field. Cutting to the center where our safety had been just seconds previously, he turned, caught the pass and ran 50-yards for a touchdown.

To make matters worse, very late in the game, McLanahan and I dropped back to receive a punt that Kirksville had to kick. He caught the ball and zigged and zagged and broke free down the left sideline with me now as an escort to block any would-be tacklers. He was racing no more than five feet from the sideline. I ran about seven feet from the sideline, ready to throw a block on anyone coming from the right. Out of nowhere, a Kirksville speedster in a noticeably clean jersey and pants passed me on the left... between me and the sideline. It still blows my mind that he actually got past me without stepping out of bounds. He tackled McLanahan on the 9-yard line preventing the touchdown.

We couldn't score from the 9-yard line, further proof of the ineptitude of our offense. Something was missing as we were shut out for the remainder of the game, losing 6-0. Our best chance to score had been on that punt return, and I had blown it by not seeing that damn speedster running down the sideline behind me and just to my left.

This is the only game I remember vividly from my junior year. Kirksville went on to win the MIAA championship that year. I felt personally responsible for that loss. I learned later from my friend in high school Nick Katsaras, who attended Kirksville, that the tackler was exceptionally fast and had not played much in that game, thus the clean jersey.

One other play in that game keeps it fresh in my mind. It involved Denny Kurre. We had met our freshman year during our two-a-days. He was from Brentwood, a St. Louis suburb. Before "official" practice began, he displayed his pass-catching skills. He had great hands and caught anything he touched. He impressed everybody and we would become lifelong friends.

In the Kirksville game, Kurre played defensive end and I was defensive back, both on the right side of the line. A Kirksville back carrying the ball ran to his left towards us. My football mindset and adrenal glands shifted into their usual high gear as I flew towards him, set on leveling his ass. I made a great hit. However, not until Monday when we watched the film did we see the whole story.

On film we watched as the ball carrier gained considerable yardage on that play. My great hit? Kurre yelled out, "Leara, #%*&, you're the one who hit me? Shit, you hit me from behind and knocked me down!" When my playing shifted into high gear, I guess I got a little carried away.

* * *

Lest you think that was the only time I made a serious "friendly-fire" mistake, let me clue you in. In another game, I was positioned out at the right flank, that's to the right and a few steps behind the line of scrimmage, to the right of our end. The play was a sweep, which meant that the ball carrier would be running to the right. I would protect him by moving left to block the opposing team's defensive lineman. This is called a crack back since I move against the grain.

The fervor from my adrenaline was at work again. (I must have had the healthiest or weakest adrenal gland at Cape—whichever results from its continual function.) I was intent on throwing a devastating block. Just before the snap, I made sure to be as sly as possible by not looking to my left where the intended target stood. In the heat of the moment, I hit the first man who came into my vision.

One of our guards happened to be pulling to the right to throw his own block in front of the ball carrier. With me heading in, that guard was in the right place but at the wrong time. I hit him hard with my head. My helmet caught him flush in his facemask, knocking out some of his teeth. After the play ended, he staggered to the sideline, bleeding, with his nose bent. I was unaware of what I had done until, once again, film day.

On Monday, we were all paying particular attention to that play. The whole team wanted to know how our guard had lost his teeth.

"Here it comes!" piped up one player.

"Yeah," I said. "This is the play."

"Okay, look, look…" said someone else.

"There it is! Shit, it's Leara!" said someone.

"Leara hit him," yelled several other players in unison. "Leara knocked his teeth out!"

How embarrassing for me. This episode gives you some understanding of the intensity and focus of some football players, not all. Probably just the crazy ones!

* * *

After the defeat to Kirksville, our team seemed to lose a little more of its edge. The previous three and four years had been very successful. The juniors and seniors on the team who were supposed to be the leaders just weren't inspiring the team this year.

Even though I had mistaken Denny Kurre for a Kirksville player, he and I were fast friends. In 1960, '61 and '62 he invited me to his home in Brentwood where I got to know his family. His parents were special people, warm and welcoming. Many were the times during the '60's, '70's and 80's that I just phoned them to catch up on their news. Or, I would stop by their house to say hello. Always they offered a drink if not a meal. When I met Dorci, introducing her to the Kurres topped my agenda.

* * *

On one football trip when we were in our motel on a Friday night, Denny sneaked into my motel room late. He woke me up by shining a flashlight at his face from under his chin. He looked like Dracula with toothpicks sticking out of his mouth. He screamed scaring the hell out of me for a good laugh. Amazing the stuff that went on the night before a football game when we were on the road. A year earlier a player lit a Roman candle in his hand in the hotel hallway. Football did have its lighter moments. Denny served as king of imagination and social life. Yet, this prankster and party planner would go on to have a stellar career in the FBI.

During my junior and senior years at Cape, Denny became my social director, setting up revelries almost every weekend. Kurre's escapades rivaled his football skills. For me, more parties meant less food, more weight loss. Denny had me attending one outing after another.

Kurre belonged to the Sigma Chi fraternity and recruited me for membership during my junior year. I accepted and was voted president of the pledge class since most of the other pledges were freshmen.

One day late in early spring, the pledges were cleaning up the yard around the fraternity house. We were on our hands and knees picking up cigarette butts and other garbage. One of the frat brothers, paddle in hand, came up behind a freshman and hit him hard for no reason. It was merely his prerogative to do so. He laughed and then proceeded to harass and yell at the pledge. In my mind he demonstrated all that was wrong with the fraternity system with his arrogance and stupidity. When I couldn't take it anymore, I stood up and walked over to the guy holding the paddle. I grabbed it away from him saying, "I'm really tempted to smack you with this, but I won't."

Towards the end of the semester, the fraternity brothers voted on membership. Only one vote was required to black ball a pledge. It doesn't take much imagination to figure out who would cast that one vote against me. And so, my brief fraternity membership ended. Having witnessed the ridiculous behavior of fraternities on college campuses later in life, I wear my black ball as a badge of honor. Following for the sake of following goes against my nature.

* * *

At one of the parties Kurre arranged my junior year, I met the girl who would take my virginity. I'll call her "Kelly." I fell hard and fast for her, probably because I had little experience with girls. As a college junior, I could recall just a few sexual "experiences," though none of them cost me my virginity. Just as I had yearned for a bicycle and a football in my youth, I had yearned for girls.

Surprisingly, my first arousal occurred at the age of seven. I specifically remember the occasion. We lived in Southbridge, Massachusetts. A bunch of us kids were playing, and four of us ended up in a pile on the ground. A cute little girl about my age lay directly underneath me. My cute little "thing" stirred. The pleasant feeling overcame me. I had no idea what was happening but I enjoyed the sensation. I knew nothing about the "birds and bees." However, from that point on, I paid more attention to the hormonal instincts.

Not until I was twelve did I actually see anything that might be construed as "sexually dirty." A buddy had an "8-page Bible." This little paperback book had rather simple drawings in it. They looked like something created by a ten year old. We flipped the pages and the stick figures looked like they were having sex.

That year, 1952, a girl asked me to lie down with her on the ground. I was totally unprepared for this "opportunity." Nothing happened because I was too innocent to understand what her invitation implied. I didn't even know how to kiss until the age of sixteen.

By the time I turned thirteen, my hormones were raging. My most daring, self-initiated sexual adventure happened on my birthday. A bunch of friends went to see a movie, and I sat next to a girl from my class. Her breasts were more developed than most of the other girls'. Breasts intrigued us thirteen-year-old boys. Feeling them was a topic of conversation among us. I thought, "It's my thirteenth birthday. I should do something special." At that, I groped her. She slapped my hand away and let me know she didn't like it. Although I continued to think about girls' breasts, I didn't try touching one again until I was a junior in high school, and then I had the girl's permission.

In high school I had a steady girlfriend during my junior and senior years. We were starry-eyed teenagers. I suspect those two years were responsible for my enlarged prostate problems at age thirty. During those two years we did a lot of kissing and necking, nothing more. All my little swimmers had nowhere to go. I picture them getting all psyched-up during foreplay and then just drowning.

During my first two years in college, I dated a few girls. But nothing serious had developed and I remained a virgin.

The "party" that Denny Kurre arranged actually was a gathering of students at a state park one Saturday afternoon, a beautiful, sunny February day. Ironically, we were walking down railroad tracks, a skill retained from Southbridge. When I first saw Kelly, I was immediately smitten—actually

I fell instantly in love, with lust coursing through my loins. I had never lusted like this before. Kelly walked in front of me on the tracks, and I was gawking at her ass. She inspired erotic thoughts. Her face was striking and her body—all tits and ass with long, slender legs. When we climbed in the back of a friend's car for the ride back to campus, she planted a kiss right on my lips. It felt so good. She knew how to kiss. Although a year younger than I, she had experience and took charge of me. I became a little, Romanian puppy in her hands.

I lost my virginity on a Sunday night in the back seat of a football player's car. Kelly and I had spent most of the weekend together. Since she lived in a sorority house, we had no way to be alone in the evening. I had spied a car I recognized and discovered that it was unlocked. She signed out of the sorority saying she would stay at a friend's house Sunday night. After everyone else was signed in, we headed to the car for some serious necking and petting. We crawled in and consummated our relationship. I never did tell my buddy we had "initiated" his car.

From then on, Kelly owned me; she completely seduced me. All that passed between us was totally new for me, physically and emotionally. In retrospect, this was the only time in my life when my big head was controlled by my little head. And, although I knew I lusted after her, I also thought I loved her. Kelly's powerful effect consumed me.

After meeting at that party, we were together as often as possible. We played tennis where I could stare at her ass. We played bridge where I could stare at her face and breasts. We were always trying to find a place to be alone. A friend would lend me his old clunker so that Kelly and I could park out in the countryside.

With all the parties Kurre arranged and all the time I spent with Kelly, I virtually stopped studying. As a result, I got a "D" in both business statistics and business law. Statistics—what a detestable class. Like most of the other professors in college, the teacher stood in front of the class and droned on and on. However, being old and senile he talked about everything except business statistics. Nothing he said pertained to the subject. The tests were based solely on the book which I couldn't make heads or tails of. Disliking it so much, I always studied it last and fell asleep reading the text. The school required a "C" average in classes for my business major. I would have to attend summer school.

Kelly and I went home to St. Louis at the end of spring semester. We visited with my family and were always looking for a place to be alone. I began working at Taystee Bread in St. Louis for the few weeks before the beginning of summer school. Kelly and I spent as much time together as we could for those two weeks before I had to return to Cape Girardeau.

* * *

When I could, I phoned Kelly from Cape. I began to sense that something had changed, that ours was not going to be a long-term relationship. Frequently, she would not talk on the phone. I realized that the relationship meant a lot more to me than it did to her. I wondered about her high school sweetheart. On one occasion when we had gone to her house during those two weeks before summer school started, her former boyfriend parked outside her house, just sitting there. Maybe Kelly was going back with him.

My life seemed to be deteriorating in front of me. I was losing my girlfriend. I had little money to take me through the coming seven weeks since scholarship money didn't exist during summer school. Not working at the bakery for the entire summer also meant I'd have little money for the next school year. Ahead of me loomed business statistics. I decided that what money I had would go to buy food, and I'd have to use my wits and personality to find a place to sleep.

For the first couple of weeks of summer school, I camped out on the floor in a dorm room. A generous friend offered it and I took it. I slept there until some busybody squealed on me. So, I took my satchel and scouted around for another place to sleep. Good thing I've never been interested in clothing and style. Everything I needed fit into an old gym bag. And besides, I was too poor to own anything akin to luggage.

Having lived in the Sigma Chi house when I had pledged, I was familiar with its layout. It stood empty for the summer. With no place to go after leaving the dorm, I thought I'd check it out. That next night when darkness fell, I found an unlocked window and crawled through.

Every day after that, I stayed at the library until it closed. I needed the time to study so as to earn a "C" in the business statistics and law classes. At around 10 p.m., I entered the fraternity house through that window and slept with one eye open.

One night after a couple of weeks sleeping there, I awoke at midnight having heard a noise. Someone had entered the house through the front door. My sleeping quarters were in the basement of this two-story house. Whoever was upstairs walked around for a long time. He scared the hell out of me. Thankfully, he never knew I lay there shuddering below his footsteps, but I decided that would be my last night in the Sigma Chi house.

With about three weeks remaining in the summer session, Kurt Diekmann came to my rescue. He belonged to Sigma Chi where I had met him. He was another person I befriended because he lacked arrogance. He didn't study much but carried a high grade point average. With a great sense of humor and upbeat personality, he enjoyed life more than most guys, definitely more than I did. Kurt seemed inherently to know the secret to living fully.

He had his own apartment that summer and offered to let me join him there with no strings attached. What a prince! He had lent me his car the previous spring for my amorous escapades and now put a roof over my head. Not wanting to take advantage of him, I planned only to sleep there.

Before Kurt opened his apartment to me, I had tried to stretch my minimal funds by looking for free food and by eating some meals in the dorm cafeteria where the food was relatively inexpensive. I saw Mrs. Stevens there. She supervised the cafeteria. I knew her through her son Gary.

When I had pledged Sigma Chi, I had met Gary Stevens, one of the fraternity brothers, a year younger than I. We hit it off, I suspect, because we were so different from each other. He was a local boy whose parents and grandparents ran a farm on the outskirts of town. He had been raised in this rural community whereas I had spent my formative years in the heart of a large city. In St. Louis, the closest I had come to a farm occurred when I went to Soulard Market downtown. Farmers took their fresh products there for city folk to buy.

Gary was brilliant. Me—I was a "C" student. But he treated me with respect. He took a sincere interest in me, asking about my life and family. In fact, one evening in April, he wanted to do something different. He said, "Let's drive to your house!"

"Gary, that's 140-miles away," I said.

"Yeah. Let's get going," Gary replied.

He and his steady girlfriend, Kelly and I drove up to St. Louis. The four of us just showed up at my house. Mother was entertaining Romanian relatives from California. Gary and I and the girls just crashed the party. After visiting for a few hours, we drove back to Cape. He was my kind of guy, spur of the moment.

Because of this summer of near starvation before my senior year, I will be forever grateful to Gary and his family. His mom worked in the school cafeteria which is why I saw Gary there a couple of times. He figured out my situation, that I was a little hungrier than the other students. On at least two Sundays that summer, his family invited me to dinner. Imagine— home-grown corn, home-grown potatoes, greens, meat from their farm. Their faces lit with joy as I kept accepting seconds and thirds on everything at the table.

"Would you like more, John?"

"Yes, thank you, Mrs. Stevens."

"We're so glad you enjoy our fresh food."

"Thank you, Mrs. Stevens."

"Would you like another helping to carry you through the evening?"

"Yes, thank you, Mrs. Stevens."

"Would you like to take some food with you, John?"

"Yes, thank you, Mrs. Stevens." Mac would have been proud of my table manners at the Stevens' home.

I'll bet Gary hasn't forgotten those Sundays. In the summer of 1965 I had to do my student teaching in Cape Girardeau. Mrs. Stevens, who supervised the school cafeteria then, gave me a job as a dishwasher. My pay was all the food I could eat in the cafeteria Monday through Friday. Seems things hadn't changed much for me even though I had earned my BS in Business three years earlier. That was priceless. Gary and his family were beautiful, generous people.

Once I began sleeping at Kurt Diekmann's apartment, I used the small kitchen. A plan evolved to stretch my money to feed myself. I could buy a day-old loaf of bread for five cents, a dozen eggs for ten cents, and, with some stolen American cheese, I was set. Since Kurt's butter was on the house, I made toasted cheese sandwiches, eating eight at a time to fill the void in my stomach. I'd scramble half of the dozen eggs and spread Kurt's butter on five pieces of toast. I got my protein but not much in the way of vitamins from fruits and vegetables. This was just about the lowest point of my summer. The emotional drain from the break-up with Kelly, my limited financial situation, the stress from the statistics class, the lack of a permanent/temporary home, and my poor eating habits seemed to be coming to a head.

With the final exams just a few days away, strep throat hit me with a vengeance. Kurt had to take me to the hospital, to the ER. A doctor administered a shot of antibiotics. Instead of staying on campus to take the final exam, I crawled into the back seat of a friend's car and hitched a ride home. When my health didn't improve after a couple days in bed, I went to my family doctor. The test results showed that I had mono. Thankfully, I recovered at home where my mother did what she did best: feed me home-made chicken noodle soup and wait on me hand and foot.

I didn't steal again after that summer. I think I only stole cheese twice. Actions taken on an empty stomach have been the stuff of great literature and real-life tragedies. As for me, I still remember the exquisite flavor of something as simple as grilled cheese sandwiches.

As for the final exams, I passed them when I returned for the fall semester. I was relieved to be finished with statistics and law classes. Ironically, all the effort and concern I had over my business classes were for naught. Taking on English as a second major resulted from my love for the subject and became the focus of my career. I maintained my business major only because I thought having a double major was cool; but, my business major didn't really factor into my future. If only I had known that before suffering through the summer session.

* * *

Senior year would be my last hurrah and I wanted to achieve peak performance on the gridiron. Even though the Canadian Football League had sent me recruiting packets, my lack of size and, especially, speed convinced me that playing professional football was a pipe dream. And so, I wanted to throw all of my effort into this final season of playing ball. With great home cooking during my recovery from mono, lots of milkshakes with eggs for extra protein, I had begun to shape up and gain back some weight for my last year.

With a little over two weeks left before football practice began, Ken Plassmeyer invited me to join him in Cape to work out to get ready for the season. He already had an apartment leased for the year and was returning early. We'd have no distractions. Ken was serious about preparing for our senior football season. This attitude propelled him to success. He was voted Most Valuable Player on the line in November.

As my strength began to return, hills beckoned. "Run up those as many times as it takes to get nauseous," I told myself. At first nausea would come after running only a few hills. However, with mid-day naps and good food provided mostly by Ken, I felt less pain from the hills. They were no longer huge dragons to be slain. Nausea had disappeared. My lungs and thighs got stronger each day.

One and only one thought dominated every minute of every workout. "I am a senior running back. These next three months will be the last three months to run a football in any meaningful game." A sense of urgency had set in. This year, my senior year, would be the culmination and the end of my childhood fantasies. I pushed and pushed for almost two weeks to be ready for when practice began.

I wasn't in the best shape of my life, having recently recovered from mono, but I was close. Another week to work out on my own would have been ideal, but time didn't allow that. I had just turned twenty-one in June. No longer a kid, a man's strength emanated in me. Great speed did not. I could bench press 230-pounds and weighed 165. I didn't know what to expect of myself. I knew the routine and what was ahead of me. "What will I achieve this last year?" kept running through my mind.

As the lack of leadership was a problem for the 1960 football team, in 1961 various cliques divided us. Friction surfaced between some of the St. Louis area boys and some of the Southeast Missouri team members. The greater influx of football players coming from out of state and the St. Louis area seemed unwelcomed by the local boys. Instead of team members appreciating the variety of distinctive personality traits, the arrogant ones assumed an attitude that separated us.

By this time, my personality had made a total metamorphose into a zealous but realistic player. I wasn't nearly as brash as I had been in previous years, and I knew my limitations. I became a much quieter person. Since many players were younger, sophomores and juniors, leadership fell partly on my shoulders as well as those of the other seniors. I wanted to set an example of enthusiasm, hard work and love of the game. But I didn't see the same desire in some of the other seniors.

Something was also lacking in the coaching that year. The coaches didn't seem to be able to bring the players together and inspire camaraderie among the local stars, the players coming in from up-state and out of state. We had talent but the coaches didn't seem able to inspire unity.

The two-a-day workouts flew by without my having any memory of them. Before I knew it, we were playing our first game against Western Kentucky. It turned out to be one of pure frustration. Playing in 90-degree heat, we did a lot of sweating. We had more first downs and more total yardage than the other team and yet lost 13-0. I gained 50-yards in fifteen carries. I felt disappointed with that performance as it was very average.

We won our second game 13-12 against Jacksonville State. This was another game played in summer-like heat and high humidity. Again, a lot of sweat. I had a major part in the 80-yard drive for the winning touchdown, running the ball in most of the plays. However, for the entire game, I only carried the ball eight times for 55-yards.

On one of the last plays of the drive, an opponent's helmet hit my right thigh causing a deep bruise, my first ever. The next day I could barely walk. On Monday the bruise still caused me to limp. I didn't practice Tuesday or Wednesday. By Friday I was well enough to run and play against St. Benedict's although my thigh was still tight. The coaches wrapped it well, padding it with foam to protect it.

Surprisingly, my thigh didn't receive one solid blow from anyone's helmet or shoulder pads during the game. St. Benedict was a much bigger team than we were and had most of their players back from a very successful previous season. Although they had received favorable pre-game publicity, we defeated them 14-0.

I must have slept well the night before that game because I gained 121-yards on eighteen carries. Most of those yards came on 5 to 10-yard runs with lots of second effort. I had no long carries. The highlight of that game for me came right after I had squirmed, twisted and fought for a decent gain. One of my teammates yelled congratulations, calling me, "You crazy Romanian!"

St. Benedict's game set the bar for the rest of the season. I figured my average gain per carry: 121-yards in eighteen carries equaled 6.7-yards. In my mind I thought, "Yes! That's the kind of play you would expect from a guy who has been a running back in hundreds of daydreams over the past ten years!"

The following Tuesday the coaches decided to have us scrimmage. That particular practice occurred fifty-three years ago; yet in the back of my aging mind, I vividly remember it and the play that re-injured my thigh. The day was hot; the sun still had some bite to it. Most everybody felt sluggish, including me.

My leg was still tight from the injury during the second game, but had not been re-injured over the weekend at St. Benedict's. In the scrimmage, on an ordinary play, I took the handoff and ran straight ahead, as the play was designed to be executed. I covered three yards until a defender's helmet hit me. Son-of-a-bitch—that helmet hit my thigh right on the deep bruise. The pain intensified, more than I had felt from the original injury.

That contusion stubbornly refused to stop hurting for the rest of the season. Even after football ended and into the Christmas holiday, my thigh always had a knot-like feeling of tightness. I played in all of the remaining games but could not perform as before. Whatever glimmer of quickness I had had, vanished. Now the entire line could out run me.

The remaining games blur in my memory with one exception. Kirksville came to our home turf and kicked our butt 26-7. In the four years I had been playing at Cape, the 1961 team ended what had been an impressive run of seasons with a dull record of five wins, five losses. The previous squads had been MIAA champs, playing impressively. Or, we had seasons with eight or nine wins. What a disappointing way to end my college football career.

The 1961 football season, like the 1957 season in high school, helped build the foundation for my own philosophy in my coaching career. As an example, when I coached in Arizona, one of my boys got blasted on the hip in a game and suffered a deep bruise. I made him wait fourteen days before allowing him to participate in contact. I easily made such a decision after my experiences. That same player won all-conference that year.

Football is a violent game, but playing when injured has always seemed self-defeating and stupid. Nobody, at least in football, is that indispensable. In other sports, like golf where no one is propelling himself at another player with the intent of knocking him out of the game, the situation is different. Coaches who use injured players in contact sports are not helping their team. Players on the bench have proven over and over again that they are capable of performing well when needed. Sometimes a star is born when the novice out-performs the injured veteran. It has happened many times. Do the names Kurt Warner or Tom Brady ring a bell?

Arrivals at college, John and "Fat Mac" Ed McWilliams

"Are you ready for some football?"

"Yes, I'm ready for some football!"

Graduates Ken Plassmeyer and John, "happy" to be finished!

After re-injuring my thigh, I wasn't about to give up on my last season. The effort and passion continued to pulse through me. I had just lost a step or two. However, to a back with average speed, losing a step or two is disastrous. No more 100-yard games. I remained the leading ground gainer on the team, but the St. Benedict's game was my last hurrah.

At the end of the season, I was given the Most Valuable Player award in the backfield. The youngsters on the team must have swayed the vote in my favor because I don't think I had the support from all the seniors. Receiving the award humbled me. Deep down, though, frustration ruled.

Sometimes I think the cliché about learning life skills through sports is correct. I certainly had to learn what my limitations were. One can learn to lose with dignity or turn the loss into something positive. A person can suffer setbacks only to pick himself up again and continue trying.

* * *

From January to May of my senior year, the burden of graduating in four years with a double major wore me down. I feared any unexpected setback because my GPA registered barely high enough for me to graduate. I was tired of student life. I wanted to work, earn money and go my own way with "freedom." I was sick of school. College life had many lessons to teach, but I had reached the point where I needed to get on with living. Although there were still many parties on the weekends, I didn't enjoy them. By the time graduation arrived, I weighed less than I had at any time during the past three years.

I joined the Army Reserves in June, 1962 to get my military obligation out of the way. The draft still existed, and I didn't want to spend two years on active duty in the Army—nothing against the Army. Basic Training started in early August. By late September I'd gained close to fifteen pounds with the three square meals a day. Nobody ever heard me complain about the food. I ate until full at every meal and drank lots of whole milk. I loved the physical challenges during the first two months: marching for miles, crawling on my belly, maneuvering through barbed wire with live machine gun fire, heaving grenades (quite different from the rock hand-grenades I threw at age six). All this played to my strengths, and I relished the conditioning with performance tests and trials. Out of the 200 soldiers in my company, only one scored higher than me in accuracy when firing the M-1 rifle. I also came in first in the physical fitness test. One of the sergeants referred to me as "Stud" and made me a squad leader. By the end of eight weeks, I looked at myself in the mirror and thought, "I should have looked and felt like this for my final year of football." In my physical fitness test I ran a 5-minute, 45-second mile in combat boots and weighed 173-pounds.

After basic training ended, I joined H. J. Heinz and worked as a salesman. A year on the road selling their products left me with few rewards and little satisfaction. I was one and a half years removed from my college days of playing football, but the memories and love of the game lingered. What should I do about my future and that connection to the game? Another memory surfaced from back in my elementary school days. I had impressed my sixth grade teacher with my grasp of English grammar while the other ninety percent of the students sat dumfounded. If I became a teacher, I could also coach. I resolved to return to Cape Girardeau to earn my teaching certificate. Thus began my true career which would allow me to combine my vocation with my avocation, my love of balls.

Reflecting on my high school and college days as a running back, I like to analyze what made me tick. Let's take twenty guys who want to be running backs. They all weigh about the same and have close to the same speed. What makes one stand out from all the others? I believe it is desire. One player's passion to run the ball is so strong that it transforms him. He becomes a being whose sole purpose is to move forward while clutching a football. In a football game, should a defender hit him, he would bounce off and continue pushing forward. When a defender ahead of him comes into view, he tries to avoid him, making moves to fake him out. If he has no other options, he runs right into him or runs over him. With no time to think, he just reacts, keeping that ever- important ball tucked into his body. Peripheral vision and balance are skills he uses constantly—as he continues to drive forward. If he gains an extra foot or many yards, he is doing his job, or rather, fulfilling his mission: advancing the ball until all options are expended.

"Fire in the belly." I had it and the drive it created propelled me like fuel. My love and passion for the game separated me from the pack—that, and second effort. Although I attained some notoriety from my actual performance on the football field, I know in my heart that it does not reflect my true potential. I honestly believe I could have achieved much more had it not been for my injury.

I was the leading ground gainer my senior year at Cape. In my best game I carried the ball eighteen times, gaining 121-yards. That statistic is impressive. However, in most of the games, I held the ball no more than thirteen times, a very mediocre stat. Since age eleven, I had dreamed of being a running back. That vision consumed me and drove me for all those years. When I estimate the time and effort and anxiety, the hopes and expectations from all those formative years, add all that up and compare that amount of time to my actual on-field experience as a running back, well, it's like for all those years I was building up to my fifteen minutes of fame. In fact, were I able to total the amount of time that I carried the football during my college games, I suspect it would amount to much less than fifteen minutes.

But that would miss the point. Being on the field, the atmosphere of the game, the anticipation of success and the success itself, were all part of the ingredients and culmination of my dream. I consider myself lucky to have played college football. I had longed to play and imagined becoming a running back. Now, I recall that past I experienced and envision the running back I once was.

CHAPTER 4

TEACHING, CEMETERIES, CRAZY AND MOVING ON

When college football players realize that the NFL is not in their future, earning their degree becomes imperative. In my case, I had no desire to work a 9 to 5 job, but I gave it a try. After graduating from SEMO and serving six months active duty in the Army Reserves, in the spring of 1963 I took a job with H. J Heinz and Co. I was 22 and began working a regular job. But, the job as a travelling salesman brought no satisfaction.

One of my elementary teacher's comments kept nagging at me. She told me in front of class on more than one occasion that I had a great knack for English. My understanding of grammar was outstanding. With immigrant parents, I had a strong desire to hang on every word during grammar lessons back in the 40's. I wanted to talk like the rest of the students and not have an accent nor speak broken English as my parents did. However, I read books and homework at a snail's pace. I wonder to this day if she had any idea how slowly I read.

Because of my elementary teacher's encouragement, in my junior year at SEMO, I decided to add English as a second major to marketing. I enjoyed the subject. In the back of my mind, I hoped to someday throw myself into a job with the same enthusiasm as I trained for football. Thus, in 1964, after attaining a temporary teaching certificate in summer school, I took a position teaching English at Ritenour High School in St. Louis. A large part of my excitement over this job stemmed from the duty of coaching the cross-country team. Ritenour was just starting its cross country program that fall. No balls involved; but, oh, to be coaching! Anticipation pulsed in my every cell.

My coaching duties commenced immediately. I had never run distances in track; but, my mind-set said, "You're an athlete, you can do anything. Right?" I had enough common sense and desire to know that I had to educate myself. The first book I chose to read, The Four Minute Mile, a biography of Roger Bannister, did the job. Bannister broke the 4-minute mile in 1954. This accomplishment had been monumental in track, a milestone chased for decades. Experts had long considered it an impossible feat for any human being. Thus, it had become more than a physical barrier; it had taken on psychological proportions. (Today, almost sixty years later, the record stands at 3.43.)

In that book, I learned that running made the runner better. Run in sand on a beach. Run up hills. Run in heat until heat exhaustion closes in; then jump into a body of water to cool off. Find any excuse or place to run. Run home from a girlfriend's house, especially after a frustrating "good night" that is sexually unsatisfying. So that's what we did. We ran.

I loved the attitude of the eight young runners. They were excited about this new program, and did anything I asked of them. There was a nucleus of good athletes. Bill Wertz, a senior, went on to run distance at SEMO in Cape Girardeau and eventually became the head track coach at Ritenour. Bob Savage qualified for state; and, I believe, could have achieved more in high school had he not had health problems. He would run so hard at times that his face looked green. "Pale" is the common term used, but he definitely looked green.

We trained in different locations since the high school's only facility was the track itself. I desired something more exotic for the team's workout. We'd travel 15-miles; I was looking for hills, for acres of grass. We went to a state park and a golf course. I transported as many as seven athletes in my car, some in the trunk on several occasions. I know I violated traffic laws. Maybe some of the things I did could have been labeled "child abuse." But with my tunnel vision, all I could see was the goal: to train so as to qualify for state competition.

One philosophy dominated my coaching. I would not ask the students to do something that I would not have done myself. I would not force a body to compete while injured. I remembered practicing in full pads with injuries that needed more healing time. I wouldn't subject my boys to that kind of regimen. But, don't get me wrong. I pushed athletes as hard as I had pushed myself at their age when I played football. I had thrown my heart into being the best I could be, especially because I knew many of my teammates could outrun me.

Coaching did not fall under the category of work for me. Teaching was work. It was my job, but it gave me the opportunity to coach. While I coached, time meant nothing to me—I wasn't "on the clock." Getting eager, young athletes ready for competition satisfied me—almost as much as my own training for football had at their age. Almost. Reflecting on all the coaching positions that I was to hold, I acknowledge the fact that I would have preferred being a participant, to run the race, throw or kick or hit the ball, vault over the bar. But I certainly found rewards in the students' success and took pride in their achievements.

* * *

After two years at Ritenour, the football bug took over. My desire compelled me to find another teaching job where I could coach football. In 1966 Belleville, Illinois, a short distance across the Mississippi River from St. Louis, had just built a second high school and needed assistant coaches. I was hired in the summer of 1966 at Belleville West High School to teach English and coach the pole vault and high jump. I had to lobby for an assistant football coaching position and was given shared duties with Bill Perry as sophomore football team coaches. He had the line and I had the backs. We did fairly well with the team.

But, typical of life, one of the great ironies of my life occurred during my years at Belleville. Rather than football fulfilling my passion and evolving into a career future at Belleville West High School, I found working with the pole vaulters one of the most fascinating of all my coaching experiences. Up until that first year at Belleville, the cross-country runners at Ritenour had been my inspiration. Then, that spring at Belleville, I met Terry Woolsey.

The head track coach gave me some youngsters who wanted to pole vault. Terry was among them. The vaulters had not achieved much. Most were freshman; one was a junior and his best height was 10-feet. The

John is first on left

Cross country at Ritenour, 1965

Clearing 13'6" in the pole vault event, senior Jeff Schwarz took first place in the Lincoln-West track meet earlier this month.

high jump didn't require much coaching, for I had discovered that high schoolers can either jump or not. Therefore, I was able to throw all my effort into the pole vault.

Terry, a freshman, slow of foot and skinny, the typical wide-eyed, right-out-of- eighth-grade scrawny kid, had all the heart a coach could ask for. I think we fed off of each other, Terry and I.

I had to learn how to vault myself. I phoned a high school buddy of mine. Jerry Smith, a vaulter a year ahead of me at Roosevelt High School, had cleared 12-feet with a steel pole back in the 50's. He told me what to do to get started with freshmen, and I took it from there. So many factors entered into a successful vault, including some speed, arm and shoulder strength, stomach strength, coordination, heavy doses of desire and maybe a trace of insanity. Actually, more than a trace. I taught Terry everything I learned in those first few months.

In order to achieve decent heights, a vaulter has to attain a certain speed while sprinting down the runway. I knew that running hills would develop legs. I had run up hills incessantly back in the summer of '61 before my senior year playing football. I had seen how running hills helped the cross country boys at Ritenour.

I took the boys to a cemetery in Belleville which had great hills, steep and long enough to make a runner feel like retching from fatigue. At first, the boys must have thought, "This is crazy." But, these were the best hills in the area. The runners became so focused on the fact that they were running in a cemetery, that the pain and fatigue were held at bay for a while. More importantly, with Terry's willingness to run, the rest of the boys put up with my shenanigans.

By the time the boys had a pole in their hands, their strength and running had developed fairly well. That first year some of the freshmen vaulted 9-feet 6-inches in competition. We continued practicing after the school year ended, and some vaulted 10-feet that summer.

As a sophomore, Terry was the leader of the vaulters. He set the standard, not of speed, mind you, but of effort. "Terry," I'd say as we stood in the gymnasium, "see how fast you can get to the ceiling climbing the rope." Up he went while I timed him with a stopwatch. Then I climbed the rope. Then anyone who wanted to vault would follow. Then I'd say, "Terry, see how many push-ups you can do." Then I'd do push-ups. Then the rest of the boys would follow. It went on and on like that. It was coach and kids having fun and seeing how far we could go.

Terry exuded a passion for excellence. He began recruiting and encouraging younger guys to try the pole vault that next year. He found a freshman named Jeff Schwarz who joined us for the second year. As a sophomore, Terry vaulted 11-feet. Most of the freshmen cleared 9-feet 6-inches, which became the standard.

The following year, as a sophomore, Jeff was bigger and stronger and faster than Terry, a junior. Jeff cleared 11-feet and then went higher. He was the strongest of all the vaulters. For fun, Jeff used to walk across the gym floor on his hands. We had a pull up contest one time—a perfect pull up contest, mind you. The other boys were rallying to do fourteen, sixteen or eighteen pull-ups. Then along came Jeff. He did 28 perfect pull-ups. With this kind of strength, it was no wonder that by his junior year, he cleared 14-feet and took third at state.

The vaulting success all started with Terry Woolsey, the hardest working athlete I ever met. (After high school, he worked just as hard at his job as he had with the vault—a truly admirable young man.) He wanted to read about pole vaulting during the summer after his freshman year. Mind you, Terry was not academically-minded and reading had never been a pastime of choice for him. He and I went to the Washington University library in St. Louis where we accessed picture upon picture of Bob Seagren clearing 18-feet and read articles about vaulting. This was before "film" became a common coaching tool. Terry was *seeing* what a successful vault looked like. I, too, learned much about vaulting. For hours I studied the pictures of Seagren. I consumed as much as I could so as to help my boys literally vault to higher heights.

Terry and Jeff became the veterans in the program: Terry as the enthusiast and Jeff as the silent leader. The boys had fun watching me get after the younger guys. They had been through it all and had developed their personal work ethic. They wanted only those freshmen who were committed to the sport. They became my "assistant coaches," backing me in almost everything we did to push the limits.

One of those freshmen was Kevin Connor, very slow afoot. I was pretty ornery with him because of his lack of speed, but I admired him as a young man. Over forty years have passed and I still have a vivid memory of Kevin plodding down the runway, noisy as hell since he wasn't light on his feet, and me on the sideline poking fun at him. Hell, if a coach behaved that way today, a parent would be complaining to a principal. In fact, in a recent correspondence, he reminded me that when he first came out for the pole vault, I had all of the boys run ten 440's. "I ate spaghetti and vomited everywhere on the track!" he wrote. His senior year, Kevin cleared 14-feet. He phoned me to tell me of his success because by then, I had moved on to a new job in New Mexico to follow my unrelenting dream of becoming a head football coach. (See Chapter 6.) I was probably as proud of him as he was. I wish I could have seen his vault, witnessed the transformation he had completed by his senior year, sprinting down the runway. His call demonstrated the bond that he had not only with me, but also with the other vaulters and the persistence and hard work we all had given to the program. In retrospect Kevin's achievement was probably the most significant accomplishment of the vaulters I coached.

One day, after a longer than usual track practice, I wanted the boys to have some fun. We started working on a trampoline in the gym. After what seemed to me a little while, an upset mother of one of the boys walked into the gym looking for her son. Practice normally ended at 5; it was past 6:30. Needless to say she was worried. No cell phones in those days!

To develop stronger vaulters, we would practice with the gymnastic equipment. As a junior Jeff Schwarz was so strong that he could do a "giant swing" on the horizontal bars. That meant that with a straight body, he would swing all the way around the high bar. At one practice Dorci saw Jeff do his swing. Since she was my new bride, I decided to impress her by doing one also, knowing that her college boyfriend had been a gymnast. "Hell," I thought. "If Jeff can do one, I can too." Great logic on my part! How many men have been undone by their testosterone? I asked the older vaulters to stop me at the bottom of the swing. I had no straps attached for protection in case I lost my grip from the centrifugal force.

I went into a handstand at the top of the bar 8-feet off the floor and just let my feet reel in an arc as I had seen Olympic athletes do in the giant swing. At the bottom of the swing, I lost my grip and slid flying across the gym floor. And now I wonder why my neck hurts! I guess I didn't instruct the guys well enough on how to spot me when I reached the bottom. Safety and common sense abandoned me whenever I could give myself up to spontaneity. I never considered the example I was setting. Hopefully, the boys had better judgment than I.

In case the reader gets the impression that I was only interested in the "star" athletes, I want to mention Tom Jones, Gary Klemme and Darryl Titchenal. They stuck with the program even though they weren't in the limelight. These boys as sophomores and juniors, sixteen and seventeen, were still gangly. Gary Klemme endured a lot of teasing from the team because he lacked speed and coordination. But, the look of determination on his face when he came down the runway is still etched in my mind. Tom Jones wobbled as he ran, looking like he would trip and fall. He became a mature, strong man after high school and continued vaulting to attain a personal goal. We kept in touch for years after high school, enjoying many laughs about our antics and relishing our achievements.

I recently spoke with Darryl Titchenal by phone. He was always talkative and interacting with me early on when he joined the vaulters. A bit brash, he could make us all laugh with his humorous remarks. He lacked the typical "vaulter's build" being short and stocky. Darryl remembers running in the cemetery. "How could I forget that? I was so exhausted; I lay down next to a tombstone and looked up at the sky. There was the moon. 'Well, this is just great!' I thought to myself. 'If I die, they won't have to carry me very far for my burial.'"

He also recalled some of the other crazy things we did. For instance, every time he and his wife drive by The National Shrine of Our Lady of the Snows in Belleville, he tells her, "My coach had us run in there one time." Just as I had done at Ritenour for the cross country team, I sought exotic locations for running with hills being the prime focus. One day I spied what looked like a great hill to run. We stopped and ran it. Later I realized the site was not the appropriate place for training, it being in a religious shrine and all.

Although I had left Ritenour to coach football, had to lobby for such a position when I was hired at Belleville West, after three years with the sophomore football team, I was fired from that extracurricular position. I guess that my personality precipitated the firing. You see, as the pole vault coach, I really felt like the vaulters were my boys and we had a personalized program; whereas, in football, I was an assistant, working with the other sophomore coach. I had to scout varsity games out of town, which I abhorred. The fact that I didn't want to be an assistant coach probably found its way into my attitude. I'm sure my intensity and centralized focus on the pole vault could be partially to blame. I had a wonderful rapport with the athletes, contrary to my relationship with some of the other coaches.

Maybe my success and camaraderie with the vaulters themselves created some ill-will. We had a sort of exclusive club into which other athletes were welcomed and encouraged to come but which also demonstrated an enviable bond between me and the boys. Add to that my "winning personality" and the mixture was complete. I didn't fit in with the rest of the football coaches.

Although the pole vault was becoming a successful venue for a handful of students, I had to fight hard to get equipment, even those things we desperately needed. I petitioned the boy's athletic club for financial support, asking if the club would contribute half of the funds needed for a new landing pit if the vaulters paid the other half. They supported us willingly.

To raise our half of the money, we decided to sell Rice Krispy Treats at basketball games. Dorci and some of the mothers made dozens and dozens. The athletes and their girlfriends sold them at basketball games. They were a big hit and we raised the money. An inflatable pit had become a necessity because of the heights Jeff was clearing. The foam we were using was not thick enough for vaulters clearing 14-feet.

I made mistakes with the pole vaulters. After Terry Woolsey's sophomore year, he wanted to vault in the summer in other towns where track meets were held. We drove together in my VW Beetle with the 12-foot fiberglass pole taped to the side. He cleared 12-feet in a meet that summer. He was ecstatic; and because of his enthusiasm and ambition, I tried to get him on a different pole. My decision ultimately hurt him.

Terry had his limitations. He lacked speed and natural strength. He was an over- achiever. His tenacity had propelled him beyond the12-foot height that summer. He wanted to improve his junior year, working alongside Jeff Schwarz as Jeff progressed. In our strategy for improvement, Terry and I concentrated on his arms and chest and neglected to develop his back muscles. Add to that the dilemma about the poles.

Vaulters quickly lose confidence with poles that are too stiff. The school owned only three poles: two fiberglass and one steel. Because I didn't think the school would purchase another one, I pushed Terry into using the stiffer, 14-foot pole. We both became frustrated with my mistaken decision. Vaulting has to advance in small increments. Terry lost his timing. When the pole didn't catapult him over the bar, he fell onto the runway. He lost his confidence. For the rest of his high school career, 12-feet was the best he achieved. However, that 12-feet still stands as the seventh best vault in the school's records. But for Terry, it was not the goal he had hoped to attain.

I made a poor decision that hurt Jeff Schwarz also. During Jeff's junior year, he kept improving at meets, going higher and higher, even though spring weather sometimes made vaulting very difficult. The 14-foot pole bent fairly easily for him; he had mastered it. Jeff became so confident, rightly so, that he would not start to vault at meets until the bar was set at 12-feet. Then, he would just fly over that height. At the end of that year, he took third place at state with a vault of 14-feet using a new, 15-foot pole, a brand considered to be the best at that time and to which he was still adjusting. The school now had four poles.

The summer after his junior year, Jeff took it upon himself to set up the vaulting pit himself and practice with the new pole. He started clearing 14-feet with ease in June and July. The new pole was a good fit. He was weightlifting and looked like a linebacker with muscles everywhere. He amazed me; he was inspired. He seemed to be at the apex of his strength and speed. I thought, "He will go to meets next April and clear 14-feet. Probably, at the important competitions, his adrenaline will carry him higher." We shared the same dream: "State Championship!" We agreed that the possibility existed for him to surpass 14-feet his senior year. To do so, I thought he should go with a slightly stiffer pole than the new, 15-foot one he currently used.

The Greek myth about Icarus who flew too close to the sun conveys a powerful message, one of *hubris* or failed ambition. Pushing the boys to get in shape is one thing. But when an ultimate goal is at hand, a coach must determine when his athlete has attained mastery and confidence and is ready to progress to the next level. I made a mistake. My competitive desires got the better of me as I began thinking that Jeff might soar even higher with a stiffer pole. However, the stiffer the pole, the more difficult it is to bend. As muscular as Jeff had become, he would have to be even faster and stronger to catapult himself to ever increasing heights. I hadn't learned my lesson with Terry.

Since the school had recently purchased the fourth pole, I didn't think they would buy another one. Instead, I thought we had to trade the new pole. With Jeff's achievement at the State Track Meet his junior year and our confidence that he could do more, the school accepted my proposal to swap the new 15-foot pole for a stiffer one. I phoned athletic directors at other schools seeking a trade: our 15-foot, 150-pound test for a 15-foot, 155- pound test—same brand but 5 pounds more resistance. To this day I regret my decision. I apologized to Jeff at the end of the season for my overzealousness. Under no circumstances should I have taken that pole away from him. It was his security and a damn good pole. Jeff had successfully vaulted with it in June and July. We saw the state championship within his grasp. I should have found some way to keep what we had, the pole Jeff felt confident with and used to clear 14-feet, and acquire a fifth pole with which to challenge him.

I should have just helped Jeff have fun until he became bored with 14-feet. He enjoyed that 150-pound test pole. Pole vaulting was exhilarating. The boys had always had fun. Now I had taken the fun out of it for Jeff. I was reaching too high. He never became comfortable with the new pole that summer. It was too much, too soon. My decision wasn't fair to him.

During his senior year, Jeff was plagued by a nasty hamstring injury. He did clear 14-feet again late in the season with the old 14-foot pole that was easier to bend. However, I never saw the same look in his eyes or the strength he exuded that summer after his junior year. If not for my ambition, I am sure that Jeff would have vaulted at least 15-feet his senior year.

* * *

Establishing rapport and nurturing the pole vaulters was the result of more than just work outs and practices. I was involved in activities that were lawsuits waiting to happen. In the summer time, Dorci and I took several camping trips with some of the boys. Southern Missouri has wonderful State Parks with rivers and clear lakes and cliffs.

At Johnson Shut-Ins State Park some of us jumped off of the 37-foot cliff. The cliff area is now closed to jumping because of an accidental death that occurred in the mid-80's. If one did not jump out far enough or slipped while jumping, he could land on rock instead of water. At Sam Baker State Park we found a perfect tree. We attached a rope to it for swinging—rather, I climbed the tree and tied the rope. Then Terry, Jeff, a couple other boys and I swung out over the water and dropped in. We had to climb over rocks with the rope before swinging. Slipping on the rocks was a risk, but we were having fun!

We sought thrills because vaulting was sort of wild. It can be scary. The first time an athlete bends that pole, he gets a rush. "I bent the pole! I bent the pole!" Vaulters know that this is the first step to becoming successful. When a vaulter bends the pole, he is upside down. He clings momentarily to his pole. His feet are pointed to the heavens. The back of his head points to the ground. He is 11, 13, 14-feet in the air. He twists and pushes his body over the bar. Can you even imagine doing that?

On another trip to find thrills, Dorci and I and Jeff and his girlfriend drove to Bull Shoals Lake to camp. The lake had several areas with good cliffs. Scaling the rocky walls was probably more risky than jumping into the water from them. Some of them were 35-feet high.

On that trip I had a brainstorm: Jumping from a high bridge might lessen any fear of heights for Jeff. While meandering around Bull Shoals Lake through the Missouri Ozarks, we came upon a bridge in Theodosia, MO. It crossed an arm of the lake 50-feet above the water. We measured it with our "swinging" rope. It was just what I had envisioned.

With no one in sight, I decided to jump first because of my belief that I should be willing to do whatever I'd ask my boys to do. Also running through my brain was the idea I could impress Dorci, my beautiful new bride. I obviously hadn't learned anything from the "giant swing" fiasco while having fun after practice with the pole vaulters.

Jeff swam around under my position searching for anything that could undo me, like rocks, fishing lines, submerged logs, etc. The water was clear, but why take chances! "Take chances? Here I am about to jump 50-feet off a bridge!"

I was standing on the side of the bridge showing much hesitancy, debating the sanity of jumping. Dorci, tired of waiting, yelled, "John, there's a police car coming!" I jumped and panicked on the way down, lost control of my breath and did not exhale through my nose properly. When I hit, the water shot through my nose, into my brain, and sideways out my ears. At least, it felt that way. When I got out of the water, Dorci assured me I looked normal—no visible bleeding and my eyeballs were still in place.

Dorci was nuttier than I for there was no police car approaching. She just wanted me to jump. My hesitancy resulted from the difference between 35-foot cliffs and a 50-foot bridge—fifteen additional feet of FEAR.

A few minutes later Jeff walked up to the very same spot where I had

On a camping trip, Jeff Schwartz (left), John in mid-air (right)

The bridge from which I jumped

Dorci and John on roadside next to bridge

been standing. He calmly stepped off the edge with perfect form and no sign of timidity. He plunged the 50-feet and emerged a few seconds later with a smile on his face.

That episode and the horizontal bar episode should have slowed my search for endorphin highs, but they didn't. Thanks to the popularity of Evel Knievel, a year later in New Mexico, I was performing jumps with a motorcycle. In the wide-open spaces there, many natural mounds made perfect ramps. I didn't need cars or busses to jump over to hone my skills and eventually jumped 30-feet. Would this madness ever stop?

I didn't realize it at the time, but I was just a mini-league thrill-seeker compared to the skydivers and cliff jumpers of today. I watched them on my TV in high definition jump from 1000-feet with parachutes and flying suits. These guys are really nuts!

* * *

The desire to coach football had never really left me; and thus, after Jeff graduated, I decided to move on. I took an assistant position in Bloomfield, New Mexico. I was expecting to assist for a year, and then get the head job when the coach retired. As it turned out, that was not where I got my first head football coaching job.

Ironically, I recall being invited to the principal's office at the end of my fifth year at Belleville West High School and being told I had acquired tenure. Obviously that security didn't mean anything to me. I had worked hard for five years, surrounded by fine young men on the track team. We had developed a successful reputation and an enviable program. Then, because of my dream to coach football, I decided to move 1500-miles away with my six-month pregnant wife, my one year old daughter and our dog. Why? I'm not sure. I know I wanted some wide-open spaces. I knew the beauty of the western mountains. I longed for change and opportunity.

I had been a football player since age twelve, and playing that game came naturally to me. I didn't have to read any books on coaching football or teaching its finer strategies like I did with cross-country and the pole vault. At Belleville I had been fired as an assistant in this, my favorite sport! Maybe I was willing to walk away from Belleville because of my unfulfilled desire to achieve success as my own boss, not an assistant. How could I possibly accept the fact that I was fired when deep down, way down,

I believed I could turn any football team into a winner if I had some semblance of control over the program?

Before I started coaching, I noticed how other coaches functioned. I saw their results and decided immediately what I would do differently to succeed. Philosophically, I believe that a coach needs to have credibility with his athletes. He must know that his responsibility is to prepare the athletes, physically and mentally. If they are not prepared, he has to correct that. The athletes must understand that they have to achieve certain levels of physical and mental preparation; they cannot fake them. Otherwise humiliation, embarrassment and injury are always lurking. For this reason a coach who is honest and patient, somewhat intelligent, and instinctively knows the sport he's coaching often will build rapport with his players because of these attributes.

In over twenty years of working with athletes, I've learned that youngsters will succeed if nurtured properly. In my estimation, no difference exists between my wife nurturing our three children and a coach nurturing athletes. I would succeed at coaching football because I had a burning desire to take on the challenge—sort of like those freshmen vaulters who worked on their bodies day after day and endured my harassment so that they could fly down that runway, clear the bar and then set it higher.

* * *

Not until many years later did I discover the legacy handed down by these athletes who participated in the pole vault at Belleville West High School. As of 2011, four of the top eight record vaults at Belleville West are still held by the boys I coached during those five years: First place Jeff Schwarz at 14' ½", second place Kevin Connor at 14', third place Hal Hall at 13', and eighth place Terry Woolsey at 12'.

Terry and Jeff were like sons to me. In fact, the summer after Jeff's graduation, he drove with me to New Mexico when I interviewed for the football coaching job. We had jumped off cliffs together at Bull Shoals Lake. We both liked the thrills and risks of doing such things. Being a coach, for me, would always be about creating a personal bond with the athletes I nurtured.

I recently received an email from Mark Wilding who reflected succinctly and insightfully on this. He is a former athlete at Wright City High School, the school from which I retired. He wrote, "You were always 'Leara' rather than 'coach'." I think he was suggesting that we had a more personal bond, one associated with using a person's name rather than his title. As an honest, ordinary person, I connected with the boys I coached. I was privileged and honored to work with these athletes. They enriched my life as, hopefully, I did theirs.

The love of playing sports grew into a desire to coach football which then led me into education. Luckily, this profession allowed me to satisfy my wanderlust, which I suspect might be credited to my father's genes. Or, maybe I could blame Emerson and Thoreau. I read excerpts from their works about self-reliance in junior English classes. Their ideas about self-fulfillment crawled into my subconscious in a perverted way. After my first teaching job at Ritenour High School, I went to Belleville West High School. I would go on to teach and/or coach at four other high schools. Between some of those jobs, I completely left education. For a while I became a traveling salesman. I was a laborer shoveling dirt. I was temporarily unemployed. I pumped gas. I built several homes. Compare my employment history to my wife who taught at the same school for more than twenty years. Or, to our three children, Beth, Matt and Briana, who have stable professional careers. Or to the gentleman I met the other day while playing golf who worked for Ford Motor Company for 35-years and then consulted for them another ten years. My life, in retrospect, appears rather unstable, to say the least.

The only period when I seemed to have "settled down" occurred shortly after Briana was born in 1978. I taught at the same school for thirteen years, the longest span of time that I worked at the same job. It seemed a lifetime to me, a person whose genes scream for change. I think an element of fear kept me there because of my age. My two oldest children went from high school to college to medical school. The youngest was seven years behind them. I sort of bided my time, getting our children through school until I would be eligible to retire. I like to tell Dorci that she is the only constant in my life, the only thing from which I won't "move on."

CHAPTER 5

MY OTHER FASCINATION

Although the title of this book is "Fascination with Balls," one other fascination engrosses me: Dorci. When we met in 1968, she managed to supersede everything else in my life at that time. Although I loved my high school sweetheart and was consumed with attraction for "Kelly" in college, what I felt for Dorci not only ran deeper, it was completely natural, easy and immediate. We liked each other and sensed the chemistry between us. The magnetism grew as we discovered values in sync with each other. Falling in love with her was as instinctive and comfortable for me as tossing up a ball and catching it.

Have you ever considered how many women a man has met or dated by the age of 28? I wasn't a ladies' man, *per se*, maybe because I had what Dorci described as "a rugged handsomeness" that combined Charles Bronson and Clint Eastwood. But, my looks aside, I was always dating or looking for dates throughout college and afterwards.

Dorci once asked me to tally all the girls with whom I had a relationship. She asked this because occasionally, out of the blue, I started telling some story about a girl I knew. These miscellaneous stories seemed unlimited. Even at age seventy, I related a "girlfriend" story about a woman I had never mentioned before. So, Dorci asked me one day to count these girls and women. She is not jealous. In fact she welcomes my appreciation for beautiful women. She doesn't worry when I admire breasts or a lovely face. She knows how deep and solid our love is. She knows I am faithful to her but admire women.

So, out of curiosity myself, I began counting. "Let's see, there was immature infatuation with a girl in elementary school; then a girl in high school before I began dating my high school sweetheart." Moving on to remember all the girls I dated during college and then the women I knew after that, I totaled about a dozen intimate relationships plus 46 assorted others. She was impressed but not surprised. One relationship became rather serious, over a year long, until the Greek father decided a Romanian "gypsy" wasn't good enough for his daughter. I knew one girl wouldn't last long when she began describing the fancy cocktail parties and entertaining she wanted to do once she married. Another woman lived in Chicago. I drove from Washington, D. C. to see her on my way home to St. Louis. That was only 300-miles out of my way for one date. For another date, I drove from St. Louis to Columbia, MO, and back in the same night. Then, St. Louis to Minneapolis. You get my drift.

One girl, whom I identified as "Florida 1" on my list, was beautiful. (Further down the list was "Florida 2" and "Florida 3.") On vacation with a friend, I met #1 in Miami Beach. She lived in Chicago. After I returned home to St. Louis, I decided to write her a letter. She had told me her dad's name. Thinking I could be clever, I looked up his name to get the address. I figured a letter would be more poetic than a phone call. When the letter arrived, the "dad" opened it. Except, this wasn't a "dad." This was a husband of an older woman. Out of the two "Steve Haynes" in the Chicago phone book, I chose the wrong one. It was the wrong address and the husband who read the letter thought his wife was having an affair. When I phoned, he started cussing me out and threatening to kill me. I was pleading with him, trying to get a word in edgewise. "Please, I'm just 25. It's not me."—whatever that meant. "I'm looking for a girl I met in Florida. I didn't have an affair with your wife!" I was thinking, "This guy has my name, my address on the envelope. He'll show up at my door with a gun!"

Since I'm counting my girlfriends, I have to relate my experience with Dorci's boyfriends after we became engaged and married. She was not dating anyone in particular at that time. Most of these male friends were acquaintances she knew from her social life. That is a euphemism for "the guys she met at bars." Now, don't get the wrong idea about my wife; she was and is a moral, upstanding woman. But, in the late sixties, living in Belleville across the Mississippi River from St. Louis, the bars in the city were another venue to meet the opposite sex--like they are today. Dorci knew quite a few men.

Once we were a couple, the phone would frequently ring in the evening. A guy was calling her. If she had to say it once, I think she must have said it at least a dozen times: "No, Jerry, I'm engaged now, sorry." Or, "No, Greg, I'm married now, sorry." I remember that as late as a year after our wedding, some guy called her. But these dozen phone calls were no contest to my 46-plus.

In the summer of 1968 I was dating a Romanian girl. Although my mother harped about my settling down and had tried to interfere in my social life, I thought, "John, you're getting old. Your dad married at 28. You have a good job. You should find a woman you want to marry." This young lady came from a good family. I had made a trip to her hometown in Minneapolis and met her parents who liked me. The relationship had possibilities.

My whole life had revolved around the Romanian and Greek Orthodox communities. My parents took the whole family to St. Thomas Romanian Orthodox Church every Sunday. Most of the time, I had no understanding of the multiple rituals, especially since the Romanian spoken in church differed from my parents' dialect. I sang in the church choir and was a cantor for four years. Our house had the traditional icons to which my mother prayed and made the sign of the cross. I often attended weddings between Eastern Orthodox couples and receptions in the church basement. In addition to the traditional food (peta and lamb), we all joined in the circle dance, Hora, and, when I was older, I joined in the drinking.

My mother and family fully expected me to settle down with a nice Orthodox girl. My sister had married a Romanian; my brother, a Greek girl, Denise Georgopoulos. Through my high school buddy Nick Katsaras and other friends, I had met and dated many Orthodox girls. However, the older I got, the slimmer the pickings. But marrying "one of my kind" was an expectation.

Then, on Friday evening, July 26 (obviously an auspicious date since I recall it so accurately) my friend Mike Schwartz phoned and prodded me to go to Joe and Charlie's. I stayed away from singles bars; I considered them a waste of time. This one, located in Clayton, was a popular destination. That night it was packed. Men and women stood shoulder to shoulder, making circulating to "check out the babes" difficult.

I spied an alluring woman with long, blonde hair. I knew her! Well, actually, I recognized her—a substitute teacher for me at Belleville West High School. Mike and I made our way over to her and then managed to find a table. She, Emelee, was with a friend, another teacher, a beautiful woman. I couldn't stop looking at her face. Her eyes—I concentrated on them more than anything else. We made introductions—Emelee and Dorci, John and Mike—and began talking. After all of the dozens of women that I had met in my adult life, none were anything like Dorci. My fascination was twofold: her beauty and her personality. Although I'd always found boobs and butts important in my evaluation of females, not to say hers weren't nice, her face and personality enraptured me.

Far from being an Orthodox girl, I would call her a "blonde bombshell." She came from German stock. To mock me in college and put me in my place, Ken Plassmeyer affectionately used to say of his German ancestors, "They took over the oil fields in Romania!" Rooming with Ken, a German Catholic, in some ways helped prepare me for life with Dorci Stieglitz of the same ancestry and faith.

I bought her a beer. She bought me one. I was impressed. No woman had ever bought me a drink before. "This is a first!" I thought.

Then, she looked into my eyes and said, "I think I can tell what kind of car you drive." I became intrigued. How would this woman determine the make of my car? She studied my eyes, seemed to be evaluating me, thought a bit more and said, "You drive a Volkswagen." Oh my gosh! Who is this woman? How did she do that? I was impressed.

"Yes," I said. "How did you know that?"

She started laughing. My VW keys lay on the table. In those days most automobile keys all looked the same. That is, except for the VW key which actually had "VW" carved on it. I was pretty gullible, but she didn't hold that against me. I liked her sense of humor and no nonsense personality.

Dorci was an English teacher at the other high school in Belleville. She asked, "Why haven't I seen you at the joint department meetings?" I told her about coaching and how it excused me from such obligations. I wonder what might have happened had I attended. Would things have taken the same turn as they did with us at Joe and Charlie's? Meeting in the bar has always made for a colorful story—certainly much more exciting than an English department meeting.

From Joe and Charlie's the four of us went back to my house. We had a few non-alcoholic drinks and sat around talking until 5 a.m. I asked her if she'd like to go to a movie and have pizza Sunday evening. She agreed. Before she left, I kissed her. After Dorci and Emelee departed, I asked Mike what he thought of her. He remarked, "She has big lips." Well, they were slightly large; but man, what a great kiss! Some forty years later women were injecting their lips with Botox to make them look like Dorci's.

I have to confess to a slight indiscretion that evening. Uncertain of if and how this new relationship would get off the ground, I had made a tentative date with Emelee... I said, "If this thing doesn't work out with Dorci, could we go out some time?" Emelee said she was thinking of driving to San Francisco and I could join her. When "this thing" with Dorci did work out, I told her about my back up plan with Emelee.

Dorci and I went to see <u>Petulia</u> starring Julie Christie Sunday night and then on to Luigie's which had a reputation for good Italian food. Now, just like Friday night when she bought me a beer, she surprised me again. As I ate each piece of pizza, she ate a piece of pizza. Piece for piece she matched me. "What is this woman all about? She's different from anyone I've ever met. All the other women are dieting. Am I going to have to order more food?" Dorci came from a family with seven children, five were boys. She was used to getting her share among her siblings.

When I took her home to Belleville, we spent the rest of the night talking and learning all about each other. Monday we went out to Emelee's lake house and swam and had dinner with her. While Dorci prepared the meal, she got this serious look on her face. (I didn't know what her expression meant then, but think I have figured it out after forty-plus years of marriage. I think it's her German genes taking over. When she prepares a meal, she is all business and doesn't want anyone in her way. The result: She's a pain in the ass.)

We returned to her house. In the early A. M. of Tuesday, I told her, "I'm already thinking of you as my wife." Now where did that come from? We had been talking about our futures, our faith, children, money, family and on and on. We had only met Friday night. Here it was eighty hours later and I felt I'd met the woman with whom I could spend the rest of my life. She felt the same way, even though I never did officially ask her to marry me in the traditional manner.

In our country, the sixties were a horrible era. Especially in 1968 everything seemed to be going sour. There were two assassinations (Dr. Martin Luther King, Jr. and Robert Kennedy); and after four years of the Vietnam War, the Tet offensive had begun and many more American troops were dying. Yet, here, into my life came this woman. I saw with her a life that included a family and a fulfilling future. With her I would take a leap of faith.

A lot of the women I had met tried to mold me into something they envisioned. They saw potential in me but wanted to alter this or that. They hinted often about the way I should behave or how I should dress. They had some ideas about what their spouse or boyfriend should be. Dorci was refreshing because she wasn't that way. She just accepted me "as is." That's the way she has always been when meeting people. She has strong values, but she doesn't force them on others. She expects proper behavior but is non-judgmental.

Tuesday we returned to my home in St. Louis. I had been living with my mother since finishing my Army obligation, paying the mortgage on her house. I needed a change of clothing, and Dorci was able to meet my mom. Later, my mother told me that she knew I would marry that girl. We "made the rounds." I wanted everyone to meet her because I thought she was so cool.

It was obvious to us and others that we were very serious. We talked about marriage and thought about a wedding over Labor Day weekend. Dorci suggested we part for a week. She went home to visit her parents who lived northwest of Chicago. Since we'd been together almost constantly for a couple of weeks, we thought a break would be good, and she wanted to tell her parents about me.

When she returned to Belleville, we decided to tell everyone we were engaged. Her parents had thought we should wait until Thanksgiving for the wedding. We agreed with that, set the date for November 30, and started making plans. There wouldn't be anything elaborate; we both agreed we didn't want to spend much money. Dorci was going to wear her mother's wedding dress. (Her mother had married in 1938; her sister had worn the dress. Later, three nieces and our oldest daughter also wore it.)

My eyes were dazzled. Dorci seemed to get better looking as the days and weeks passed. My hormones kicked in whenever I looked at her. She was 23 then. By the time she was 27, not another face could match her beauty. By then she had begun a regimen of walking and running and was as fit as she had ever been. In my eyes, she radiated more beauty as the years passed. Recently, a friend of our daughter saw a picture of us from the early seventies and said, "Wow, John, your wife was a babe!" (Must have been her husband's nurturing!)

A couple of things to be said about Dorci's beauty… I'm sure you've heard people say that some couples grow to resemble each other. Rest assured, that did not happen in our case. What Dorci called my rugged good looks remained distinctly my own. Her beauty, which she seemed oblivious to her whole life, barely diminished over the years. Once she reached her sixties, I began kidding her about her "jowls." But compared to women even ten years her junior, she retains her beauty. We were on a house tour with friends one time and got separated from them. They came looking for us. A realtor in one of the homes asked them, "Oh, are you looking for that short, dark man who is with the tall, lovely blonde?" We have our distinct looks, no blending for us.

Occasionally during our married life, people have compared Dorci to various blonde movies stars, those with large mouths. Names like Diane Cannon, Linda Evans, and Candice Bergen were mentioned more than once. My brother said she looked like Bo Derek when the movie 10 came out in 1979. A young girl we offered a ride to during a family vacation kept calling her "Meredith Baxter-Birney."

And then there is the story about the guy, so struck by her beauty that he tried to pick her up when she was about 33. She was teaching at Wentzville High School and stopped at central office on her way home from work. A salesman in the office saw her and managed to follow her as she drove away. When she stopped at a gas station, he got out of his car, introduced himself and asked her to go out for a drink. "I'm married," she said.

"That's okay. I still want to have a drink with you. Can't we go somewhere?"

"Sorry," she said. "I'm happily married and not interested."

In addition to her beauty, Dorci had attracted me by her values. One of the things we had discussed during those first few nights together was family. She told me she wanted a large one, and I agreed with that, maybe five kids. We both shared similar attitudes about raising children. Although the number of children that completed our family changed, we were always in sync in our approach and dealings with our three. The two of us were one, co-conspirators, when making decisions or confronting the kids for any reason. For this I am most grateful after some of the things I witnessed as a teacher. Many families are in shambles because the husband and wife cannot work together.

Although Dorci became a new fascination in my life, I did not totally abandon my other love. True, some of my sports interests were put on the back burner, to use a trite expression. Dorci superseded golf and handball. However, throughout the summer and fall, as we dashed towards a Thanksgiving weekend wedding, I sought out information about the Cardinal baseball team. When I had time, I tuned the radio dial to KMOX, the voice of St. Louis. Dorci came first, but the Cardinals still drew my loyalty. Life was good that summer, the best of both worlds for me—a beautiful wife-to-be and the Cards headed for the World Series with Bob Gibson pitching.

My love affair with the St. Louis Baseball Cardinals had begun in the summer of 1949 when my father listened to their games on the radio. My fascination with balls has not been limited to physically playing with them. I enjoy watching and listening to professional teams play. In '49 the exploits of Enos Slaughter, Stan Musial, Marty Marion, Red Schoendienst, and Harry Brecheen piqued my interest immediately. I relished learning about the great players the Cardinal teams had in the 1940's. They earned their way into four of the five World Series from '42 to '46, winning three of them.

Unfortunately for me, the voice of the Cardinals on the radio from 1945 to 1969 totally frustrated me. Harry Caray made listeners think the world came one step closer to the abyss any year the team didn't win the pennant. My impressionable mind followed the gamut of his emotions. For example, Caray would denigrate Ken Boyer. Boyer played for the Cards from 1954 to 1966 and won the 1964 National League Most Valuable Player award. During that time, Boyer earned impeccable defensive and offensive stats—led all National League infielders in fielding percentage, from '58 to '61 won the Gold Glove awards, and in several seasons drove in ninety runs. Yet, with a disparaging inflection in his voice, Caray would utter, "Struck him out!" on Boyer's third strike with runners in scoring position. By the time I reached high school, I barely tolerated Caray's emotionally judgmental style. I didn't like listening to him, but he was the only one calling the games.

When Jack Buck took over the broadcasting, around 1965, I was pleased and relieved. Here was a man with class. His style and intellect brought a breath of fresh air to the games. His wit and on-the-field interviews topped any of the other sports' commentators I heard in the '70's, '80's and '90's.

I was so enthralled and faithful to the Cards that players on other teams seemed like the enemy. If Bob Gibson had been on any other team, there's a good chance I would not have liked him. However, since he was a Red Bird, I loved reading about his accomplishments, especially in 1968. His stats that year posted 22-wins and 9-losses with an ERA of 1.12 and thirteen shut outs. Wow! He pitched 304-innings; today managers worry when their pitchers go beyond 220-innings.

I have distinct memories of the 1985 baseball season, even though it resembled so many others that I experienced before and after that year. The players' names would change and scores and statistics varied, but generally, my emotions and behavior were the same. When things went wrong, when mistakes were made, I would yell and cuss at a player or manager or umpire as I sat by the radio or TV. Or, I wouldn't watch televised games because losses were so upsetting. Sometimes I purposely avoided listening or watching, hoping that they might win, as if my lack of awareness might propel them to victory.

In 1985 the Cardinals had a successful season and found themselves pitted against the Los Angeles Dodgers in the playoffs. During one particularly close game, I became so distraught, sensing a loss on the horizon, that I grabbed my golf clubs and headed for the course to play nine holes. I hoped to calm my churning stomach. While walking the fifth hole near some homes, I heard the roar of fans coming from a television. I could tell they were screaming with delight. I discovered that Jack Clark had hit a home run to beat the Dodgers.

Another vivid memory from that playoff series that few Cardinal fans could ever forget occurred when Jack Buck yelled, "Go crazy, folks, go crazy!" Ozzie Smith had just hit a game-winning home run left-handed, his first-ever homer from the left side. The moments and memories go on and on and on.

My marriage to Dorci, the births of our three children, moves from Missouri to Illinois, New Mexico, Arizona and then back to Missouri, some career changes—my life marched through the end of the twentieth century and into the twenty-first, and I remain faithful to the St. Louis Cardinals. If I wasn't listening to KMOX radio, then I was searching for a TV station that televised the game. Dorci, busy with the tasks of wife and mother, absorbed players' names and baseball stats through the radio or TV announcer's voice as I followed season after season. Our children grew to become fans just as I had. Even though Matthew now lives in Hawaii, we continue to discuss the latest news about the Cardinals.

Nothing has changed since our move to Arizona. Well, one minor change. When a game is televised, I will phone Beth, our daughter who also lives in Arizona, and let her know. She and the grandkids watch the games, and the kids have become fans and know the veteran players by name. This wasn't the case a few years ago. Then, the grandkids' major exposure to baseball came from their personal experiences on co-ed "T-ball" and "coach-pitch" teams, not from major league baseball. One evening three years ago, while watching a Cardinals' game, the children were commenting on Pujols and Carpenter. Bella, age 6, said something about Molina the Cardinals' catcher, that "she" had made a really good play picking off a runner. Nick, age 9, and Jack, 4, agreed, saying "she" was a good player. Now, Yadier Molina could be described as having a "girlish" face; and, there is a lot of on-line discussion about his looks, specifically his eyebrows. It was easy for the kids to think he was a "she." Beth chuckled and phoned us to relate the conversation.

Part of my daily routine since moving to Arizona includes reading about the Cardinals every morning on my computer. While we lived in the St. Louis area, I faithfully examined the sports pages of the local papers. Today, via the internet, I pull up the St. Louis Post Dispatch web site and enjoy the latest Cardinals' baseball news, commentary, statistics and interviews. I absorb the stories about each player's personal life, his past, his family, and obstacles he has overcome. (Stan Musial in his mid-eighties was diagnosed with Alzheimer's.) When there's a game scheduled on television, I've programmed my DVR to record it. Unfortunately, not much has changed with my behavior; I still get distressed over inept ball handling and yell at the players or managers on the screen. I care about this team as though they were an adopted child.

So, in the summer of 1968, my loyalty and interest in this team hovered in the background as I met, fell in love with and planned to marry Dorci.

When we both returned to teaching in September, Dorci at Belleville

East and I at West, we announced our engagement to friends and co-workers. After a few weeks Dorci told me her fellow teachers were beginning to doubt that she was engaged. She had no ring and she wanted to know when we were going to get one. With my "unconventional" proposal behind us, Dorci thought it was time to return to some standard behavior. She also told me what she expected.

Apparently, several of her friends had married shortly after high school or during college when money was especially tight for them. When the girls proudly displayed their engagement rings, holding forth their left hands, Dorci was not impressed. The diamonds seemed hardly more than chips. She told me she required a diamond that could be seen across the room. Since I had connections with a jeweler, her request didn't faze me. I had some investments and saved money. We could afford a nice diamond. Also, I had a little ego going and wanted to give her a large ring. After shopping for several weeks, we purchased a 1.5 caret diamond in an interlocking band setting.

I had impressed Dorci the night we met with my talk of investments and plans to retire at age 45. She thought I was "on my way" to making a tidy sum and living comfortably. I wasn't lying to her, but the reality of investments going sour loomed in our future, unbeknownst to us.

Dorci's dad had been a successful business man. He had earned a good living while supporting his wife and seven children. I'm sure she looked forward to a similar life. She didn't know what she was in for! She didn't know how cheap I was. A good clue would have been the automobile situation.

When we met, Dorci drove a fully-loaded Ford, LTD that her father helped her buy when she graduated from college. It was a comfortable, luxurious car, about two years old. I drove a Volkswagen, an old Volkswagen. When we married, we sold her car.

Another clue early on in our marriage was our budget. We both brought in a good salary, and I wanted to live on just one and save the other. We agreed to a spending regimen which had a limited food allotment. Dorci always clipped coupons and shopped the grocery ads. She got very creative with tuna fish which cost only 25-cents on sale. She had to since we ate it several times a week.

We learned to take advantage of "free" offers. We used not one but several 8mm cameras for the "two week free trial, postage paid return."

"Free 8 x 10 portrait" offers relied on people who couldn't bear to see all the other pictures thrown in the trash can. That didn't bother Dorci because the next week there were two more "free 8 x 10 portrait" offers. This was helpful when Beth and Matt were young. We managed to save a tidy sum which we invested in several ways, none of which proved profitable. Ten years later we had to start over with our savings' endeavors.

The first Christmas after our marriage, I wanted to buy Dorci a nice gift but nothing too expensive. I thought "underwear." Notice I didn't say "lingerie." I had a lot to learn and words like "lingerie" and what it meant were among those things. I'd say that regarding finesse, I had none; which is why I went shopping for "underwear" for my bride of four weeks. I did know that black was supposed to be sexy on a blonde so that became the color of choice. When she opened her gift Christmas Day, there were six pair of black underwear, "grannie-panties"—the full leg-to-the-waist style. Also in the box lay a nice, full black slip. Once again in the "grandma-style." With my pride dashed, I realized what I had done, but it's been the source of many laughs over time.

For many years, ever the skeptic, I kept waiting to discover some awful secret about Dorci. I just knew that nothing could be as good as she seemed to be. There had to be some "thing" from her past that would eventually surface. I knew that somewhere there had to be "skeletons in her closet." Haven't we all seen those movies where an unsuspecting husband or wife is oblivious to the fact that the spouse is a killer or sociopath or leading a double life? Not to say I thought something that bad would turn up—but who knows? I wasn't going to be one of those unsuspecting victims.

After we'd been married about eight years and without discovering anything, I asked her about her past. "Isn't there anything you want to tell me about yourself that I need to know? Something bad from your past?" She looked at me like I was crazy. This look had become familiar to me; she knew after eight years that, yes, I was crazy. But this particular question added a new dimension to my eccentric nature.

"No, John. I'm not hiding anything from you. You are not going to discover anything about me that you don't already know." Well, of course she'd say this. What was I thinking? "How long have you been worried about this?" she asked.

"Well, I don't know... A while, I guess." Eventually, I admitted that I'd been waiting for years to discover something. And I still waited. And waited and waited. When we'd been married twelve years, Dorci asked me one day, "John, are you still waiting for some skeleton to come out of my closet?" She looked intently at me. What could I say?

"You think it's time to give it up?" I asked. I got the look. "Okay, I guess there is nothing bad for me to discover about you." I meant what I said. After twelve years, I decided I could trust that Dorci was what I knew her to be and there weren't going to be any surprises in the negative.

Another incident about Dorci being as good as she seems to be comes to mind. About twelve years ago I attended the funeral of a high school buddy. Various memories were narrated by relatives and friends. I listened with interest to expressions of admiration for the deceased and to assorted recollections. The ideas were eloquent and touching. A thought struck me: "I need to prepare for the time when Dorci dies, should she precede me in death. I don't want to leave anything out—there are so many great things I want to recount. I don't want to rely on family or friends. I know her better than anyone else." That very evening I found a clipboard and began writing a list of attributes and skills that typify this woman. So many pictures and incidents flashed through my head; the fervor of inspiration, something usually reserved for my sports' passions, consumed me. In less than thirty minutes, I easily composed an inventory that filled one page. Over the course of months and years, I have returned to that clipboard to note a few additional thoughts. It is a work in progress. It may prove to be a gratuitous task as I fully expect to die before she does. Then, it will serve as my fond farewell, my memories of our life together, specifically how I saw this woman I married, the chief fascination of my life. What follows is the list, as written, that I keep tucked away in my bureau drawer to serve as her eulogy:

"1. Drive in a 16 penny nail.

2. Was she good with a shovel! The only time I saw her give up on a task was that tree along the service road that she wanted to transplant. It had a five foot tap root. She gave up because I insisted that she stop. (That's probably what hastened the degeneration in her hip requiring a replacement ten years later.)

3. Fix just about anything in our house – use a power saw or screwdriver.

4. Devotion to God, to church, to children, to siblings, even to mother-in-law.

5. Smile every day for 45-years and counting. She'd walk in the door

with a smile. And what a smile! She had a lot of fun pointing out my attempt at smiling with my teeth hardly showing.

6. After her hip replacement she had energy galore when healed.

7. After her hernia surgery she was using a wheelbarrow a week later.

8. Installed the underlayment in our first house. Tile in another house.

9. Laid brick hearth and wall in first house.

10. Installed a paver patio—resulted in hernia surgery from loading and unloading the pavers.

11. Built houses with husband, side by side five times.

12. So beautiful and photogenic yet her character so outshined her beauty.

13. Remained passionate for entire marriage. (Am I delusional?)

14. Strange fit, she and I. We liked each other immediately. Still trying to figure that out. Somehow, we filled each other's needs. Not 50/50, more like 70/30. Some friends thought it was more like 90/10!

15. Sin of pride—accused herself of it. I think that is a joke.

16. Wally (a student I had who transferred into Dorci's class in Wentzville, then returned to Wright City, all in the same school year)—he asked me what it was like living with a "perfect woman."

17. Skeletons in her closet when we were early in our marriage—a futile expectation because she seemed just too good to be true.

18. Many student letters or phone calls after graduation expressing appreciation for her teaching skills

19. Some of her talents: hammer, screwdriver, power saw, calking gun, paint, plumbing, wiring, cooking, baking, gardening (food and flowers and houseplants), untangling string or rope or wire or garden hose or Christmas lights, upholstering numerous pieces of furniture (chairs and couches), sewing clothes for herself and children, drawing (pictures, art), landscape design and installation.

20. When a migraine would hit, sometimes two or three times in a month, the only way I knew was by looking closely at her face. No complaints. She must have figured I complained enough for both of us.

21. After witnessing her genius interacting with Beth when Beth was an infant, I decided she knew a heck of a lot more than I did. She did not work during the early years of parenting with Beth and Matt. She was inventive, creative, loving, marvelous in handling parental skills. Dorci nurtured the children, motivated them with love and intelligence.

In addition, her German heritage provided the discipline necessary to instill responsibility, gratitude and humility in them. They are not brats. If I have any regrets, it's that we were both working once Briana was nineteen months old. However, Briana can tell you that her mother was still brilliant in helping her grow when the world was throwing more and more 'crap' in the direction of young children and teens. Easter of 2011 I saw her using those same skills with the grandchildren, incorporating fun and learning in the Easter egg hunt. Caught up in the grandchildren's excitement, I told Beth, 'I wish she had been my mom.'

22. Beyond pettiness

23. Architectural drawing (house plans for our six homes and kitchen designs—plus floor plan and kitchen of Beth's house in Prescott)."

Dorci and I credit God with bringing us together. We thank Him often for the gift of each other. He must have been in control during our whirlwind engagement and wedding which seem a bit rash in retrospect. But our marriage has been solid due to our faith and commitment to God, to each other and to our union.

My other fascination, Dorci, in her mother's wedding dress (1968)

Jumping in the desert in Bloomfield, New Mexico

Beth joins Dad on motorcycle, 1972

CHAPTER 6

A DREAM DEFERRED AND A BAG OF GARBAGE

My search for a football coaching position through the placement service at Cape Girardeau began in the spring of 1971 after track season at Belleville ended. I found a vacancy for an assistant's job in Bloomfield, New Mexico, and set up an interview. In late June, Jeff Schwarz helped me drive the 1550 miles straight through, leaving Belleville, Illinois; crossing Missouri and Kansas; heading south in Colorado to enter northern New Mexico. Straight through both ways, typical John Leara-travel-style—brutal.

During my interview, the head coach told me that he had already spoken to my college coach. My record impressed him. He also said that the coming season would be his last and that I made a good candidate to fill the vacancy after he retired. Confident of this future, I accepted the position. I thought, "I'll assist for one year and then I'll be the head coach."

I accepted the job at Bloomfield as an assistant, motivated by that thought—becoming head coach. But other factors contributed to this decision. Restlessness was one, the desire for change. I had been teaching in the St. Louis area for seven years and wanted a new challenge and environment. New Mexico was about as different from St. Louis as any other place. The mountains of the west lured me. How could they not? Add to this the idea of westward migration, the very stuff of heroic, romantic stories.

At last, a longed-for dream might come true. In a year's time, I might be a head football coach. The seed of this desire had been planted when I played high school football. Within me for so many years stirred the confidence and longing to take a group of boys and lead them to a successful season.

The belief that I could do in football what I had done with the pole vault in Belleville came from my inherent understanding of the game. My grasp of football seemed to be genetic—like it was part of my DNA. Whereas with vaulting, I had had virtually no knowledge, football coursed through my veins.

In August with the help of athletes and relatives, we spent a full day loading a U-Haul truck. Typical of American families, we had lots of "stuff." Dorci, the organizer, oversaw the placing of furniture and boxes. I gladly ceded this duty to her. She's very much "a place for everything and everything in its place" kind of person; whereas for me, any flat surface or doorknob makes finding things easy. That loaded truck resembled a Rubik's cube when the packing was concluded. Everything was so tightly stowed that we had to tie my Suzuki motorcycle to the outside on the back of the truck.

When I began unpacking in New Mexico, a surprise awaited me. My esteem for Dorci's talents suffered just the slightest of chinks when the first item out of the tightly-packed truck that had traveled 1550 miles was—a bag of garbage. "Dorci," I thought, "where do you plan to place this item?"

Around 7 a.m. the day after packing, I set off for the long drive in the U-Haul. Since Dorci was seven months pregnant and Beth only a year and a half old, they would board a plane to fly to the Farmington, New Mexico, airport two days after I left. The excitement over this, our first, really big move, kept me alert for the long trip. I had no problem driving most of the night because I was so psyched. My traveling companion, our cool Rhodesian Ridgeback named Tarbu, gave me an ear for listening. Although a dog, his presence in the truck and the one-way conversation elevated my mood.

The beauty of the Colorado and New Mexico mountains awed me. This was my second time seeing them, the first time being when I came out to interview. However, driving through Wolf Creek Pass got my adrenaline pumping, and not because of its beauty. In 1971 this pass was a steep, winding, two-lane switchback which took hours to negotiate. Here I was in this strange truck, driving a road barely two lanes wide. Forget shoulders. At times, if I looked to my left, a sheer drop-off of 500-feet met my gaze. The ascent seemed safer than the descent which required almost constant braking.

"What if the brakes fail?" I thought. "What if a tire blows? What if the steering fails?" Ever the pessimist, I've always been able to conjure a plethora of the worst scenarios. "I need to be prepared. I need a plan." My door was not locked. "If a problem occurs, I'll open it and jump."

Then I remembered a movie I'd seen. The hero couldn't open his door when he needed to escape his car. "What if that happens to me? My plan needs more options." While cautiously manipulating the switchback, I rolled down the window of my door. "This will give me another avenue of escape." With one hand on the wheel, I unlatched the door, and held it open just a crack. "OK, John," I told myself. "You have an open window and open door. You should be able to escape. Good thing you saw that movie. You're smarter than that character was." For the rest of the drive through the pass, one hand held the steering wheel while the other clutched the open door, ready to push it should catastrophe strike.

"Poor Tarbu!" I thought. "He has no idea what I'm planning. I'm leaving him to his own devises. All I know is that I'm jumping! He's on his own." Of course, I would be successful only if there were no 500-foot drop on the driver's side. "On my way out, I'll yell for him to come and hope he follows." Tarbu, although weighing some 60-pounds, was still a bit of a pussy. He might not follow his master's command. As Providence would have it, no exit was required, no emergency occurred. The possibility of danger had kept me watchful through another stretch of the trip.

Dorci had packed food and drink for our journey. What with stops for gas and restrooms (or bushes in the case of Tarbu—okay, sometimes me, too), we arrived in Bloomfield around 1 p.m. the next day, some thirty hours after leaving Illinois.

When I picked Dorci up at the airport and drove her to our new home, she was totally surprised to see an empty truck. Our new neighbors, adults and kids, had lined up to introduce themselves and help unload everything. Several were teachers who knew I was joining their ranks. Their help gave us a sampling of how nice the folks in the area would treat us. They had placed everything inside the house but hadn't unpacked, although they offered to.

"If you put stuff away, Dorci will just move it when she arrives." I knew better than to try to organize anything for her. She would just change it all around. She likes everything in its proper place, including her husband. Of course, soon after her arrival, I informed her of that bag of garbage that traveled from Illinois. I can't let opportunities to point out her flaws pass without note—she seems to have so few.

Bloomfield is located near the "Four Corners," where the states of New Mexico, Colorado, Utah and Arizona meet. Aesthetically the area is not very attractive. The arid climate produces sparse vegetation. This barren, high-desert environment, however, became a great playground for me on my motorcycle. With the wide-open spaces, I could experience an adrenaline high, jumping "sand moguls" and climbing the dunes.

Another "playground" lay only an hour away from our home at the Purgatory Ski Resort. During our first year in Bloomfield, neighbors and parents of my students encouraged and welcomed me to join them on one-day ski trips. I missed Dorci's company, however. Matthew had been born in late October, and she spent the winter caring for him.

I recall one of those excursions specifically. After skiing all day, I was sitting in the lodge drinking a beer. Moods were high among the Bloomfield folks. Upbeat music played. Conversation was lively and friendly. The only thing missing for me was Dorci. I thought to myself, "If only I could use the transporter on <u>Star Trek</u> and beam Dorci up. She would materialize in the chair next to me to share the moment."

Besides spending leisure hours on my motorcycle or weekends skiing, I used to spend hours kicking field goals. After football practice was over and all the players and coaches went home, I would go out on the field with a tee, place a football on it and start kicking. I still had a pretty good leg. I didn't kick soccer style, off the side of the toe, just straight ahead a la Dempsey, the 63-yard field goal record-holder.

Eventually I could kick goals from 50-yards. I began dreaming. "I'm thirty—not over the hill. Look at Mac Percival the field goal kicker from Chicago. He's a former teacher and now he's playing for the Chicago Bears. That could be me!" I talked to Dorci, telling her about my fascination with kicking field goals, about Mac Percival. Talk about excitement!

After discovering that the NFL didn't use tees, I began practicing off the ground. Dorci came out and helped by holding the ball with her fingers. When she wasn't available, an assistant principal in Bloomfield would risk his fingers. He was a wonderful man who later wrote a letter of recommendation for me when I applied for head football coach at a different school.

Before long I could regularly kick a field goal from 50-yards from the ground. In 1971 that was very respectable, though today, goals are made from 60-yards in practice. I thought, "If I weight lift and strengthen my leg, I'll be able to kick a 55-yarder." That is, without linemen rushing me. "Surely that will attract the attention of a pro team."

Throughout the fall and spring that year I kicked field goals. Then, my right knee started giving me problems, my kicking leg. Although I iced it, rested it, tried my own therapy, the pain remained. I thought, "What am I going to do? Be a field goal kicker with a sore knee or become a head football coach?" The dream to follow in Mac Percival's footsteps had been exciting, brief but enjoyable.

In addition to coaching at the high school, I had been hired to teach English. Many of the students in my classes were Navajo. This was my first personal contact with Native Americans. They were fun-loving boys and girls, always laughing and joking whether in class or in the hallways. Despite the problems of alcohol and drugs on the Navajo Reservation, these kids had a great sense of humor.

One Navajo boy constantly talked and joked in my class. Maybe he wanted to test the new, Anglo teacher. The high school had a "paddling policy." A student could choose his consequence when he stepped out of line, either a swat or a detention. When I told the boy he was out of line, I gave him that choice. He chose the paddle and after his swat, never misbehaved again.

After the academic day ended, I headed for the football field. Having been assigned the defensive backs, I concentrated on teaching strategies. I did not focus on hard hitting. My goal was to make sure the backs could read plays and take the right positions. Being out of place was unacceptable. I wanted aggressive players. We practiced moving without hesitation. We drilled so as to react instantly to the opposing quarterback's movement. Some of the boys were good athletes with lightning speed. In the first game, the left defensive back responded just as we had practiced and positioned himself perfectly, enabling him to intercept the pass. I beamed with gratitude over his success. "Wow," I thought. "This is fun!"

I felt assured of my coaching talent and style, particularly after my success at Belleville with the pole vaulters. The rapport I developed with the athletes instilled confidence in me. The athletes at Belleville and Ritenour had all become "my" boys. I never had to worry about feelings or coddle anyone. My boys knew me and I knew them. This approach was innate for me—a confident, straight-forward relationship of coach to athletes. My manner would never change, whether in high school football, or, many years later, in second-grade soccer.

However, several factors in Bloomfield stifled my natural approach to coaching. The feeling of being an outsider was one. This was a small town. All of the football staff had lived in the area for a long time. Some had actually graduated from Bloomfield High School. I, as an assistant, the new guy, seemed to be an intruder from 1500 miles away.

The intensity of my passion for football may have been another factor. It felt out of place in Bloomfield. Because success was so important to me, I knew I would use all the tools available to attain it. My approach would emphasize teaching the game's intricacies to the players. I would stress drills to produce agility and strength to out-maneuver opponents. But here I felt constrained as I did not want to step on someone else's toes, especially since this team and program had proven to be successful in previous years.

Off the field, I felt viewing film of previous games was a way to learn. Film allowed coaches and players to find their mistakes, to plug holes and develop strategies. I well-remembered studying game films in college. Coach used to re-wind the 16mm tape to find mistakes and who made them, to discover our weaknesses and develop a plan for overcoming them. Yet, to the coaches and players in Bloomfield, it seemed to be merely entertainment. We viewed it. The players joked around, laughed. I had hoped to discover ways to improve our play. We didn't study the film.

As a newcomer, I felt uncomfortable with the camaraderie between some of the players and assistants. I was meeting these boys for the first time and missed the familiarity of the vaulters in Belleville. These coaches and players had worked together, lived in Bloomfield for years and, with typical small town flavor, knew everybody and everything. Everybody, that is, but me.

That football season in Bloomfield required adjusting on my part. I was coming down from the high of my experiences and success with the Belleville vaulters. Being an assistant football coach required a different mindset and more accountability to the larger picture that included the other coaches. With the vaulters, I had separated us from the rest of the track team for workouts. With them I created competitions and drills that were fun and unusual.

My assignment under the head coach was to work with the defensive backs. For the first time in my coaching experience, I did not feel totally in charge of the boys under me. In my head I felt the need to throttle back. I did not want to teach or introduce something that ran counter to what they had previously been told or learned. They weren't "my" boys. I had no tenure with this team. I had to answer to the head coach and be a team player.

Lacking the security of familiarity and longevity with the players, I felt a need to tolerate a few boys with wise-ass attitudes that I would not have tolerated had I been the head coach. They'd make comments I couldn't hear. Or they snickered. Maybe I was being myself—paranoid; I just wasn't comfortable.

I had a good relationship with most of the other coaches. I liked them but I had my way of doing things. I had a different temperament and a hands-on approach. The coach handling the offensive backs was bright and, like me, athletic. We both got physically involved with coaching. One day he commented, "You and I make a good coaching combination." I coached his younger brother, one of the backs on the team. In fact, this younger brother was the player who had the interception in the first game.

The season ended with a winning record. True to his word, after the last game was played, the head man retired from his position. I was one of several who applied for the job. Before spring break, the next year's contracts were released. The head job went to a local guy from the middle school, not any of the assistants at the high school. Although disappointed, I was not surprised. I knew that things just hadn't "clicked" for me in Bloomfield. I had suspected I wouldn't be asked to step up.

This did not change my determination and commitment, however. The past season would be the last year that I accepted an assistant's position. I resolved to find a head job anywhere on the planet. There would be no more waiting. My dream would not be deferred any longer. Time was passing; I was 31. That is how Sells, Arizona, became one of the most important chapters in my life. In retrospect, I suspect that Sells was probably the only place on the planet that would have taken me as a head football coach. But Sells and I were meant for each other.

CHAPTER 7

A DREAM REALIZED... OR NOT?

     Imagine this scenario for a TV movie. The setting is a reservation in southern Arizona, in a small, remote town. The main characters are an Anglo football coach and the Indian boys on his team. Not only is the Anglo new to the reservation high school, this is his first season as a head football coach. The Indian high school has a dismal record, never having won a conference competition in any sport. In his initial season, the new coach takes the football team to its first win. By the end of the second season, the team is 7-2 and the coach is nominated for Arizona prep football coach of the year.

Such is the stuff of Hollywood and TV-land. Dreams don't get any better than that unless they come true. In 1972 when I took my wife and two children to live in Sells, Arizona, the dream began. The plot for the imaginary TV movie comes right from the events of my two seasons with the Papago Indian boys at Baboquivari High School.

* * *

Having accepted a head football position, I felt confident that my coaching would nurture the boys I was to meet. As my desire to coach had grown, so too had my commitment to prioritize the safety of my players. In my coaching program, "inflicting pain for pain's sake" had no place. The memories of practices from the new coach during my senior year at Roosevelt High School solidified my principles. Yes, I would work my players hard. Yes, they would experience pain, but it would come from training, building strength and developing skills. I sought a goal of cohesiveness through teamwork. These would be the standards by which I would lead athletes to success when given the opportunity.

No doubt existed that my instincts were right on. I had confidence in the conclusions I had drawn as a player. They would form the successful foundation for a coach's philosophy: 1) Take care of the athletes; 2) Demand hard work from all; 3) Understand the importance of offensive and defensive strategy; 4) Communicate intelligently on a daily basis about the team's and the individuals' progress; 5) Prepare myself so that players have the highest probability of success.

* * *

My dream to become a head football coach was coming to fruition. I left New Mexico where the head job I had hoped to gain after one year as assistant had been awarded to someone else. A head-coaching job had opened in the remote town of Sells, Arizona, sixty miles west of Tucson on the Papago Indian Reservation. (The reservation has since been renamed Tohono O'odham Nation.) I was 31 years old. My resume was impressive enough that the superintendent phoned me, told me the board liked my credentials and wanted to hire me, pending an interview.

Within a few weeks, Dorci and I and our two children drove the 500-miles from New Mexico to Arizona for the interview. In my mind, all I could think about was becoming the HEAD FOOTBALL COACH! Two people that I talked to during that first trip to Sells told me it was a "no win" environment. No one had anything positive to say about the football program. Someone told me that the Baboquivari High School football team had never won a conference game and never more than one game, ever. In fact, I heard a rumor that that was the case for all the sports teams at Baboquivari. I really did not care about the situation or what challenges lay ahead. I really wasn't listening; the words meant nothing to me.

The teachers in Sells comprised a wide spectrum. Compared to the three previous schools where I had worked, Baboquivari High School had a much wider assortment of teachers. Some had massive beards, others dressed in what might be called anti-establishment clothing—the guy who wore a tie fastened with a paperclip instead of a tie-clasp. I had never met anyone, especially teachers, who openly used drugs until we moved to Sells. A myriad of reasons existed as to why people would choose to teach on the reservation. Dorci and I with the two toddlers landed in Sells for only one reason: I wanted to coach football and Baboquivari was the only school that offered me a head football position.

Dan Crawford, who taught shop at the middle school, lived in our neighborhood, in the same compound of houses. Dorci and I connected with him and Lori, his wife, immediately: children of the same age, pretty much the same values, Dan a football coach and good athlete to boot. During the very first week we arrived, he took me fishing. At 5 am, no less! We began by collecting grasshoppers. Then he helped me bait my hook with them. I had never done anything like that before.

Dan and I both had motorcycles, and we went riding together in the desert sometimes. On one return trip, our competitive juices kicked in and we raced. Outside Sells, on the two lane highway that ran through the town, we marked off a distance about the length of two football fields. We went at it. I jumped out ahead with my semi-dirt bike only to be overtaken by Dan's street bike. We raced again with the same results. We were both going almost 80 m.p.h. I conceded.

Dan and Lori would remain our friends for the rest of our lives. (In 2004 we returned to Arizona and now live eighteen miles from them.) It is as easy for me to talk to Lori as it is to Dan. Lori, who was one of nine siblings, is a kind-hearted, wise person. She knows that I can be harsh, and yet she still enjoys my company—for which I am very thankful.

Sells was a very small community. The Papago tribe supervised the Baboquivari School District. Sells had a hospital administered by the Bureau of Indian Affairs. One general store offered a limited assortment of items at high prices, including some food. High desert surrounded the town, typical Arizona with a variety of cacti including saguaro. This was a pleasant contrast to the barren, virtually colorless desert in the Bloomfield area.

Another difference I discovered between Bloomfield and Sells was in the nature of the Navajo and the Papago students. In Bloomfield the Navajo were integrated into the high school with the Anglos who were in the majority. They were fun-loving and out-going; a few tended towards arrogance. In Sells, where the classes were 95-100% Indian, the Papago were passive and non-competitive. In my physical education classes at Sells, the boys would exhaust themselves playing basketball, running up and down the court for the full period. At the end of class, when I asked what the score was, they had no idea. Winning wasn't the objective.

In my English classes many were very bright and wonderful writers. However, these very same students were hesitant to speak up in class. With pen and paper, they communicated one on one. In front of a class of students, they did not like to speak. Some told me it was not the thing to do, to answer questions and draw attention to oneself at the expense of others who did not answer. They seldom did anything to shine a positive light upon themselves. One might wonder how this lack of competition and desire to shine would translate onto the football field. Initially unaware of these factors, I would learn to consider them as I interacted with the players.

One of the contrasts between the two communities proved ironic. Bloomfield was primarily an Anglo town with a minority of Navajo. However, I never felt like I "fit in." But in Sells, a town on the reservation where 99% of the population was Papago Indian, I would be accepted and bond with the athletes. This difference was spawned by the fact that I was the head coach rather than an assistant and could run the football program as I designed it, not answering to any coaching superior.

* * *

"Football! I am going to coach football the right way!" Euphoria consumed me. My thoughts were all about the opportunity to test my coaching philosophy, bring cohesion to a group of athletes and watch them develop into a good team. I still carried with me the gratification and camaraderie of my success with the pole vaulters from one year ago. I was optimistic that I could now experience the same thing coaching a team of football players.

I suspect I was experiencing an emotion taken from my father's and mother's lives in 1932. In coming to America, they were consumed with optimism. Their thoughts while crossing the Atlantic Ocean focused on starting a new life in America. They weren't thinking about poverty or failure. I, too, was traveling to my "new world"—starting a fresh chapter in my coaching career. Should I worry about how bad the Baboquivari football team had been? No way!

I wonder how many first generation children feel the same way I felt back in 1972. Was it just me, or was it the result of living in the Leara household where I saw my father forever striving yet failing to become a successful businessman. Witnessing that had prepared me to work every day as many hours as necessary doing what I loved to do.

* * *

Unfortunately for me, I moved to Sells with a few pre-conceived notions. At the age of fourteen, I had read Jim Thorpe—All-American. Thorpe, a Pottawatomie Indian, excelled in football, track and baseball. His feats in football and track left an indelible impression on me. In football he was almost unstoppable as a running back. In track, he could long jump 26-feet! In college he ran the 100, 200, and 400-meter and the mile and frequently won. He was like a one-man team. Along with a few other Indian boys, he brought victory after victory at track meets to Carlisle, an Indian school in Pennsylvania. In the 1912 Olympics, he won a gold medal in both the decathlon and pentathlon, setting a record that stood for over two decades. In 1950 the Associated Press named him the greatest, overall male athlete. Later, ABC Sports named him the greatest athlete of the century. My imagination easily conjured visions of this great athlete, an Indian of superior physical skill, with toned muscles, light and fleet of foot. The image in my head became an expectation.

"Shock" is the best word to describe my reaction to meeting the members of the Baboquivari football team in August of 1972. "Dismay" followed close behind. I had never seen so many soft bodies. "Dim" best described my prospects. Where was I going to find athletic bodies to field a team? The boys who told me they were linemen, "linemen" being those players who have to force open holes in the opposing line for the running back to charge through, could barely do one push-up. "Wake-up call" is what that first meeting was for me. Many more "wake-up calls" were to follow.

Baboquivari was a small high school with about 250 students. All the football players were Papago, a close reflection of the student body. (Most of the few Anglo students were children of employees on the reservation.) Until coming to Baboquivari, I had been surrounded by fine athletes. However, these young Papago men, who would touch my heart more than any other athletes I had worked with, were almost devoid of muscle tone. "Tone"— no. Devoid of muscle, period. What had I done to my family and myself in taking this job?

With just over one month to game time, I needed a plan. I had to accept the fact that no matter how much we worked on building bodies, the boys weren't going to change much physically during the first season. I also had to choose the coaching staff.

Dan Crawford had been the assistant varsity coach the previous year. He told me he wanted to take the JV squad. He'd had enough of the varsity. Dan wanted to be left alone with his own team. His desire resonated with me. I couldn't blame him after he described the ugly losses that the varsity had suffered under other head coaches. Dan went on to have a winning season that year and the next. I needed another coach. Gary Tom joined me. He was a new teacher, a fine athlete younger than I.

What was my plan? I had twenty-one youngsters wanting to play football. Most were not very fast and not very strong. I had been a running back, but Gary Tom had also been a back in his youth. Who was going to coach the line? I wouldn't ask Gary to do it; I gave him the backs. So it fell to me. I decided to go with my instincts, go it alone and not phone linemen or line coaches I knew.

I seriously doubted that we could achieve much our first season with so little time to build bodies. There was only one goal in my mind: Start working from day one and for the next twelve weeks get stronger, faster and smarter and come together as a team. I knew nothing about the competition. I only knew that the past losses had been lopsided: 50-0, 60-0. The rumor about the team having won only one game in the previous four years turned out to be true. (It was confirmed by a writer from the The Arizona Republic.)

That first year I relied on Dan Crawford, Gary Tom, Father Holly (the principal of the high school) and my wife. I mention Dorci because she filmed our games, home and away, sometimes as far as 200-miles away, even though Beth and Matt were three and one respectively. The film was vital because I had to study it every evening and weekend to decipher blocking schemes for the linemen. All of my life, I had run and caught the ball; and, thus, I knew everything necessary to coach backs. And now, although the responsibility to teach the line challenged me, I knew I could prepare them for their duties. My confidence stemmed from the pole vault. Without knowing anything about it initially, I had developed record-breaking vaulters in Belleville.

* * *

My best "friends" in the equipment department as a line coach were the seven-man sled and a whistle. These two "friends" developed cohesion, attentiveness, body strength, timing and a sense of cooperation. I am amazed to this day that these young men were willing to push that piece of metal all over the field, day after day. I purposely used it for many of our practices. I discovered that the sled was considerably safer than scrimmages or other contact drills which I had experienced as a player in college. Most of my football injuries had occurred during practices, the result of a helmet hitting me in a vulnerable area. We could ill afford injuries with only twenty-one bodies available, especially since some were just there to take up space. Some would probably never play in a game, but we needed bodies for practice. With twenty-one boys, we couldn't even field two complete teams for scrimmage since that requires eleven boys on each side.

Angelo Listo and Earl Francisco had good size and gradually developed strength through weight lifting during the winter months after the first season. Dave Miguel, of average size, started getting stronger. Our smallest guard, Phil Lewis (130 pounds) was very bright. I had these and most of the boys in English III for their junior year. Phil amazed me with his command of the written word. His intelligence helped him immensely as an offensive guard. Can you imagine a lineman his size going up against a 190-pound opponent?

Gilbert and Gary Two Two were brothers who played basketball. They were in pretty decent shape, albeit thin as rails; but they lacked speed. Gilbert Two Two had good hands as an end. Roger Antone, a senior, played fullback in the "I" formation in front of Timmy Siquieros our tailback. Alan Antone was tall, lean and quite strong. Not a "natural" running back, I still used him in the backfield and any place else, sometimes at defensive end. Kenny Antone was a small back with a fluid running style. He almost broke a few kick returns for touchdowns and started in the slot position because he could catch a short pass and gain yardage. Neil Miguel, about the same size as Phil Lewis, (130 pounds) was our quarterback. Neil was also bright and physically talented. He handled the ball smoothly and moved gracefully while playing his position.

Max Chavez was a senior who played defensive end. He was intelligent with an amiable personality that made him stand out from the other boys, more outgoing and talkative. Because the girl he was dating became our babysitter, I developed a personal relationship with him off the football field, one that lasts even to the present. When he graduated, even though he was fifteen years younger than I, I saw him as a peer. Max had foresight and maturity.

His out-going personality separated him from the reserved nature of most of the Papago. He smiled a lot and had a genuine appreciation of opportunities that were available to him. Not that there were many.

* * *

In that first season, conditioning was crucial for two reasons. First of all, many of the boys played both ways, offense and defense, and needed the stamina to do so effectively. Secondly, losing had become a tradition which had to be overcome. The team would initially play well but quickly tire because the boys covered both offensive and defensive positions. Tired and discouraged because they couldn't maintain a competitive pace, they would lose heart. The result—scores like 50-0. Every day at the end of practice, I reminded the boys of their plight. I told them that their losing tradition resulted from their lack of stamina.

After practice they ran wind sprints and did push-ups in between the sprints. Some of the bigger linemen had a terrible time. I thought they would give up. Angelo and Earl, both juniors, really nice boys with not a trace of arrogance, were our two biggest linemen, fairly tall and thick but with little muscle. I knew they would be needed the following year, but I had to risk pushing them that first year. Hell, at times when they were trying to run, their pace was no faster than a brisk walk. But they kept trying.

Their push-ups were actually funny. When I coached the pole vaulters in Illinois, some of them could walk across the gym floor on their hands, then do sixty push-ups easily. These poor boys didn't know the correct form for doing a push up. They would arch their backs and sort of wiggle their way up into the correct position. They begged for leniency, heaved and gasped for air, and continually looked in my direction for a sign that we were finished for the day. But, they had tenacity. I always talked to them while they were working their butts off. Sometimes, I chided them with my words and sometimes I stroked them.

I taught them techniques, everything I knew about blocking and shedding blocks. At thirty-two, I was in excellent shape and often demonstrated how to use the arms on defense and keep the feet moving, especially on end-runs where staying upright was so important. On offense we worked incessantly on timing. On defense, even though I was in charge of the line, I made sure defensive backs knew when to come up fast to stop the run and where to cover during passing plays.

I was adamant about reducing penalties, primarily those resulting from "false starts." When any player on the offensive line moves in any way prior to the snap of the ball, the penalty "false start" costs the team five yards. I didn't want to lose that yardage. We weren't good enough to overcome mistakes like that. The boys fought hard to gain each yard. Any penalties could destroy their momentum. After the first game, I decided that for the rest of the season, the ball would be snapped on the first sound after the word "set." Even into the second season, we continued with that strategy.

* * *

None of the boys could kick. One of my favorite things to do as coach before practice officially began was to have some of the players kick field goals for about fifteen minutes. We also worked on passing then, before practice started. All twenty-one of the boys would be on the field, but this was informal time when we'd have fun and just do whatever the boys wanted. I'd kick field goals and then ask if any of them wanted to kick. It looked like fun so several wanted to try it.

Leroy Antone had a size 17 "lead" foot. A good, husky fellow, he had some feet on him! That's what people saw when they first looked at him— his feet and wild hair. When Leroy started kicking balls, I saw considerable force in his leg. He began to practice willingly, kicking incessantly. In that first season we were to score few touchdowns. Leroy didn't have an opportunity to show off his potent foot. But, in the following year, he was automatic at scoring extra points. I still remember his kicking a 35-yard field goal in one game; it was a thing of beauty.

Today in high school, it's nothing for the kicker to boot field goals. Many are soccer players with great legs. But picture Sells, Arizona, where football was almost non-existent. Here was Leroy, prancing onto the field and booming a 35-yard field goal with lots of room to spare. It may have been a 50-yard goal. That was one of the intangible rewards of coaching: being around young men who developed an intensity to excel, who developed skill that enabled them to succeed and experience pride in their achievement.

* * *

Remember my friend the sled? Every day I stood on it with seven players lined up. I'd yell, "Set." They would wait and then I blew the whistle abruptly. I used the whistle instead of "hut" because talking across the field during wind sprints made me hoarse. The boys would explode with power and enthusiasm. At first in the early season practices, they made a dysfunctional attempt to move it. But watching the boys on the sled proved fascinating. They improved from disjointed motions to spontaneous unity.

We diversified extensively on that sled. Sometimes the players were challenged to pop it with their right shoulders at the sound of the whistle, immediately get back into a three point stance and pop it again on the next whistle until five perfect pops had occurred in unison. "Popping" the sled actually refers to the sound of the seven boys hitting the sled together and the thrust of that contact which moved the sled. Then they used their left shoulders. Sometimes, after the first whistle, the players drove the sled some two to four yards before I sounded it again. Then all of the players would roll right one slot and be ready to repeat the drill. The player on the far right rolled off the sled and a new player filled the vacated spot on the left end.

In 1972 when the players hit the sled, it merely jostled. As hard as they tried, they barely moved it. By the middle of the next season, standing on the sled became exhilarating. Being on that sled when the boys pushed it all over the field was as thrilling as any ride in an amusement park. The bigger boys could really pop it, and I think they actually plotted to knock me off the sled and run me over!

* * *

Going on the first sound after "set" became a source of pride. We were, in so many words, telling our opponent, "Here we come—first sound!" This technique worked well in our second year because all of the players had one full year of working with weights and getting stronger. No doubt existed in anyone's mind: "Set" meant explode on the next sound; hit the man assigned to you.

When the boys became more confident with this system, I decided they were disciplined enough to try something else. It would become a play we might use just once in a game. We called it the "Penalty Play"; no fancy numbers for this strategy. We would use it in the second half of a game when we needed up to four yards to make a crucial first down. Instead of the usual explosive movement after "Set; hut," we practiced staying still. Nobody moved a muscle; each player stayed frozen in one spot after the quarterback yelled, "Set; hut." We actually didn't even have a play to run, for we hoped to draw the other team off sides. It worked beautifully. The other team's defensive linemen, conditioned to our "Set; hut" during the first half, would lunge forward. They'd make contact with one of our offensive men. The referees would call a five-yard penalty, and we'd have our first down.

If the Penalty Play didn't result in an off sides call, our intention was to signal for a time-out. It was a fun strategy. The boys loved it because it was successful so many times. Probably, previous to 1973, Baboquivari had not been scouted by opponents. Why should they be when they would lose 50-0? But during our second season, the other teams paid more attention to us. They became aware that our linemen moved on the first sound after "set." But they also knew that once in a while, we didn't. If that created doubt in the minds of the opposition, then Baboquivari had just developed an offensive weapon.

One particular time, I remember that the Penalty Play failed in reverse. In the first season, before the play had been "drilled" into the head of each lineman, we needed a crucial down of only a few yards in one game. I called for the Penalty Play. The quarterback yelled, "Set; hut." The ball was not snapped but a Baboquivari lineman surged forward. Flags were thrown. We were assessed a five yard penalty for a false start. I was totally frustrated that one of our guys had moved. Remaining still had been stressed repeatedly.

Our team members teased the lineman after the game. But they did so in a gentle way. Although these boys wanted to beat our opponents and worked hard to play well, by their very nature they were not all-out competitors. Even if the lineman's mistake could cost us the game, they would not deride him. Tease him, yes, but without malice. Joke about his moving, yes, but without spite. Remind him of it later, yes, but without rancor. They would not become angry or burden him with blame. This trait, this lack of anger in these Papago boys, was one of the many rewards I enjoyed while coaching them. They were much more forgiving than the white culture; less arrogant. They did, however, resolve that no lineman would ever move on the Penalty Play again.

* * *

That first year was the most tormented of my life. I had never faced a situation that looked so bleak. I threw my heart and soul into coaching, and yet our football team lost the first game and went on to lose every other game until the very last one, a meaningless competition which we barely won. A few inspiring episodes and the fortitude of some of the boys could not counter the effect of the losing tradition, the blowout losses and the arrogant opponents. I knew in August that this would be a season of roller-coaster emotions and events, but it surpassed my expectations.

One of the strangest moments of my whole coaching career occurred at Baboquivari in that first year. Our third game was against Thatcher. We were losing; but in the second half of the game, the Baboquivari boys started moving the ball. The momentum of the game began to change. The boys got fired up. I saw real teamwork. We scored several touchdowns but ran out of time to win. It became our third loss, 33 – 26, but the boys were in a good mood because of their rallying effort. As we were leaving the premises for the 170-mile ride home, a spontaneous outpouring of emotion erupted on the bus. The boys got louder and louder as they saw opposing fans and players. It was a burst of pride from these young men who had been doormats for so many teams. That night, they were not pushovers. They were demonstrating pride in their efforts.

This noise was like the sound you hear at an NFL game when the opposing fans keep a sustained level of cheering right before the visiting team's snap of the ball. There's no profanity, just pure emotion. We had lost, but we had executed plays well. Towards the end of the game, we had actually believed we could win, given a little more time. As we left the Thatcher school parking lot, the noise level was exhilarating for its spontaneity and volume. Their excitement after a loss made me think to myself, "The boys are coming to life!"

However, the fifth game of the season came within a nanosecond of destroying my confidence as a coach. Our opponent was winning and running up the score. Physically, the players were humiliating us and taking cheap shots with no fear of the penalties. We endured painful injuries. My boys limped off the field. Throughout the fourth quarter, the opposing team celebrated with a carnival attitude along the sidelines, with self-glorification and obnoxious behavior.

Years after that game, I read an editorial by Dan O'Neill in the St. Louis Post Dispatch about un-sportsman-like behavior. He described the self-indulgence which disrespects not only the opposing team but also shows no respect for the game, whatever the game may be. He could have used that fifth game as a good example of his topic.

In this particular game, at halftime, we were in total disarray. Players and coaches used to losing this way will just shrug their shoulders. However, nonchalance went against my nature at the age of 32. Distress overcame me and I could not talk to the team at halftime. Having witnessed the debacle of the first half, the only thing I wanted to do was cry. I asked Gary Tom to speak to the team in the locker room. I went outside and wept. It was nighttime and I found a dark corner where I cried hard. When the second half started, I was able to get through the game without bursting a blood vessel or going into cardiac arrest.

I honestly believe the boys knew how emotionally tied I was to them. They knew I internalized their success or failure. My inability to communicate to them at halftime indicated how committed I was to them. My assessment in August had been right on. We were in for a long, difficult season, especially against conference teams.

I coupled my distress with resentment for other teams and coaches. I'm not proud of the attitude and feelings I had for those outside our community. I did not like opposing coaches. I did not like officials. I loved the twenty-one football players on our team, my wife and two children. Whenever I saw an opposing coach in his coaching attire—the school-colored jacket and matching hat, whatever—I disliked him even more. You see, when the opposing team is beating the brains out of your team or about to do so, how can an ordinary human being accept that debasement with grace? Hell, I'd be close to sainthood if I could deal with it correctly. My competitive fire made me care too much and behave badly. I was neurotic; but, then, aren't we all, a little. Well, not my wife. Dorci is not neurotic.

The beating we took in the fifth game was difficult to swallow. In the third game we had played hard and were especially proud of rallying in the fourth quarter, playing competitively. We could build on our effort in that game. But then the 45-0 loss in the fifth game caught me off guard. The rest of the weekend consisted of my studying film, hour after hour, trying to discover a flaw in the coaching aspect of the game. I concluded that physically we were still badly out-manned against some teams. Also, the boys still hadn't escaped the burden of their losing record; they needed an emotional boost.

Therein lay the dilemma. If I worked them too hard to improve their strength and skills, I might lose them. Somehow, gradual improvement had to come from my short talks with them and my honest evaluation of where we stood as a team competitively. Dedication to each other during the grueling wind sprints and push-ups after most practices might build pride.

I admit that, at times, anger filled my thoughts. Why did the school even have a football team when most of the athletes were in such pathetic condition? Did the community even care about their football team? Hell, all season long, I had to fight for small things other schools took for granted—like having clean towels for the boys.

Some of the players were good athletes. They became the leaders during the worst of times. Because of their attitude, I pushed and pushed the team, always explaining my feelings and letting them know why we had to work the way we did. Whenever an out-of-shape player showed signs of giving up, my first thought was, "If you were in any kind of decent shape, you wouldn't be so sick and fatigued."

That kind of thinking can be poison. Players can sense arrogance and indifference to their pain. There's no credibility with that kind of coach. Credibility comes when players know the coach is committed to them and their success and has the sensitivity to understand what they are going through. When players and coach feel the disappointments and experience the difficulties together, cohesion and camaraderie result.

Coaches have to balance their empathy for their players with the demands of conditioning. Two years previous to moving to Sells, I had spent five years as a pole vault coach and developed a program, which, after the first two years, almost ran by itself. This first year in Sells was a hurry-up, do-or-die situation. If we did not get better quickly, the other teams would continue stomping us physically and running up the score. In a boxing match, the referee will stop a fight when one fighter is in danger of harm. In football, the game is rarely stopped to protect players from injury.

That has always been my major complaint of football officials during a blowout in high school football games. If a player on a dominating team takes a cheap shot at a player on the losing team, the officials should kick him out like they do in soccer. As a high school student, I called those players "punks." They are often mean-spirited individuals who get pleasure out of punching any defenseless person. Why allow a player to inflict more pain on a team suffering a humiliating defeat?

Some of the skill players, Timmy Siquieros, Gilbert Two Two, Kenny Antone, and Neil Miguel, had speed and good hands. However, backs and receivers need the support of the rest of the team. They can do very little when eleven opposing players are bent on stopping them, smashing them, whatever. No fault exists. Simply put, some teams have no business playing against other teams that are far superior.

* * *

Our next game came against Benson at home. Somehow we picked ourselves up off the ground. Maybe we were looking to redeem our previous performance. Benson was good. Baboquivari managed to keep the game reasonably close. While our boys competed, Gary Tom and I harped at the officials from the sidelines. In no mood to see our guys defenseless on the field again, I felt a responsibility to challenge the officials.

In the third quarter, a play occurred which we contested. Gary Tom went on to the field to complain about the call. During the exchange, he threatened the official. Gary was ejected from the game. We were assessed

45-yards in penalties for a myriad of reasons. I was incensed over the penalties called against us and those not called on the other team.

By the fourth quarter, we were losing, 15-0. The boys were competing reasonably well, playing hard. One of Benson's ball carriers broke loose and was running in the open field for a considerable gain. Then I saw a nasty clip on one of my boys who was pursuing the Benson player. No flag was thrown. That set me off.

I charged on to the field and yelled at an official, "Call the damn penalty!" There is a rule against coaches doing that—charging on to the field. My competitive juices were in full flow. I was so irate that the official threw a penalty flag on me; and when he did, I went further onto the field to give him more lip. Smart coach, huh?

The scene came to a head when the official threw his hat on the ground. I'm not sure why he did that. Maybe he was assessing another 15-yard penalty. I have no idea. My first thoughts were, "Screw your officiating, screw your penalties, screw this game, and screw your hat!" With that last thought, I kicked the hat as hard as I could. Remember now, I could kick a 50-yard field goal. I kicked his hat twice and then threw it at him.

That was my final act of disobedience because the officials called the game. We forfeited to Benson right then and there. The officials asked for a police escort off the reservations saying that they felt threatened. Not by me—I had only manhandled a hat!

No Arizona newspaper had bothered to write anything of significance about our team previous to this game. Certainly our name had not appeared in any headline. The next day, The Arizona Daily Star printed its first article about Baboquivari football. It was entitled, "Coach's Hysterics Cause Baboquivari to Forfeit." (See Appendix #2) My "fifteen minutes of fame" in Arizona focused on my "hysterics."

You know, I still don't remember if I was embarrassed by what had occurred. I know I was really pissed and down in the dumps at the same time. We had made great progress from the previous week's game; and when I saw one of my players go flying and landing hard, awkwardly, on the clip, I just did what any parent would do for his child. Only, these boys weren't my children. But the team knew I empathized with them and would do all I could to back them.

In college in a pileup, I had had players scratch me. I'd been bitten; I'd had my testicles squeezed; but I had never really become too upset. I would forget about it when the next play was called. I had concluded that the players who did those things were just lowlifes. I planned to dish out any payback against them in the next play. But as a coach, the situation was totally different. I couldn't release any anger by ramming my helmet into an opposing player after the ball was snapped. So rage took control of me.

I remember that a week later, as we were on the bus returning home from our seventh loss, I was sitting next to Bennie Conde. He was a senior, short, skinny, bowlegged, had a huge Afro and weighed maybe 125 pounds. He was bright and I enjoyed talking to him. I was telling him how lousy I felt about the season, especially last week's forfeit. I'll never forget what he said on that ride home. "You know, Coach, before you came, nothing different or exciting or interesting ever happened on the reservation. You have changed that. I thought what happened last week was great!"

A few years after I left Sells, Max Chavez told me that Bennie had died. I was traveling in Iowa at the time, a salesman, and I felt like I'd lost a son. More crying by myself in a motel. I'd only known him for his senior year, but I saw his willingness to perform; with so little size and weight he would throw his body into much larger opponents. And his conversations on the bus rides were so pleasant.

* * *

As the evening wore on after the forfeit, my emotions went numb. Dan Crawford sensed my weakness. He was wise enough to suggest that his family and my family get in our vehicles and drive down to Rocky Point in Mexico the next morning. Normally, Dan did not make a habit of telling me what to do. Remember, I was the head coach; he, the assistant. But he handled the situation beautifully by saying, "Let's get the hell away from here. It'll do you some good."

Bright and early that October Saturday morning, both families drove to Rocky Point, Dorci's and my first trip there. We camped on the beach; the weather was perfect; we had our children. Who cared about the mess back in Sells? We didn't return home until late Sunday evening. What a Godsend that trip was. No phones, no football, no film to study, just family, friends and ocean.

Dan had the wisdom to know this. It has been one of the things that I admire about him. Almost from day one of our moving to Sells, he seemed able to read me and sense my motives and needs. His insights in Sells in 1972 and even today are still right on.

Had we not gone to Rocky Point the very next morning, who knows what state of mind I would have been in? Dan, his wife Lori, Dorci and our kids were the support group I needed. Makes me wonder about people who have no friends or family for support. How do they make it through hard times?

* * *

On Monday I received the bad news: My principal (Father Holly), the superintendent and I were told we had to go to Tucson for a meeting with the officials. Someone in the Arizona high school athletic association conducted the meeting. I knew I was wrong and apologized. I expressed my feelings honestly, about being debased by other teams. The committee told me I'd be "Out" if anything like that happened again. By "anything" they meant any small infraction. They were going to keep a sharp eye on me.

To my surprise, the official whose hat I had kicked complimented me on the improved play of Baboquivari. That meant so much to me because it came from someone in the trenches. Seeing him in his "civilian" clothes put him in a different light in my eyes. I saw a working man, like myself. Had he appeared in his striped shirt at that meeting, who knows what stupid thing I might have said or done. His compliment of the team's improved competitiveness made me realize how immature my behavior during the game had been. I had been a jerk. Nothing close to that episode occurred the rest of that season or the following year. I still had distaste for opposing coaches, but was able to restrain myself.

* * *

Sometimes I reflect on that first season and wonder how each incident, each game contributed to the second year. Were the seeds of the second season sown at the Thatcher game with the boys' spontaneous noisy outburst of pride in the possibility of winning? Were they sown the night of the forfeit or the night I couldn't face them at halftime because my emotions were spent? Maybe the first season was a process. I was always honest with them, brutally so at times.

Some coaches are meticulous in their methods. They have everything mapped out: where, when, how, etc. I, on the other hand, made decisions almost day by day and at times by the moment regarding what we would do and how we would do it. For example, when the forecast predicted inclement weather for a home game, after the rest of the team concluded practice, I had the quarterback, center and running backs stay. They worked in the rain handling the ball. At a feverish pace they snapped and handled the ball as many times as they could in the wet conditions. They were good sports, knowing instinctively that what they were doing made sense.

I read a newspaper article about Missouri coach Gary Pinkel and what he experienced during his first seven years as the University of Missouri's head coach. I concluded that those years were part of a process and that process resulted in the program's ascent to a top-five ranking in the country. He had a plan which had succeeded in the past, and he believed in that plan. Seven years later, Missouri was playing championship football, the kind of play which had been missing for over thirty years. His personality sparked love and loyalty. That's hard to beat. There are other ways to win in sports, such as outspending your opponents, but Coach Pinkel's way, to me, is the most admirable.

In that first year, 1972, we lost our first eight games with scores that ranged from 15-0 to 45-0. The number of hours I put in after teaching five classes cannot be counted. The coaches and team suffered countless aggravations. The players were without towels frequently after practice. On one Friday afternoon, we were waiting in front of the school for the bus for a game some 200-miles away. No bus showed up. One of the players indicated that the driver was probably home, hung over, and I needed to wake him up. Sure enough, I found him as the player described. Knowing our lives would be in his hands that evening, I kept my cool. I actually drove a bus home from one game; why, I cannot remember. At one away game, we were locked out of the visiting team's locker room at halftime. In my usual mild manner, I just kicked in the door.

* * *

My "mild manner" was not limited to circumstances related to the football team. We, my family, lived in a complex of attached houses for teachers. It was some 200-yards from the high school. Since Dorci and our two children were so close, I would walk home for lunch each day. On one occasion as I was returning to school, I heard noises coming from a neighbor's camper, parked outside the back fence. I suspected that a crime was being committed. "John, you're paranoid," my wife has said many times.

Well, a crime was being committed, typical high school "crime": students smoking pot. I knocked on the door, and my neighbor's thirteen-year-old son, an Anglo, opened it. I saw several older kids, Papago, inside and yelled at them to get out. Realizing that they were almost in my backyard, I lost it. I grabbed the boy who looked like the oldest and virtually carried him to the principal's office. He resisted the whole way. Luckily, I was stronger; otherwise we would have ended up in a fistfight. Some students saw me man-handling him and yelled racial epithets and remarks about abuse.

When it was all over, everybody knew why I had reacted that way. I'm sure many didn't appreciate my physically taking the student to the Principal, but I needed to demonstrate my commitment to kids who were straight or trying to be straight. I would not allow anyone to use any illicit drugs right next to my home—not while I was alive. This episode and the other incidents drained me emotionally. But what would eventually get the best of me was my ill health.

* * *

The last game of that first season was at home against Fort Grant, a fairly weak team. In fact, according to an article in a Phoenix paper a year later, Fort Grant dropped interscholastic competitions the year after we played them. In the week before the game, after coughing hard for days, I went to the BIA (Bureau of Indian Affairs) hospital in Sells. The doctor said I had a cold. Well, it wasn't a cold as I later found out; I had pneumonia. The last game was pure torture. I felt so horrible with a high fever that I can only remember one play.

We were ahead and were driving for another score. Obviously my feverish mind was in total disarray because I called a screen pass to the left. Baboquivari was about twenty yards from another touchdown, and Fort Grant wasn't really hitting very hard. The last play a coach should call with a weak defense is a screen pass. The boys executed the play the way it was drawn up but there was one problem. Fort Grant's right defensive end gave little effort to rush our quarterback when he dropped back to pass. The end looked like he was lethargic, just standing around waiting for the game to end rather than rushing the passer. Later, on the film, I saw our quarterback finally throw the ball to the left to our back. The lethargic end, a rather tall boy, stood directly in the path of the screen pass. On impulse, with the ball headed toward him, he awoke from this lethargy, stuck his hand up, deflected the pass into his arms and took off running down the sideline. I can't remember if he scored, just that he ran a long way.

I almost lost the game with that play, a decision made in the delirium of pain. I vaguely remember Dan and Gary giving me a strange look when I called that screen pass. No doubt they knew we could score with just basic hard-hitting football instead of a pass.

That's all I remember of the only game we won that first year. Dorci and the kids savored the victory at a small party at Dan's house. The players, the school community and the whole town reveled in the win. But, as exciting as winning was, it was a meaningless victory to me.

I went home and straight to bed where I stayed for the rest of the weekend. The following Wednesday, after incessant coughing at work for two days, I drove to Tucson to the University of Arizona Medical Center to see a pulmonary specialist. The doctor told me I had atypical pneumonia and gave me a prescription.

While at the hospital, I decided to show him my left foot which had recently turned purple. I told him my story:

"Way back in September a small red spot by my little toe got so itchy I couldn't stand it anymore. I regularly use Desenex on my feet to keep my athlete's foot at bay, but it wasn't helping on that spot. I had even cut a hole in my shoe, for air to circulate, knowing athlete's foot thrives in warm, moist areas. I decided to try various other over-the-counter remedies. I bought Absorbeen Jr. and used it for about a week. When it didn't work, I bought Tinactin which was supposed to be the 'cure-all.' That spot continued to itch. It was driving me nuts."

In typical John-Leara-fashion, I was desperate to try anything but also very impatient. That impatience is a life-long trait. Just ask Dorci how many different vitamins, to use just one example, sit unused in our kitchen cabinet. I hear an ad or someone recommends a vitamin for memory or pain relief and I tell her to buy it. After three weeks, when the pill hasn't achieved anything, I stop taking it. Dorci repeatedly tells me to continue with the vitamin for two to three months since most require that long to affect a change in a person's system. I can't wait that long.

Ironically, there's a flip side to this impatience. I am very methodical and patient when it comes to finding the best value for a possible purchase. I'll save newspaper ads on automobile tires for a year knowing I have about 10,000 miles left on my current set. Or, I'll keep automobile ads. I can easily accumulate a paper grocery bag full, although Dorci is the one to bag them. I just let them pile up in a corner somewhere. Do I care that at the time of purchase the advertisements might be up to twelve months old? The prices are a point of reference from which I hope to negotiate. My family and friends are familiar with this practice of mine and sometimes call on me to help them find the best value. But, I have no tolerance for pills, creams or other products that don't work within a couple of weeks' time. Thus, I searched for relief from the red spot itching but kept switching treatments

I continued recounting to the doctor the saga of my foot:

"Being impatient, I asked my friends for ideas. One of the Papago suggested using a natural solution. My wife went into the desert field by our home and picked greasewood branches. She boiled the leaves and I soaked my foot in that water once a day for about four days. I had no relief.

"Another friend had suggested soaking in a solution of water and bleach. After doing that a couple times, my foot erupted, turning purple."

The doctor had listened intently to my story which appeared to entertain him. He looked at me. He looked at my foot. He called in several other doctors to see my foot. He told them my story. Hardly able to contain himself, the doctor said, "Well, Mr. Leara, what we have here is a classic case of over-treatment." Then he and his colleagues broke out laughing.

He told me I needed daily treatment for my foot. I had burned the skin. The dead skin would have to be removed piece by piece. He suggested I have this done at the BIA hospital. And, that's what I did. With pliers in hand, the doctor in Sells pulled the skin off, a little at a time according to what had pealed most. The pain was excruciating. The treatment sent my skin into trauma. I broke out in hives all over my body and had to get another prescription.

My foot smelled like dead meat. Hell, it was dead meat and I had been the one who killed it. Dorci made me sleep in one of the kids' rooms while they slept together. I ate in the living room while they ate in the kitchen. Then I sat in the kitchen to watch the TV in the living room. So, not only was I suffering from pneumonia, I had a rotten foot and my family deserted me—for about five days until the dead meat smell dissipated.

The doctor said that soaking it in a peroxide solution would facilitate the healing. My foot mended slowly. But, heal it did, eventually. And it did return to normal, normal being its original condition, little red spot and all, right there where it had been before I began my self-treatment many months ago! And, to this day that spot itches, but I have learned better than to attempt any more home remedies.

As for the pneumonia, I suffered until sometime in March. Without antibiotics for the first five days, my lungs were set up for bronchitis for the next three years. I coughed up phlegm for over two months. In December and January, Dorci taught my three English classes in the mornings, and I would go to school for my two afternoon PE classes. I was slow to heal. The eight losses topped off by a dead-meat-foot and pneumonia took a huge toll on me.

* * *

One difficulty doctors had in arriving at a diagnosis for my respiratory problems arose from my temperature. Unaware that my normal temperature is 97.2, I was unconcerned when, each evening, the thermometer read 99.4 or 99.5. I actually had a fever of more than two degrees. My chest hurt like hell every day for many months. Earlier in the school year I had had a positive reading for Valley Fever, which is indigenous to the Southwest and is like tuberculosis. I'm sure that set me up for respiratory problems.

My immune system remained weak for many years. When we returned to the St. Louis area a year later, there was, amazingly, a bright side to my frequent infections: my doctor Melvin Goldman. He really knew his patients and treated each person according to that understanding. I could phone him while traveling out of state, describe my symptoms, and he'd get me on antibiotics. Always a gentleman with my wife, with me he was a bit bawdier. Like the time I questioned him during a rectal exam and Dr. Goldman said, "What d'ya think? I'm gonna do a half-assed job?" He looked at me in 1975 with my muscular physique and gave me hell for allowing stress to get the jump on me. He gave me a steroid shot because I was run down and told me to appreciate my beautiful wife. He said, "Screw as often as you can. It's good for you." I loved the man. He was "old school." Then there was the time I had a bad sinus infection. He darkened the room so as to shine a light up my nose. When I tilted my head back, the tickle I felt was unstoppable. I let out a large, wet sneeze right in his face. In his typical no-nonsense manner as he headed for the sink to wash his face, he said, "Oh, for Christ's sakes! Four years in college, four years in medical school and this is what I get!"

* * *

During Christmas break in 1972, Dorci, Beth and Matt and I took a short trip to Las Vegas, just six and a half hours away. We had signed up for a land promotion presentation in return for two nights at a hotel on the strip and free tickets to the "Folies Bergere." We asked Max Chavez and his girlfriend Sylvia to accompany us. Max, a senior, seemed more like a peer to me once football season had ended and we were no longer coach/player. Sylvia had babysat the kids a couple times and the plan was that she and Max would watch them when we went to see the show.

The trip to Vegas was my first and Dorci's second. When we arrived, the lights overwhelmed me. I stood in awe of them and the splendor of the new motel with its fancy décor. I was surrounded by glitz and glamor and, I assumed, a lot of wealthy people. I could not feel comfortable in this kind of environment. These feelings were repeated one summer some twenty years later when we took our daughters to a 5-Star restaurant.

That summer in 1992, Dorci and I drew up a list of things to do with the kids. One of those things was to take the girls to a fancy restaurant. (I can't remember where Matt was at the time.) We researched to find a 5-Star restaurant but had to settle on a 4-Star that had previously been ranked higher and was known to be quite swanky. Our table was served by five waiters, all wearing white gloves. They pulled out our chairs, placed our napkins on our laps and catered to our every whim. Dorci and I agreed

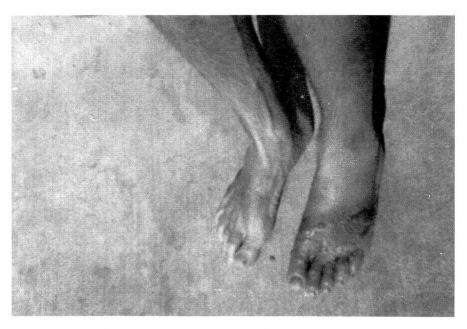

"Let's try seven ways to get rid of athlete's foot!"

Max & Josie Chavez

later that evening that we weren't comfortable with all that attention; it made us feel like we had to be on our best behavior to impress the waiters. What a way to feel in a restaurant!

Well, here I was in Vegas, having driven up to the door of a gorgeous hotel on the strip in our "Plain-Jane" Chevy Cargo Van that didn't even have air conditioning. Unloading only added to my embarrassment. We pulled out assorted suitcases, a crib, our own pillows (motel pillows are always too fat), a cooler. Dorci held Matt, and Beth toddled on her own, carrying some favorite stuffed animal. I thought we must look as conspicuous as the Beverly Hillbillies. The only thing missing was a yelping dog.

Then, to make matters worse, Max pulled out a humongous duffle bag. It looked like a World War II remnant. It must have been five and a half feet long. I said, "What the hell, Max. Did you bring all of your belongings? Couldn't you find a suitcase?" Max looked at me. Then he looked at Dorci who was beginning to giggle. Max cracked a smile and then they both started laughing. They were laughing at me, seeing my distress over our appearance. And, they were laughing at our appearance, knowing we did, indeed, look like we'd come right from the backwoods—or rather, right off the reservation.

When we'd left Sells for Vegas, I was still running a two degree fever in the evenings from pneumonia. Once in Vegas, it did not subside but increased, as did my coughing. We did not go to the show but spent the evening in our room. The next day I saw a doctor who gave me a shot of antibiotics in my rear end and a prescription for more antibiotic pills. The fondest memories that remain of our Vegas trip revolve around our arrival at the hotel and unpacking our van.

* * *

For the rest of that first school year, the only real positive for me was the bodybuilding that the players, especially the linemen, elected to do. Beginning in January with the new semester, the team began working on the weight machines. The boys were enthusiastic through June, doing everything I asked.

Then, at the end of that school year, when grades were due, a dilemma confronted me. I taught two hours of PE and several English classes. One of my football players was in my PE class, a really nice kid. I liked him a lot, but he would skip my class. He was very capable and not a troublemaker. Like many of the other students in 1973 on the reservation, he just didn't want to go to school. I decided that I had to fail him, even though he was an outstanding football player. I realized that everything I stood for as a teacher would go down the drain if I passed him. It would have been easy for me to give him a "D." But I failed him. That "F" turned out to be a big mistake that haunted me the next season.

* * *

That summer of 1973 our family took off in our van and traveled. I needed to get away. That previous school year, weekdays I had been on the football field until dark; weekends were spent studying film; in the spring I was recuperating from pneumonia. In June we went to Mexico, parked on an isolated beach. We saw dolphin and sting ray, and snorkeled while our kids floated in little inner tubes.

From there we drove all the way to the East Coast, stopping in St. Louis to visit family, my mother, sister and brother. On the East Coast in Massachusetts and Connecticut we visited a host of cousins, aunts and uncles. All were wonderful, so glad that we came, dishing out not only great food but old-world hospitality. We ate lots of *peta*, a standard dish of the immigrants from Korce, Albania. The summer travel was exactly what I needed before returning for the next season at Sells, a season that would be a mind-boggling experience.

CHAPTER 8

THE THRILL OF VICTORY; THE AGONY OF... STRESS

With the arrival of August and my family back in Sells, I was ready to start the second season. Practice began in the summer's heat before the opening of school. Most of the boys from the 1972 team were back. I was delighted to see their muscle tone. They actually had "muscle tone." They had continued to work out and were a much different group of athletes than they had been one year ago.

In addition, we had a few new faces. Just having additional bodies (remember we had only twenty-one last year) would give us more depth. We lost four boys to graduation and picked up seven. With twenty-four players we had enough bodies to field two teams for a scrimmage in practice.

That number included the PE student whom I had failed. Officially, with two failures, he was ineligible to play ball. But, I now thought like a coach. I really liked this boy. He was a talented football player and the hardest hitter on the line. He seemed to know football instinctively. So, I let him practice with the team. Even in 100 degrees he gave his all. I decided I couldn't let the team down and would play him.

(In my next twenty years of teaching, I was to learn that had I given him a "D," I would have been following an acceptable practice in education. There have always been principals who pressure teachers to pass students for one reason or another, sometimes for athletic teams. There are also principals who actually go into the teachers' grade books and change "F's" to "D's" so that students can graduate or move on to the next grade.)

The 1973 team was comprised of a good mix of athletes. The seniors were very strong physically. Many of the boys were very smart. Juniors were able to fill in vital areas so that just a few boys would have to play both ways, offense and defense. Although some of the linemen weighed in at only 128 to 140-pounds, they were intelligent, disciplined and skilled. Versatility was common for many of the boys who played several positions, especially on offense. The team boasted two different tailbacks, three different fullbacks and two different slot backs. I wanted lots of mixing and matching. The defensive line and linebackers were constant. From the beginning of the season, this team was much stronger than last year's. I wondered with great anticipation what difference this would make for the coming season.

During the first year, the seven-man sled taught the players to work together on timing, alertness, and quickness. In the second year, they were prepared to move the sled and effectively did so from week one. No learning this year; it was a tool for conditioning and cohesion.

My assistant coach that second year was a former pro basketball player, Pat Frink. In college and the NBA, running was the life-blood of basketball. He thought nothing of running ten to twenty sprints after practice. Because of this, he made the boys run harder and harder each week, and he would run with them. That took pressure off of me. I had pushed them so hard the first year; I felt unsure of how hard to push them now. Coaches have to know where the fine line is so as not to lose the players by demanding too much.

After several practices, one of my best ball players told me that he was going to quit. He didn't say why. I knew that many of the Indian boys lived with a variety of problems. Their homes were disheveled. Some lived in hogans. Many had no running water, no indoor plumbing. Families were unstable with single parents trying to keep the children together. Alcoholism and drug abuse were rampant on the reservation. I had no idea what this boy was experiencing.

I felt compelled to talk to him at his home. "____, think of all the effort you put into conditioning with the other boys. From January to June you worked with them. You are all much stronger." I went on to list and emphasize his talents and the team's need of his skills. "You will be a key factor if we are to be successful this year. The team really needs you." Something I said touched him, for he stayed with the program for all of the season. Some twenty years later, I received a letter from him telling me that I was the best coach he'd ever been around. His letter stated that the year he had played football was one of the most memorable of his life.

For this season, I adopted different philosophies for both the defensive and the offensive sides of the game. Defensively the players practiced to go like hell to get into the backfield; mayhem was our goal. If five guys could tackle the ball carrier, I would be deliriously happy. This approach tended to inspire the defense because a lot of the opponents could miss their blocks by not knowing what we were going to do. We wanted to knock the opponents for losses, not just hold them for minimal yard gains forcing punts. The boys were fired up with this new idea, seeing themselves pushing the opponents back. Emotion played an important role in our defense. This technique proved successful because of the talents of our two linebackers, one of whom, by the end of the season, had more tackles than any other player in the conference.

On the offensive side, efficiency and hard hitting were just as important as they were on defense, but a mental mistake could be disastrous. Our offensive strategy had little trickery except for the Penalty Play which we hoped to continue to use effectively. We wanted precision and execution in our passing, basic runs and reverses. If our blockers made mistakes, our quarterback could get slammed from the side or a running back take a brutal hit while taking a hand off. We could then suffer an injury or fumble the ball. Sustaining an effective offense would be hard if we incurred penalties or missed blocks, or stumbled, or committed any slew of other foibles. Timing was so important to the offense.

There was nothing sophisticated about this plan. It originated in a brain with a 112 IQ. I did not claim to possess any unique or masterful strategy. Usually, the smarter a coach, the better the team. But I knew my limitations. The philosophy reflected a simple approach. After all, I claim to be only an average man. We would work hard to strive for perfection of the simple tasks and mistake-free execution.

One day, five practices into our second season, Ollie Antone didn't attend and didn't notify anyone of his whereabouts. This became an opportunity to drive home a point. We would not succeed with less than total commitment. I would have to act for the sake of the whole team.

The next day was hot, as usual. When Ollie arrived on the field, I decided to discipline him. Everyone was in pads. I told him he had to meet each of the other players as they ran into him. He could not back off. I kept the distance between them short so as to avoid injury, remembering the dangerous drills I had experienced in high school.

After the last player hit him, he fell to the ground, saliva dripping from his mouth—but no blood—thoroughly humiliated and exhausted. I really felt sorry for him. I knelt down and looked him in the eyes. "Ollie, are you okay?" In anger, he shoved me.

I lost my balance and fell over. I went berserk. I looked at the whole team thinking, "Is there anyone out there who doubts my commitment and philosophy?" In the heat of the moment I said, "All right! I'll take on each one of you, just like Ollie did, here and now. I'll take you one at a time, here and now. Let's go!" I acted like a juvenile. I lost it. I don't know if it helped the season or not. It was a knee-jerk reaction for me, my typical "mild mannered" self.

During all of my coaching years, in the recesses of my mind lurked the "all-in" mentality, as in a poker game. Should I be challenged, I would throw the challenge right back at the athletes. Either they trusted and believed in me or they didn't. Here was one of those moments, and I willingly put our entire season in jeopardy. Either every boy would be in, or we wouldn't go forward because I had lost their commitment. It was a sort of "line-in-the-sand" moment: We wouldn't proceed half-assed. Fortunately, at this particular moment in Sells, Arizona, these 24 boys knew me and my emotions well enough—remember they had seen me kick open a door. They recognized the fleeting anger and did not accept my challenge. During the rest of the season, no one missed a practice without notifying me. Also, we never repeated my "one man against the rest of the players" scenario.

Ollie went on to become an outstanding defensive lineman that season, all 130 pounds of him! Sometimes Ollie played the monster position which meant he was a roving linebacker. He seemed to enjoy it because of the unpredictability of his actions. I gave him a lot of leeway on the scrimmage line. He could position himself behind the line, way off to the left or inside. Sometimes, if I thought the opponents were going to pass the ball, I'd send instructions to Ollie that he would be the pass defender against one of the receivers, or he should blitz the quarterback and try to flatten him. He rarely disappointed me.

One of the new boys this year was Paul Hendricks, a senior who had been ineligible the previous year. Paul, too, would become one of the key players during this season. He was the most talented athlete on our 1973 squad. His moves as a running back were instinctive, knowing when to cut back across the grain. He had good speed for both the short burst and the long run. He would float out to the left to catch a screen pass. When he received the short pass, he used his blockers, cutting to the right and then to the left, completing a 50-yard run into the end zone. He was beautiful to watch. He was also our best linebacker.

Paul was good natured, joked and liked to have fun. I wasn't sure how he felt about me then, but many years later in a letter he told me. I was shocked when I received it. That letter made it clear that he had nothing but good feelings about our short relationship. His comments and sentiments in that letter brought tears to my eyes.

One of my fondest memories of Paul and one of the funniest moments of my two years at Sells occurred on a bus trip. We were headed towards Tucson from Sells. I sat next to Paul. Nothing unusual about the ride, just the normal bumpy bus and undercurrent of boys talking.

Paul pointed out the window and said, "Hey, coach, look over there." I turned and looked out the window to our left. Paul had pointed to one of the many mountainous hills that were silhouetted by the waning daylight. All the boys on the bus stopped talking. Somehow they knew where this was going. Paul continued, "That's Carol's tit!" The temporary silence broke with a roar of laughter that erupted from all the boys. I saw that the mountain's peak contoured like a woman's breast. I knew Carol (not her real name), an employee at the high school, young and attractive. I couldn't help but laugh with them. Apparently that particular hill had been dubbed "Carol's Tit" by some imaginative boy.

We used this route many times, anytime we headed to Tucson. From then on, we all chuckled as we drove past that particular hill. As a group, the team and I, we had developed a good relationship.

More than any other player that second year, Timmy Siquieros had intensity. He loved football. The look in his eyes said, "Let's win, coach." As a tailback he ran with one thought: "Go as hard as I can even if I have to run headlong into a tackler." Desire was an important component of his success. An additional inspiration for Timmy came from his brother who had been a fine running back and took an interest in his little brother's performance.

I received letters from Timmy for quite a few years after I left Sells. Like many of the players, Timmy had his problems. The letters helped me. For a long time I maintained an emotional tie to the boys in Sells. Timmy's letters were upbeat. I was relieved to hear that he felt like he was improving his life.

Phil Lewis played as one of our offensive guards. He still weighed in at 135 pounds soaking wet. He was very quiet on the field, and I wasn't sure how he felt about me. Sometimes, I think he just put up with me, but he never missed a block in a game. Although not very strong, he got the job done efficiently with little bravado.

Morris Antone also played offensive guard and also was small like Phil Lewis. He blew my mind with his wit. I can still hear him saying, "Win one for the gipper." The context of his remark eludes my aging brain, but I distinctly remember laughing loudly with Pat Frink when he said it.

Our two good sized tackles were back as seniors—Angelo Listo—"the rock," and Earl Francisco—"the cat." Angelo was quiet and Earl was just the opposite. The first year I had hounded them because they had such good size but needed to develop their bodies. Anything but shy about complaining, Earl whined about being worked too hard. This year, finally in shape, he moved very quickly thus earning his nickname. Defensively he became effective at disrupting the opponents' offense. Angelo, on the other hand, was harder to read. He committed himself to doing his share as one of the anchors on the line. He played both offensive and defensive tackle, a challenging and fatiguing assignment. He didn't complain even when he was exhausted.

Calvin Wilson joined us this year. He filled the slot at center that Earl had played, thus giving Earl the rest he needed to play more effectively on defense. Calvin was broad, very broad and smart. He did the job; otherwise, I wouldn't have left him in there.

Dorci continued to film the games in the second season. I had to study them over and over because I still didn't have a lineman's brain. I didn't want to make mistakes. My linemen needed to be prepared as best they could be. I had to play and replay the film to find any mistakes we might avoid.

The film was developed seventy-two miles away in Tucson. One of the teachers would drop it off after the game on Friday night. Then, either I drove in to pick it up, or Dorci did if she were doing her bi-weekly grocery shopping. Thus Sundays found me studying the film before Monday practice.

* * *

We opened the season at home against Gila Bend on September 14. It was a hot, sweaty night. The boys were wound tight because it was our first game. We couldn't get on track offensively. Gila Bend scored a touchdown but failed to get the extra point. Finally, we scored a touchdown, and "Mr. Money," Leroy Antone with his size 17 shoe, kicked the extra point. His extra point gave us the lead.

The rest of the game was a "nail biter." The boys knew they were good and playing on a level above previous years. But knowing you're good doesn't automatically result in success. Our one point lead was tenuous.

In the last quarter of the game, the score still 7-6, we had the ball, and we were deep in our own territory. With the clock ticking down, we were afraid of any kind of miscue that would allow Gila Bend to score—a fumble, a safety, a penalty at the goal line. We were running the ball because that was safer than passing. However, Gila Bend's defense was doing a hell of a job at stopping our running game.

We managed to get a first down on our 20-yard line. However, if we couldn't get another first down in the next three plays, we'd have to punt the ball from close to our own goal line where any number of things could happen, most of them bad—a blocked punt, a bad snap, a poor punt, a fumble by the punter, a good return by Gila Bend. If any one of these occurred, we'd lose the game.

To run out the clock while maintaining possession of the ball, we needed one more first down. Gila Bend had called several time-outs after our plays, stretching out the final minutes, making the time seem interminable. Now they were out of time-outs. With so much at stake, I'm not ashamed to admit that I was afraid to pass. A dropped pass would stop the clock. On third down we had five yards to go on our own 25 with too much time left. At that point I decided on what might be construed a stupid play, should it fail.

The offense had 30-seconds to snap the ball once the referee signaled for the play clock to begin. I shuttled in a player who told Neil Miguel, our quarterback, to let the play clock run down and in the last second, call for a time-out. I signaled for Neil to come over. The play would be a run, but the formation should look like a pass. The linemen would step back as though they were going to defend Neil as he dropped straight back to pass. This would allow our line to move with the opponents' linemen and steer them to the outside just enough to open a hole in the middle for Neil to run through for a first down. Our players needed to call on all of the strength and skills they had developed in practice to force the defensive line to the outside. The receivers were to run down field, enforcing the illusion of a pass play. They might lure more defenders to follow them. However, the key to the success of this play fell to the line.

The ball was snapped. Our quarterback dropped back. The line stepped back. Our receivers ran down field. The defensive linemen charged after Neil. Our linemen moved like they had practiced this play a dozen times, opening a hole right in the middle. Neil's timing was perfect. The shortest distance between two points is a straight line, which is how to describe our quarterback's run. When Neil knew he had gained enough yardage for the first down, he went to the ground to avoid a tackle and possible fumble.

Two snaps later, the game ended. Our first game was a victory! We were starting our season with a win! In the ensuing celebration, my eye-glasses were trampled—a small price to pay for our success.

* * *

The first paychecks from the school district were processed shortly after that victorious game. I didn't receive a paycheck. I was told that the state would not allow me to be paid because I hadn't passed the test for the Arizona Constitution. Here I was into my second year of teaching and coaching, having spent the winter trying not to cough up bits and pieces of my lungs, working in good faith, and I wouldn't get paid. Any paychecks that I missed would be lost—as in "forever"!

My thoughts ran to the towels that were always missing for the boys after practices last year. That "screw-up" was a precursor for this. Someone had forgotten to tell me that I needed to pass the Arizona Constitution test while I "busted my ass" coaching and teaching. Passing that test was a requirement for teaching in Arizona; yet, no one had informed me of that stipulation. Apparently, I had been unqualified to teach during all of my first year, but they couldn't very well take that money back! So here I was, the only "breadwinner" for my family of four, plus one dog, facing the possibility of not getting paid.

My annual salary amounted to approximately $8000. What were we going to do without an income? I had already forfeited the first month's check. If I didn't pass the test soon, I'd miss the second paycheck. This was 1973, the year of the oil embargo. The cost of gasoline, after one waited in line for almost an hour, had sky-rocketed. Unless we wanted to increase our food expenses some 50% or more at the local store, we had to travel seventy miles for food and other needs. Dorci shopped every other week. The van had no air conditioning and the temperatures in August and September frequently reached 100 degrees. She'd load three large coolers and the two children into the van. One of our necessities included powdered milk since fresh mild wouldn't last the two weeks between grocery trips and all of us drank a lot of milk.

So, on top of trying to learn the intricacies of playing the line, blocking, and defensive positioning, I had to study for the Arizona Constitution. I had failed a course in high school and one in college because I had no interest in them. Was I interested in the constitution? No. But the motivation to get paid and to continue coaching became a top priority.

I studied for ten days and then Father Holly administered it. He showed me to a room, checked that I had no "cheat sheets," and left me alone. I was sweating. Four mouths to feed. Eight more games to play. Winning these games required a lack of distractions on my part. When I finished the test, I hadn't the slightest idea if I had passed or not. Fr. Holly sealed the test in an envelope and sent it back to the state bureaucracy to be graded. I went back to work not knowing if I would be paid. Hell, if I failed the test, the football season would probably be over before a paycheck would be forthcoming.

* * *

Our games after that first nail biter against Gila Bend were very rewarding. Our first win of 7-6 sounds more like a baseball score. Given the fact that we could have lost that game in the last few minutes, the next four games followed a path that any coach would drool over. Our margin for victory continued to increase from that one point: 6, 8, and 14. It was a coach's dream.

Our second game against St. John's Indian School was a 6-0 shutout. Our third game against Thatcher improved to a 14-6 win. (See Appendix #3 "Baboquivari Win Opens Grid Race") In our fourth game we increased our margin of victory again by winning 20-6. (See Appendix #4 "Warriors Find Key to Success") The point spread of fourteen was remarkable in that our leading tailback, Timmy, injured his right hip in the first half. He didn't play at all in the second half. Paul Hendricks and Alan Antone kept the running game going with 78 and 55-yards respectively. We gained 214-yards rushing in that fourth game against Duncan. In the first season we would have been lucky to gain 75-yards in one game.

Before our third game, Pat Frink, my assistant coach, took the team and coaches to a pro basketball, exhibition game in Tucson. This would be my first NBA game ever in person. Kareem Jabbar played. He was 26 years old and huge. We sat courtside. My adrenaline was pumping.

Later that week, Pat invited Oscar Robertson, the "Big O," to our home game against Thatcher, whom we defeated for our third win. I stayed in the locker room to talk with the boys, as usual, and was the last one out. Typically, a few neighbors and the coaches socialized after the games, more so this season than last. When I got to the neighbor's house, there sat the Big O on the couch, looking relaxed, visiting with folks.

I had read about Robertson years before and knew that, as a kid, he took a basketball everywhere he went. Now, at age 34, he was one of the all-time greatest guards in the history of college and professional basketball. He looked at me and said, "Good game, coach." I wanted to go shake his hand and tell him how much I admired him. Instead, I stayed calm and reserved, said "Thanks." I did not want to make a fool of myself by acting like a groupie. I didn't tell him how much I had admired him over the years. I thought he just wanted to relax and blend in with the rest of us, you know, enjoy some private time without all the hoopla that goes with being a famous sports hero. Would you believe I didn't even have my picture taken with him? I'm an absolute idiot!

Mr. Robertson, if you are reading this, do you even remember going to Sells, Arizona, to watch a high school football game? If so, please call me, John Leara, in Prescott, Arizona. I'll fly to see you so as to have my picture taken with the Big O some 40 years after the fact. And, I have to tell you, even though I don't fly to family weddings, I'd fly to get a picture with you.

In our fifth game against Clifton, we won 21-6, once more increasing our margin. (See Appendix #5 "Baboquivari stays unbeaten with 21-8 victory over Clifton"—the newspaper recorded the wrong score.) The team just kept improving offensively, a difficult task, most coaches would agree, because offense can easily break down. It's analytical and technical, as opposed to the emotion and strength that can drive the defense. Offense requires all eleven players to function simultaneously, without mistakes. Most penalties are called against the offense. Offense is harmony; defense is disruptive.

After the Clifton game, Paul Hendricks told me that he wished I hadn't emptied the bench on defense. We had a shutout late in the game at 21-0. After I sent in the boys who never got to play, Clifton scored a cheap touchdown on a very long pass because of our broken coverage. I agreed with Paul. The shutout late in the game was impressive since Clifton had totally humiliated us the year before. Paul felt frustrated because he was well aware of the past performance of Baboquivari teams. Our seniors had never experienced the pride of shutting out a good conference team. I could have preserved the shutout but chose, instead, to play everyone.

* * *

In the middle of the season, I got a wakeup call from a surprising corner. The football team was winning games and seemed to be getting better by the week. Life was good. Phoenix newspapers were writing weekly articles about the little Indian school's team being undefeated. I felt pleasantly surprised by this.

One of our neighbors, Harley Cox, hosted a celebration of the team's success. The party was a nice way for a few friends and neighbors to relax and enjoy each other's company. Only eight families lived in our little neighborhood. Our block consisted of four adjoining houses on either side of a single street. These were homes supplied by the school district for teachers. The party was fairly quiet. For me, I thought, "What a difference a year makes. Last year was pure hell and this year I get to enjoy the fruits of my labor."

The season was becoming something I had dreamed of, but I knew it could be short-lived. The school was small. The town was small. Who knew what the next year would bring with our talented seniors gone? One hopeful glimmer on the horizon arose from the freshman team that Dan Crawford coached. It, too, had not lost a game thus far.

Dorci and I stood next to each other at the party, each of us with a beer in hand. People were chatting, laughing. Harley interrupted everyone, saying, "A toast to the football team. They are still undefeated and having a great season. Way to go, coach!"

Just as I began to take a drink, a full glass of beer abruptly hit me square in the face. The cold liquid flooded me. It felt like twelve ounces in my hair, down my shirt. When I looked at who had just drenched me, standing close to me was an elementary teacher, empty glass in hand.

Within a nano-second my original impression that some prank had been pulled changed when I looked at her face. Her unfriendly expression caught me totally off guard. Hateful resentment seemed to consume her. I gained my mental equilibrium. I remember saying, "What the f___ is wrong with you?" I was totally perplexed. Harley and most of the folks at the party seemed to want to celebrate the team's success. But, obviously, not everyone relished our victories. I've never wanted to be around people socially who didn't want to be around me. With that in mind, I took Dorci's hand and walked back to our apartment. With negative emotions surfacing, I just needed to leave. Right then I needed my wife and children. Flashing through my head was the reminder that we had moved half way across the country to fulfill my dreams, but Dorci and the children would always be the only priority which couldn't be compromised. Somehow, the beer in my face seemed like a personal attack.

Later that night, as we lay in bed discussing what had happened, Dorci told me she felt the same way. She was confused and surprised by what the neighbor had done. The party had been a wonderful gesture of celebration for the teachers in a school district that received little notoriety. Later we were told that the beer thrower resented the money allotted for the football program. Obviously, in her mind, the money should have been spent in the classroom.

I also concluded that the success of the team and the appreciation I was getting for that success created envy. This was probably especially true on the reservation where there was little opportunity for fanfare. People who achieve have their detractors. I'm not talking about myself. I'm referring to others I've met in my lifetime who have reached lofty goals and lived exemplary lives. I have witnessed jealousy in the eyes of others who envy or resent their accomplishments.

How many kindergarten or elementary teachers find themselves spotlighted because of their achievements? What opportunities do they have to claim victory? They establish the very foundation for students and yet seldom are recognized when, some twelve years later, those same students graduate from high school.

In John McCain's acceptance speech as the Republican candidate for President in 2008, he talked about being self-centered in his youth. He was full of himself and his desires. But he learned through his military experience that serving others is the highest calling. I plead guilty of wanting to shine as a coach. However, my success would never be determined so much by winning games or setting records as it would be by the enrichment that occurred between me as coach and the athletes with whom I worked. I always wanted to give as much as I could to them. To contribute in a positive way to their development and growth. When I no longer coached, I maintained that same philosophy in my classroom as I taught my students. Indeed, serving others is the highest calling.

* * *

In our sixth game of the season with our record at 5-0, we met Benson, also undefeated. On Wednesday, October 17, two days before meeting Benson, one of the headlines in <u>The Arizona Republic</u>, a Phoenix newspaper, read, "Patsy Baboquivari Pushover No More." (See Appendix #6) I had gotten a big kick out of all the print the team received this season in the Tucson paper up to this point. However, this article was fourteen paragraphs in a Phoenix paper. We were only sixty miles away from Tucson, but over 120-miles from Phoenix. Most of that 120 mile space between Sells and Phoenix I would describe as no-man's land—very desolate.

I was inspired and so was the team. We were being complemented on our success in this season. We well remembered that one year earlier our game with Benson had been forfeited at our stadium because of my behavior and that of my assistant coach. But this year was different. We were on a roll. Remember, our margin for victory was ever increasing.

The reporter for the Phoenix paper had done his homework. He mentioned that Baboquivari had won just two games in the last four years. Those victories were against independent Southwest Indian in '71 and Fort Grant in '72, '72 being my first year. He also mentioned that Benson was ranked fourth statewide in schools of similar size. The article recognized Paul Hendricks as one of the reasons for our success.

This was certainly true; however, Paul was out with a leg injury. He and one of our best blocking, offensive linemen were out for the Benson game. Without these two boys, we needed a great team effort to win—especially since we were playing in Benson's stadium.

An unpleasant encounter before the game probably became one of the top three reasons I would never coach another football game for the rest of my life once this season ended. Dorci, my "Cecil B. DeMille," was there to do her usual filming. She had no previous experience using a movie camera. Nor did she claim any expertise at knowing our plays and following the ball. However, she had learned quickly, and in the first season and this one did a hell of a good job capturing our every move. The films became an invaluable tool for me to study our weaknesses.

About thirty minutes before the game, she was standing with two men, a look of consternation on her face. She called to me that Benson's principal or superintendent, I'm not sure which one, would not let her up in the crow's nest to film the game. If I remember correctly, their objection stemmed from her gender. In front of them stood a woman who, when told one time by a bricklayer, "Women don't lay mortar and bricks," built a wall 4-feet by 10-feet and laid a brick hearth. Of course, they didn't know that; she was just a female, and a blonde to boot.

Their objection set me off. At that moment, hatred started building up. I was already prepared for a difficult game, what with last year's embarrassing forfeiture on everyone's mind. Any sort of "glitch" would not surprise me. Along with these usual pessimistic expectations, I also felt the challenge of proving ourselves worthy of our current 5-0 season. Poor Dorci was caught in the middle. Had I come to blows with these men, I would have ended up in jail. With the adrenaline and resentment pumping through my veins, I probably would have broken somebody's bones.

The crow's nest allows camera operators to get great angles on the action of the game. Denying access to it was totally outrageous. I wouldn't stop arguing and yelling at the men. That is, until Dorci, from about thirty feet away yelled for me to stop; "John, you can't fight the whole world!

You're driving yourself crazy!"

Right then real doubts entered my mind about continuing in the career of head football coach. I was not happy. I knew that I would never work as an assistant again after the connection I had made with this team. I had twenty-four young men who trusted me. Not five or eight. A whole team. As pole vault coach back in 1966-71, my boys succeeded. Their results were not subjective and could not be denied: My vaulters cleared 13-feet and 14-feet. Now I was the head coach of the football team that had won five games, and yet I felt insecure. There were no guarantees we could continue winning and every possibility that the team might lapse back into its losing mode. Inside me the lows hurt too much and the rewards did not compensate for them.

I saw Dorci's face. She was yelling at me, pleading with me. We had two little children, and I stood ready to tear into another human being over a crow's nest! I was crazy with emotion. But Dorci's warnings finally registered. I backed off and walked away. She managed to climb to the top of our team bus and filmed the game from there.

Something was missing for me. I appreciated our success, that the boys were playing well. Maybe I had come here to coach for the wrong reasons. I had waited so long for the chance to become a successful head football coach. I was wholly convinced that I could inspire and train a team, that with me as the head coach, success would follow. I wasn't vain. My love of the game, my commitment to it would bring victory. It meant too much to me. Add to this mindset the reality of these Indian boys and their losing tradition. As the son of immigrant parents, I felt great empathy with them. I was out there taking their hits and fighting for respect. Hell, in one game at halftime I had said, "Let's go out there and beat those white boys!" With these emotions pulsing inside me, no wonder neurotic behavior surfaced.

Ten years later my coaching would evolve into a totally different attitude. Two of my boys would be competing in the state track finals. We had worked hard, and of course, they had carried the bulk of the load. I knew that I had done my best to prepare them for their events, but I allowed their own motivation and talent to carry them to the end without internalizing the results. I know this for sure: my emotions weren't tied to their performance like they were in Sells in 1973.

The Benson game was a dandy. Both sides hit hard and defended well. Early in the first half our quarterback, Neil, sprained his ankle badly on a sprint out to the right. It swelled and I re-taped it as best I could. Not until the end of the game did I find out just how badly he was injured. By then his ankle was the size of a grapefruit. Neil had a talent for sprinting out fast to one side while looking for a receiver. If he couldn't find one and there was an opening, he'd run through it. He had a brilliant mind and great instincts. I left him in the game and he played well, as did the rest of the team. I saw passion in their eyes during the entire competition.

During the game we got down to Benson's one yard line several times but were unable to score. We were missing Paul. I had brought up Mike Miguel from JV to play middle linebacker and shuffled some of the other guys around to make up for Paul's absence. Mike did a good job, but he wasn't Paul. When Paul and Timmy were on defense together, both linebackers, they were all over the field making plays with speed, anticipation and hard tackles. With our line playing as well as it did defensively, Paul made over a hundred tackles in eight games. We missed him dearly against Benson. With Paul on the field, we would have stuffed their runs, forcing more punts early, creating better field position.

For the first three quarters the game was scoreless. Once again, had Paul been playing offense, the team would have been more explosive and we would have had a better chance at a touchdown. Then, we fumbled the ball deep in our own territory. Benson pushed the ball in and led 7-0. Less than nine minutes remained in the game.

We took control of the ball deep in our own territory. We had about seventy yards to cover to tie the game. But time was running out. The boys still had that passion in their eyes, knowing they had possession and control of how the game would end. I had remained calm throughout but was still hateful and paranoid toward the officials. Remembering the forfeit kept me in check. The game belonged to the Papago boys, ranging in weight from 128-pounds, to 135-pounds, to 140-pounds with only a couple over 175. I knew what was in their heads and hearts from having read their writing in English class. I loved them dearly. We had come together in just fourteen months.

We were moving the ball well, mindful of the clock. If we rushed too much we might not execute well enough and lose the ball on downs. We advanced into their territory almost to their 40-yard line. I looked at the clock and decided this was the right time to call the Kansas City Special. We needed a jolt, a big gain because there wasn't enough time to continue with small gains. The clock had become our enemy. All of the sled work, the wind sprints, weightlifting, the attention to detail, were rewarding us right now, near the end of the game, with everyone near exhaustion.

The Kansas City Special! I had given the play that name when we practiced it on the field. I had seen it one time on TV. The Kansas City Chiefs ran it to perfection, but they couldn't run it often because it was an interception waiting to happen. I loved that play even though it was dangerous. It was one of our specialties, just like the Penalty Play.

Like the Penalty Play, we used it rarely. And when we did, we gained good yardage. Timmy was our best running back. He positioned himself on the right side just behind a lineman. When Neil took the snap, he started sprinting to the right side. Our linemen knew that they were to block to the right as though Neil were going to pass in that direction. The whole defense moved in the same direction as our quarterback and receivers, to our right. In the meantime, Timmy, as inconspicuously as possible, slowly moved along to the left, close to the line of scrimmage, but not too far. He was trying to blend in with all the bodies that were beating on each other.

Timing was everything. Simultaneously, Neil would pull up and steady himself while Timmy would break hard for the left side line. By this time, all twenty-one players were moving hard toward the right sideline; and Timmy ran just beyond and parallel to the line of scrimmage in the opposite direction. Neil sold the play brilliantly, convincing the defense of a sprint out right. In Benson's defensive haste to pursue our quarterback and all the receivers moving right, a huge void developed in front of Timmy.

Neil's pass was perfect; and when Timmy caught the ball, he was nearing full stride, probably only ten yards from the sideline. Our whole team knew what to do as soon as the pass was thrown. They immediately turned downfield, looking for any defenders to block so as to escort Timmy to the goal line.

Timmy grabbed the ball and turned towards the goal. It was beautiful. The defense was out of position. As he made his turn, his toe caught the turf and he stumbled. He didn't go down, but he lost all of his momentum. By the time he was back in stride, a few defenders were dashing madly back in his direction. Timmy made a wonderful run, made a good cut; but because he lacked great speed, the defenders closed on him and kept him from reaching the end zone.

We ran mostly pass plays in the waning moments of the game so as to conserve the clock on incompletions. We kept moving the ball, but we had used up all of our timeouts. The clock was the only thing that could stop us; Benson couldn't. On our last play we got to the one yard line, again; and time ran out.

The emotional pain I felt over the loss was so different from physical pain. Seventeen of the twenty-two players on that team had shared two seasons with me. We had played this game short-handed with a hobbled quarterback and had fallen just one yard short. I can still see the "Kansas City Special" developing beautifully, the boys moving exactly as they should. And then, poor Timmy, exhausted from expending so much intensity, was slowed by the turf, not a defender. If anyone deserved to race down the field for a late game touchdown, Timmy Siquieros was the man. He was voted all-conference tailback at the end of this season, votes cast by all our opposing team coaches. He ran with all his heart and single-minded purpose. I'm sure tacklers did not enjoy being hit by him.

I stayed just outside the locker room for about fifteen minutes. I had to compose myself before seeing the boys. When I went in, I shook each boy's hand; I had to touch them physically. That contact superseded anything spoken at that moment. They had heard enough of my words. Twenty years later, David Miguel, a very conscientious person, would tell me that we had been like family. His words reflected the emotions we all felt at this moment. Having to face the team now, I felt like I was consoling my own children.

We loaded onto the bus for the long drive home. We stopped at a McDonald's for Big Macs. Swallowing was very hard for me; the burger just stuck in my throat. I sat with various players just to talk. Their spirits were admirable, more so than mine. Probably because they were fifteen years younger than I.

I wasn't too interested in watching the film Dorci had taken, since she didn't get the height from the crow's nest. In my heart, no doubt existed as to the proficiency with which the team had played. They put forth an immense effort against the eventual conference champion Benson. We had played under several disadvantages: the game was at Benson; we played without Paul Hendricks who had a knee injury and without our best tackle who was ineligible; Neil, our quarterback, sprained his ankle in the first quarter and played the rest of the game hobbled by the swelling. All this, plus the fact that we were on their one yard line when the clock ran out.

(See Appendix #7 "Benson Takes Showdown")

Three games remained, two conference and one against Orme Ranch coming up the next week. Monday we were on the practice field to prepare for the match against Orme on their turf. This was the first really easy opponent we faced this season. We won 39-14, without Neil whose ankle remained swollen. Leroy Antone showed off his size seventeen foot with a booming 38-yard field goal. The kick was a beauty, straight, with perfect trajectory. I think he had 10-yards to spare.

While we were beating Orme, Benson was winning another conference game. With just two games remaining, we had a terrible let down against Sahuarita at home. We just couldn't get anything going and were trounced 42-0 in front of our own fans! That loss can be placed on my shoulders. I think I had looked into the future and knew I'd be leaving Sells at the end of the semester. There were too many lows, too much anger, too much coughing and too often the feeling of despair because of the living conditions which included alcohol and drug use in the community.

But I owed these kids one last effort for our final game against Tombstone at Tombstone, about 150-miles away. Most of the game was played in a lethargic manner. And then, Mark Puella intercepted a pass and ran it back a long way. That was the spark we needed. We won 34-7, finishing our season 7-2.

Some weeks later, another article appeared in a Phoenix newspaper. I was surprised to learn that the The Arizona Republic had nominated me for an award. The paper listed me as one of eight candidates being recognized and considered for the state's "prep football coach of the year award." (See Appendix #8)

In August, had you asked me what price I'd pay to finish 7-2, I'd have offered up a finger or a toe. However, I still had a bitter taste in my mouth that actually didn't go away for years. The most devastating part of my experience in Sells was actually to come in the years after I left, as I learned of one death after another of the boys I had coached. A couple of them died before they reached the age of 25. A few more before they were thirty. Too many early deaths—as of 2010, ten of the 27 boys I coached in two years. Whenever I talked to Max Chavez and he told me of another death, that pain would refresh itself in my chest. I am not as strong as many who can accept that pain. I'm too emotional, too intense.

Ironically, our success in 1973 and the publicity we received, especially in the Phoenix newspaper, probably attracted one of the best running backs ever in the history of Arizona high school football. His name was Alvin Leon and he transferred to Baboquivari the year after I left Sells. Max Chavez subscribed to the <u>Papago Runner</u> and had it mailed to me in Missouri so that I could read about the football team. Alvin's ability was being compared to Benny Malone who played for Arizona State University and was drafted by the Miami Dolphins in the second round and played seven years in the NFL. The high school team had good seasons and high scoring games with Leon. A statistic in that article from the <u>The Arizona Republic</u> about our team stated that, after our fifth game, when we were 5-0, our defense hadn't allowed more than one touchdown in any game. Our scores for the season were, chronologically, 7-6, 6-0, 14-6, 20-6, and 21-6. When I reviewed that article many years later, I was taken aback. Oh, would I have loved to coach Alvin Leon. But, with my personality and emotions, a stroke would probably have killed me or put me in a wheelchair.

The year and a half in Sells, which included two football seasons, was a real roller coaster ride. The first season saw a forfeit forced upon us by officials who felt threatened. We suffered humiliating defeats. The second season, with its well-played games, produced joyous victories. Yet its success did not result in personal peace for me. I cried too much during both seasons. In a recent conversation with Max Chavez, who still lives in Sells, we laughed about my kicking in the locker room door. I'm reminded of one definition of "humor" – "tragedy plus time." I can laugh about my tirades now, but I suffered emotional trauma while coaching football during those two seasons. It meant too much to me, being head coach, succeeding, watching the boys achieve beyond their expectations, and watching them totally defeated. The night I kicked open the door, I made the boys get on the bus without showering and told them we weren't going to stop to eat. Max also recalled the game when I flipped off some of our own fans. Imagine, flipping off my own fans!

* * *

Max has maintained his sense of humor through tough times. His career has involved him in the court system and law enforcement on the reservation. Drug and alcohol abuse are problematic. Even though the two of us are very different, regarding drugs, we are of the same mind. In the

Neal Miguel, John Leara, Paul Hendricks

Gilbert and Gary Two Two

John Leara, Allan Antone, Pat Frink

Leroy Antone, John Leara, Ollie Antone

Earl Francisco, Phil Lewis, Angel Listo

Timmy Siquieros, John Leara

Morris Antone, Dave Miguel

John Leara, Kenny Antone

39 years that we've known each other, we've always abhorred illicit drug use. He has a strong commitment to his family and God. He married Josie Murrietta, who was a cheerleader in 1972, and they have two daughters.

Twenty years after leaving Sells, I decided to return for a visit. In the fall of 1993 I flew to Tucson and drove to Sells to spend two nights at Max's home. The itinerary for my stay included a football game, a visit to the high school and a pot-luck dinner that Max arranged inviting some players from the team.

At the football game I met some of the former cheerleaders who were now mothers, just a bit older than I had been those twenty years ago. The 1972 – 1973 football players were now men with sons involved in sports in middle or high school. My emotions at our meeting startled me, the depth, acuity and familiarity. Their mannerisms and genuine warmth hadn't changed in the interim twenty years. There is a purity in these people that makes them unique in their relationships to each other and to me. They, themselves, were the reason I had been unable to detach myself from Sells after I left.

My decision to leave Sells is easy to understand. I wasn't happy, couldn't maintain any internal peace. I had proved to myself that I understood how to develop a successful football team and how to relate to the players. But I also believed that having accomplished those tasks, they were not important any more. I was 33. It was time to be a husband and father.

Ironically, everything I suffered through impacted me in a strange way. As passionate as I was about coaching during this time, I never coached another football player for the rest of my life after my second season at Baboquivari. After leaving Arizona, some years later I did coach other sports. But, by the time our children were playing on high school teams, I did not want to coach anything anymore. Watching our children play soccer, baseball, volleyball and softball was more enjoyable.

No other experience from my professional life had impacted me like my time with these boys, now men with their own families. As much as I loved the heart in Terry Woolsey and the drive of Jeff Schwarz, as much as I relished the successes of Mark Wilding and Steve Baldwin (chapter 9), what happened to me in Arizona went to the depth of my being. I had been able to detach myself from previous experiences rather quickly, but after I left Sells, years would pass before I felt detachment from these men.

CHAPTER 9

THE FULL CIRCLE OF TRACK AND "ON TO STATE"

In 1981 Wright City hired me to teach high school English and coach the boys' track team. I was forty-one and hadn't coached high school students in eight years, since Sells in 1973. Having spent four years on the road in sales from 1974 to1978 (see chapter 12) and then two years at Vianny High School teaching typing and business law, and then building two homes in 1980 and '81, my resume began to look rather flaky, or maybe even shaky. I felt insecure and believed Wright City was being kind to hire me. I'm not sure any other school in the area would have. I had taught at four schools in ten years; then I had taken a five year hiatus during which time I sold dresses and built homes. Whoever did the hiring had to be broad-minded to choose someone with my credentials. My record in the four schools looked outstanding, especially as a coach, but still…all of those job changes.

So, I was back in the saddle, so to speak, teaching English and coaching track. I started off with a bang. I had energy galore and remember those first few years as something special. A friend during that era told me that I had a presence in the classroom akin to an entertainer. Teaching was fun again, and quite often I'd get vibes from the students that they were getting something valuable in English class.

In addition to the coaching success I was to have at Wright City, I met

Harry Toll who would become a life-long friend. Harry taught math in a classroom just down the hall from mine. We had many of the same interests and immediately connected politically. We were always laughing or commiserating over the antics of high school life and the trials of teaching. In our classrooms, we both did handstands and walked on our hands, challenging students to a competition. One year, as sponsors of the senior class, we went to the prom "together."

I've enjoyed Harry's company because he doesn't need to bolster his own ego at the expense of others. He hasn't a jealous bone in his body. Instead, he revels in the success of acquaintances. Many times when he introduced Dorci and me to his friends, he would start bragging about our children—that's right, *our children*. He is a generous, compassionate person. As an identical twin, he donated part of his liver to try to save the life of his nephew.

And, Harry is forever joking around. Unfortunately for me, a third to half of his one-liners go right over my head because I mistakenly take him seriously. Or, I don't actually hear his jokes (with my 74 year old ears). I'll be thinking we are having a serious discussion when Harry will actually be cracking jokes. He was recently in the checkout line at a store where two women were discussing their marriages, and Harry was pulled into the conversation. "I've been married for 31 years," said one of the women.

"Well, what do you know! I've been married for 31 years also," Harry remarked. "To six different women!"

"Six women?" you may ask. No, once again that was a joke. He has been married four times.

He has visited us often in the last ten years since we moved from Missouri to Arizona, driving 1500-miles in two days. For a couple of days, Dorci and I will enjoy his company, talk of the current state of the union, and laugh until our sides hurt. Two days is about all we can tolerate because Harry talks non-stop. But, I can easily tell him he's talking too much. Between his constant yammering, his continual joking, and his ever-changing topics of conversation, I've concluded that he probably has attention deficit disorder. An example of this occurred when I last stayed at his home. One morning we were talking. His computer was close by and his eyes would occasionally dart to the screen. Finally, I took his chin and turned it towards me saying, "Harry, am I boring you? Can't you pay attention to me?"

He laughed and said, "John, I think I have ADD." My thoughts exactly!

We both enjoy investing in stocks; however, Harry is more successful than I. Harry and I will be at our computers in the morning and talking to each other on the phone as we see what the market is doing and banter back and forth over the merits of one stock or the other. What a great way to start the day because there are many laughs to be had.

During the years at Wright City High School, we both were always ready for an adventure. He is one of the few people I know willing to drive cross country, sometimes on a whim. Harry would invite my family on outings with other families he knew. We'd float the streams and rivers in southern Missouri or hike different trails throughout the state. Once we took a short hike to a 100-foot high cliff to rappel. Harry, the person at the top, was in total control of each person who chose to rappel the bluff. This scared the hell out of me. I think at age 53 I'd lost a step in daredevil activity, what with our kids there and all. I opted out of rappelling. Besides, I wasn't convinced that Harry knew what he was doing. The day ended with no casualties; maybe Harry did know what he was doing.

That first year at Wright City in English III, I met Mark Wilding and Steve Baldwin. They were juniors, both excellent students. In the spring they joined the track team which had some laggards on it. In fact, it wasn't much of a team and reminded me of the first year in Sells because of the ineptness of many of the boys.

Midway in the season I kicked one fellow off the team because of his behavior. He would pretend to be running, if such a behavior is possible. When he did do the drills, he became sick. His behavior irritated me. I wasted little time in finding who wanted to run and who didn't. "It IS called 'track', boys, after all! You have to run! Otherwise," I told them, "you should go out for baseball or archery." One day, really pissed off, I told the boys that if they wanted to stay on the team, they had to run 5-miles on our quarter mile track. That's twenty laps. It was ugly watching the malingerers. If I had to, I would see the season to its end with just two or four or six boys—not knowing who those boys would be. I can't remember how many stuck it out with me but it wasn't very many.

Steve Baldwin was a sprinter (and became a long jumper and triple jumper), yet he could keep up with (or almost keep up with) Mark Wilding, a distance runner. I was surprised that Steve didn't quit when I told the boys to run 5-miles. That's not the kind of thing a sprinter will readily do.

But Steve and Mark were special. Hard work was their friend.

Mark came from a very large family with twelve children. I knew his sisters Debbie and Sandy, and two of his brothers, Danny and Edgar. This family exemplified the power of successful parenting. Mark's siblings were all really nice kids. When I think of the snarling faces of many of the students I coached and taught and then think about the Wilding family, it's like the difference between night and day. No snarling in that family! On the contrary, Mark was fun to be around, fun to coach. His joviality was contagious. The first time I saw him, he was actually making a lewd gesture to the band director; but they were both laughing and giggling over some shared joke.

Steve, on the other hand, seemed more sober than Mark. He gave a thoughtful speech about his grandfather in Junior English, serious, touching and well-delivered for a sixteen-year-old. During workouts his introspection surfaced. Whereas Mark seemed always on the verge of a smile or laugh, Steve's smile was reserved. He intrigued me. He was such a likeable young man that I invited him to dinner. Afterwards, we all went to the city tennis courts to hit balls. Steve had never played tennis, yet he proceeded to put on an exhibition against me. His lightning speed and hand-eye coordination challenged me.

With Steve and Mark willing to put forth great effort, I looked for creative ways to train. Off of the service road next to I-70 about a mile from the high school, we found a very steep hill—Boulder Hill. I ran it a couple of times. I felt like vomiting. I was 42-years-old. Running that hill hurt, if the runner exerted himself; but it was a good hurt.

I have remained in contact with Mark Wilding, and, to this day, he still remembers it vividly: "I chased Baldwin up and down that hill until my hearing went out, never once beating him." Evidently, with his over-exertion, Mark's heart seemed to be pumping inside his ears. "Steve seemed oblivious to my plight. On he ran, back to school. Meanwhile, after running up and down Boulder Hill, my head was spinning. With my head pulsing, the sound of the passing trucks on the interstate throbbed in and out of my ears with each stride I took."

That first season ended with little fanfare; but from the time track ended until the beginning of the next season in 1983, Mark and Steve stayed very active athletically, Steve with basketball and Mark with his running shoes and earphones. What a sight to behold! Mark would run through the streets of Wright City listening to his favorite music with his earphones. He'd run 10, 15, 20-miles. Who knows how many miles he covered? He ran so many that he incurred stress fractures in his legs. However, he healed in time for the '83 track season.

And, wisely, I went to a track seminar in St. Louis. One clinic was given by Carl Lewis's coach—Carl Lewis, a track and field legend with 10 Olympic medals. The clinic described how to prepare an athlete for the triple jump. "Click!" A light went on because I realized that Steve might be a perfect candidate for the triple jump. I mean, let's get real. Most sprinters want to shine in the 100- or 200-meter dash. Maybe they'll try the long jump or high jump. But who in his right mind would want to suffer through the triple jump? It's an awkward event. Steve would have to run down the track, jump off one foot, land on that foot, then hop to the other foot and leap as far as he could into the sand pit. Watch it on TV someday or YouTube. A person can tear a groin muscle, sprain a knee, twist an ankle, get an ugly stone bruise on the heel or any combination of these injuries. It is truly a grueling event.

What an opportunity for Steve, "Mr. Hard-worker." Many of the athletes involved with the triple jump probably don't enjoy the difficult event. Advantage Steve. He believed me when I suggested he'd be good at it. He chose to do a myriad of exercises to enhance his jumping and hopping ability, and he seemed to relish them. He loved training and the opportunity to hone the skills for this event. At least, I think he did. I had come back from the clinic in St. Louis loaded with these drills; and to Steve they seemed to be presents from Santa's bag.

As the 1983 track season progressed, so, too, did Steve and Mark. Mark had a breakthrough in Centralia when he raced against a very good miler from Wentzville, the son of the Wright City High School counselor. Mark was a senior and this particular opponent was a junior and an excellent runner. Naturally, Mark got pumped up and proved to be a little hungrier than the Wentzville boy. He won by only one stride. However, his time, a remarkable 4:37, blew us away. No doubt, Wright City had a thoroughbred with heart. Mark was a self-made runner whose body language while running conveyed pure enjoyment. Smart and disciplined, he could run each 440-yards in times that were to his advantage.

Because I had been a sprinter and jumper in high school and not run distance, I decided to contact a friend in St. Louis, Tom McCracken, who coached cross country at Lindberg High School. I would rely on his guidance. Tom had run distance in college; so, I phoned him. He gave me explicit instructions on how to prepare Mark for the district meet, the workouts, the schedule of days, etc. Coach McCracken would go on to take six track teams to state titles.

Mark trained like a frisky horse. His energy level bubbled over. He had to be reined in. When he ran 220-yard repeats, he always met his times to the second. He developed a clock in his brain, knowing exactly the precise pace of those intervals.

The Thursday before District, when he walked down the school hallway towards me, I saw something different in his face. His demeanor lacked the normal joviality. I said, "Go fishing." In a recent email to me, Mark described this suggestion as "the all-time best coaching move." As he tells it:

"The Wilding household had a strict rule: 'No board games on a school night.' Fishing fell under that category. The rule had been tested many times to no avail. I remember in the kitchen asking if it was okay to go fishing, expecting an argument that I would lose and then defiantly go anyway. Instead I got a nonchalant 'Go.' Mom knew everything. As I stood on the bank of the nearby farmer's pond with absolutely no intention of catching fish, the chalkboard of pressure was completely erased. It would stay clean until that damn curved, staggered start at the District meet."

By the time District arrived, Mark was ready. Everything he had done set him up for a spectacular performance. On a cool, misty day at the meet, he ran each quarter mile in exactly the time we had planned up to the last lap; and then he let fly with a remarkable kick for the last 300-yards, vaulting him into first place with a winning time of 4:27. That was ten seconds faster than his previous best! What an accomplishment! It's not like Mark held back earlier in the season and just tried harder at District. He just kept pushing and pushing for two years, enjoying himself; and the reward came at a perfect time.

While Mark ran the mile and 2-mile at District, Steve jumped his way to State in the long jump, high jump, and triple jump. With all of that jumping, Steve ended up with a stone bruise on his heel which plagued him right through state competition. He had spent months bounding like a whitetail deer. He bounded on his left leg, on his right leg. I saw his bounce increasing week to week. Steve was a natural athlete who excelled in many sports; so it was no surprise when he qualified for state in the three different events. His agility coupled with his work ethic assured success.

At State, Mark won the mile in 4:30 and placed third in the 2-mile. Steve won the triple-jump, tying the state record. Officials measured his jump several times to confirm the record tie. He placed second in the long jump. Throughout his jumps he suffered pain from the stone bruise. I remember telling him, "If you don't take your final jump, no big deal." However, he took it, and made his best jump of 45' 10 ¾".

These two, fine young men, youngsters with heart, Wright City's Class 2A representation at the State Track Meet, won third place for the boys' team—a "team" of two! True to form, as I looked in the rear view mirror while driving the bus back to Wright City, Mark and Steve sat in the back (we were sharing the bus with the girls' track team) laughing. With both arms surrounding it, Mark clutched the State Trophy, holding it for the entire ride home.

I coached track at Wright City four more years, but after Steve and Mark graduated, my passion began to ebb. I felt that my real coaching lay behind me. Beth and Matt were getting more involved in sports in middle school and high school. I wanted to attend our children's competitions. While coaching Mark and Steve, I had demonstrated more maturity and control than when I had coached in Sells. Because Mark and Steve were doing most of the work, I suffered no stress. When I had coached football, I took failure too personally; losses hurt deeply. With Mark and Steve, coaching was fun. That's the way it should be. These two high school athletes traveled to state competition to represent their school and came away with a team trophy. I had approached this event hoping for their individual achievement with no thought of a "team" win. But with their passion and my knowledge they won third place. A fitting and fulfilling ending to my formal days as a coach.

1983 STATE TRACK CLASS 2A

BOYS THIRD PLACE

WRIGHT CITY HIGH SCHOOL

WRIGHT CITY, MISSOURI

My Kramer impression in the Wright City classroom

CHAPTER 10

HANDBALL, GREEN BANANAS AND "THE CODE"

"Damn! He's killing me!" Sweat poured from my frame. I could have wrung out my shirt and shorts, they were so wet. "I can't get him to move! He's got ME running all over the place. He's more than twice my age. I've got muscle and agility but he barely takes more than a few steps. Why can't I do that?"

The final score of that handball game was 21-8. I lost to Bill McGreevy, Sr. He was 50-years old to my 23. But, he was an experienced handball player compared to me.

In college at SEMO, I became acquainted with the game of handball. It is played on a court (a room) 20 by 40-feet with a ceiling 20-feet high. With their hands, two players hit a hard, rubber ball that is slightly larger than a golf ball. They use all six surfaces of the court (four walls, ceiling and floor) making it a game of geometric angles. Some facilities, like parks, may have one-wall or three-wall courts.

Playing handball had been part of my physical conditioning for football during the off-season in college. Although I played frequently during those years, I wasn't mastering the skills or strategies of a serious player. Finesse didn't figure into my game then. My football mentality ruled: "Hit the ball hard; run into walls trying to dig opponent's shots."

After college and once I fulfilled my active duty in the military at Ft.

Leonard Wood, MO, I began my work life in St. Louis. Playing handball became my leisure time activity. I joined the YMCA on South Grand Avenue. Ever the penny pincher, I thought, "I can play handball free at the Y."

One day, I ran into Bill. I knew him as the father of Myra, a girl who had been my schoolmate from the fourth grade through high school. With him was his fifteen-year-old son, Bill Jr. Bill Sr. liked his beer and his belly showed it; but, oh, could he play handball! He should have been a physicist; he understood all those angles and how to use them to his advantage on the court. As soon as an opponent struck the ball, Bill knew where to position himself—usually in the middle of the court.

That day we met, I brazenly thought, "I'm young and fit. I'll give him a run for his money. We could have a good game." And so I had asked him to set up a match for us. I wanted the challenge of competing with an experienced player but didn't realize the intrusion of my request. The finesse of the game still eluded me, the bold, gauche novice. Experienced players are challenged by others who have the same skills, not former college football jocks with swelled heads.

Although grinning, in his head Bill was probably thinking, "What a schlep! He's not in my league." That's what I was to him—a muscle-man with brawn and no brains. It wouldn't have been his choice to compete against that kind of opponent. But, being a nice guy, Bill willingly humored me. "Sure, John," he said.

And thus began my endurance test. Bill easily placed the ball where I wasn't, causing me to run from front to back and side to side. With either hand he could hit the ceiling or propel kill shots—impossible for me to return. Not only did he understand the physics of the game, he had the dexterity to successfully deliver his shots. What a display he put on. What a lesson I learned.

Lest one mistake handball as a game easily mastered with just an understanding of its physics and dexterous ball placement, Bill Jr. serves as a good example of the lean and limber, powerful player. To make a kill shot, he would seize an opponent's ball coming off the back wall in any number of positions. He'd whack it into a laser shot that stayed just four to six inches from the floor heading for the front. There, it hit the wall so low that it ricocheted immediately to the floor and rolled away. An opponent cannot return it. That is the ultimate kill shot. In addition to his dad's skills, this young man had speed and strength. I witnessed him defeat an "A" player in his prime because Bill Jr. combined his youthful power with the game's finesse.

After playing Bill Sr. and watching Bill Jr., I began to refine my game, attempting to emulate this father and son. In all candor, however, my football instincts continued to dominate my thinking and style of play. Being in such good shape, I persisted with the belief, "If I run, run, run and play at a frenetic pace, I can force my opponent to play my game."

The high point of my playing handball occurred in 1966 when I participated in my first "A" tournament where all the best players competed. Having won some "B" tournaments, I knew the time had arrived for me to move up.

Anxiety coursed through my body that weekend at the YMCA. It probably hindered my performance in the first match. I overpowered my hits and set up my opponent to win points. A handball player who hits a shot too high and too hard in a rush of adrenaline simply sets up an easy kill shot for his opponent off the back wall. What a waste of energy just to lose a point!

During that match I heard a small cheering section. "Come on, John!" A few friends were watching and rooting for me, the upstart, to defeat my seasoned opponent. More adrenaline pumped through my veins. But, I began to tire.

Good thing, because I started to play smarter, expending less energy, strategically placing the ball. The successful kill shot not only uses less energy, it causes psychological damage to the opponent. It earns a point or a serve out. I won my match two out of three games.

This victory inspired my passion for the sport. During the next four and a half years, playing handball consumed me.

In 1966 the Jewish Community Center Association (JCCA) held the national finals for the US Handball Championships. In the first round, I competed against a fellow from Florida. We were evenly matched and I played my heart out. Although I lost, I prided myself in the fact that the score was close. My play in that first round inspired me, as did what I witnessed during the rest of the championship.

One could say that I became a 25-year-old groupie that weekend. Still attracting news at the age of 36, Jimmy Jacobs was competing at the JCCA. He was THE powerhouse in handball, his reputation unmatched at the time. A 1966 <u>Sports Illustrated</u> article had described him as possibly the greatest athlete of his time in any sport. Jim Bouton, a retired Major League Baseball pitcher, claimed that Jacobs could have been a .400 hitter in baseball. With typical groupie behavior, I followed Jacobs around and watched every game he played. My lower jaw ached from dropping in amazement over his mastery and proficiency.

* * *

My passion for handball suddenly ended in 1968 when I met Dorci. The time and attention I had given to perfecting my finesse on the handball court was now diverted to wooing my bride-to-be. Unbeknownst to me, I would never play another game of handball.

The sudden demise of my five-year fervor for playing handball falls into a pattern I've observed of my passions. For a number of years, coaching football totally obsessed me. However, after the second season in Sells, Arizona, I never coached that game again. As a youngster I loved hopping on and off of trains. It was my favorite activity during the years 1946-47. My train jumping was cut short once we moved away. Otherwise it might have lasted until the age of twelve had we remained in Southbridge. For five years I poured over films and read articles trying to master the art of pole vaulting. With my vaulters clearing 14-feet, this endeavor proved quite successful. However, even though I taught at several other schools and could have coached pole vaulting again, I never returned to it.

Once I retired, golf became my passion. Since 1995, playing golf has remained so, defying the pattern. Possibly that's because the only thing to move on to is a nursing home. I've thought about taking up Bocce ball. But it, like horseshoes, hurts my right shoulder. The nursing home looks ever ominous.

Maybe this abrupt severing of passions relates to another aspect of my personality. Throughout my life I've been a "spur-of-the-moment" kind of planner, in other words—not a planner at all. This has occasionally been very frustrating for my wife. For example, in 2008…

"John," Dorci said in March. "We need to make plane reservations for the Indiana wedding in June."

"I can't plan that far in advance," I replied.

In April Dorci repeated, "John, "we need to make reservations for the wedding in June."

"I can't plan that far in advance."

"John," Dorci asked in May. "When will we reserve our flight for the June wedding?"

"I don't think I'm going. You better make your plans without me." As it turned out, I had to have hernia surgery in June which prevented any travel for me.

This scenario has been typical not only of the past six years but for much of my life. When I've made commitments to attend not only weddings but family gatherings or trips with Dorci, I've had to cancel them. I vividly recall one of many bronchitis episodes that struck just before we were scheduled to leave for a ski trip. Feeling like I was going to die, I moaned from bed, "Dorci, I can't go." Accidents or illness or surgeries have caused repeated interruptions in my life. Maybe that's why I've never been one to plan long-range. But, illness or pain aside, I just don't like commitments.

In retirement I've concluded that my mantra is five simple words: "I don't buy green bananas." Friends and family know that I don't like commitments. In fact, I proudly point out, "The only long-term commitment I've sustained is my marriage in 1968 to Dorci," (with golf coming in second place at twenty years).

* * *

Some of my spontaneous decisions have resulted in taking, rather than canceling, trips. In 1966 I took a trip that ended in tragedy. A teacher I knew, two other guys and I decided on the spur of the moment to travel to Acapulco over Christmas vacation. The temperatures in St. Louis hovered around 15-degrees. One of the guys had a refurbished hearse, and we joked about four bachelors traveling in a hearse. Two of us slept and two shared the driving for eight hours shifts. We traveled non-stop to Nuevo Laredo, Mexico, right across the border from Laredo, Texas. We spent one night there, for R and R. Since this was my first trip to Mexico, my companions forewarned me of the stark difference in living conditions from the US. My heart went out to the youngsters and other Mexican citizens I encountered.

The next day we continued heading south and stopped in Taxco to purchase silver. It was a beautiful little town in the mountains, famous for its silver mines. I bought several items that I planned to give to my future wife, whoever she was, whenever I should meet her. Then we were off again, driving the rest of the night to reach Acapulco where the temperature was 85-degrees. The bright sunshine hurt my eyes but I welcomed the pain, knowing the ugly weather I left behind in Missouri.

Of course, we couldn't hit the beach without first drinking margaritas in our hotel room. I purchased a bag of limes at a nearby store. Our rooms were on the second floor; and as I returned, I saw my friend on the balcony, grinning, knowing margaritas were only minutes away. I threw him the bag saying, "Hey, Fred, catch!" Up went the limes towards him. Out stretched Fred's arms. Flash! He touched a live electric wire. Who would have expected high voltage two feet off the corner of the balcony? At the flash of his arms touching the wire, his face looked stunned-surprised-dismayed-astounded, all in the briefest instant, a look of helplessness. In a second or two he was dead; his limp body no longer in contact with the wires, draped over the metal railing.

I stood aghast for just a brief moment. Then, screaming his name over and over, I ran up the flight of stairs and administered mouth to mouth for a couple of minutes. The other teacher friend relieved me, also giving him mouth to mouth, to no avail. A local called an ambulance. We carried him down the winding stairs and into the ambulance. The doctor worked feverishly to revive him, but he finally gave up after considerable effort.

I spent most of the night in a Catholic church. I was afraid of nightmares or sleep-walking off the balcony. I felt depleted, unstable and vulnerable. The church gave me a semblance of safety.

The body was flown home. The three of us returned to St. Louis, driving non-stop for close to 48-hours.

Within a day of returning to St. Louis, we attended his funeral. The expression on his face in that split second before death is etched in my mind even today.

* * *

Fortunately, other last minute travel plans have not resulted in tragedy. In 1978 Dorci and I had planned a vacation to the Oregon coast and then a visit with my brother Angelo and his family in California. We cancelled that plan when we discovered Dorci was pregnant. However, within weeks of canceling the family vacation, and with the Missouri summer heat and humidity bearing down on my "antsy" nature, I decided to travel the route alone.

We had recently purchased a Datsun B 210, a 4-cylinder, two-door, hatchback model. I don't think a smaller automobile existed in 1978. Not quite what you'd call a "family car," this vehicle fell into the "sub-compact" classification. It looked like a torpedo with the sloping hatchback. I was attracted by its claim of 40 m.p.g. rather than any consideration of comfort for our family of four. The car had a radio—no air-conditioning, no power windows or locks, no cruise control. Those "luxuries" cost more. Saving dollars was ever foremost in my thinking.

In fact, would you believe that the next summer, in 1979, when Dorci's youngest brother got married in Florida, we drove to the wedding in the Datsun? Now, there were five of us that summer, Dorci holding six-month-old Briana for the whole trip. Also, her brother Dennis had driven down from Chicago to ride with us since his car was somewhat unreliable to make the journey all the way to Florida. Not only would he join us for the drive, but he offered to help pay for gas! Dennis and I split the driving duties. Dorci, holding Briana, Beth and a cooler were in the back seat. Matt "stretched" out beneath the hatchback on top of the suitcases. So, let's see, that's three adults (none of us slight of build) and three children traveling over 800-miles in a sub-compact car. Sounds like the ingredients for a comic foreign film—but, no, it's just another example of John Leara's frugal life.

Getting back to my trek to Oregon, with Dorci's blessing, I headed out on I-70 around noon with my pillow and a few hundred dollars. I needed the "fix" of new sights and cool weather. Dorci had packed a cooler filled with food and drinks to last a few days. The Datsun would be my bed for five consecutive nights.

The first leg of this trip was the most uncomfortable, driving through the heat of Missouri and Kansas. I drove with the windows down. By midnight the Colorado mountains gave me the perfect sleeping weather. The temperatures sank into the high 50's. In fact, every night on this trip the temps were cool because of the destinations I chose.

The next day I took I-80 to Salt Lake City where I gassed up and added ice to the cooler. I was anxious to get to the West Coast but wanted to travel roads I had never previously taken. Since Sun Valley Idaho was known for its ski resort, I decided to sleep there the second night. I expected it would be cool enough that I could again curl up in my sleeping bag.

Having covered 1600 miles in two days, I decided to go running once I arrived in Sun Valley. I limited myself to 45 minutes. I didn't want to run too hard since a shower was not part of my itinerary. I was feeling like a cowboy. They didn't shower, did they? My Datsun B 210 substituted for my horse and chuck wagon.

After a good night's sleep, I decided to drive less on the third day. Covering about 300 miles I arrived in Bend, Oregon, a gorgeous little city. Summer temperatures here might reach 80 but cooled down to the 40's at night. I was so impressed with the clean mountain air that I began considering this as a possible new home for the John Leara family. I spent time talking to realtors and doing research on the area. Mt. Bachelor ski resort was an hour's drive away. What else could anyone ask for?

After another 45 minute run, I settled into my "limousine" for my third night's repose. Although the back seat folded down flat, I couldn't stretch out as my foot was always banging against something, the cooler, the front seat. But I slept well because of my relaxed frame of mind and the cool nights.

Oregon impressed me. I spent all of day four exploring. Downtown Salem looked well kept. Corvallis was also very clean although the nearby nuclear plant was a negative. After spending an hour or so in Eugene, the coast beckoned. With lots of daylight left, I drove west sixty miles to the coastline I had never seen. The ocean mesmerized me. I got out of the car and spent time just enjoying the view.

I drove south on 101 which gave me many opportunities to see the water. I think my eyes were on the ocean as much as I watched the road. I might have died on that highway except for my super hand-eye coordination. There were many campgrounds and areas that wanted to charge a fee to park for the night, but I managed to find a spot perfect for John Leara— i.e. no charge. I met two Canadian college students there who were of the same mind as I. We talked until the chill got to me, and I hopped into the Datsun for my fourth night.

On the road again the next day I picked up a hitchhiker, a Hispanic fellow. This would be the first and one of only two times in my whole life that I ever picked someone up. I am still amazed that I did—with my paranoia. But I forgot to mention that I had armed myself for this trip. Knowing I would be traveling alone and hoping to traverse new, less-traveled roads, I wanted the security of being able to defend myself. Thus, should someone attack me, I had packed a weapon. Not a knife or hand gun—nothing so easy to pull out and use. In the Datsun wrapped up in some clothing was my 30-06. For those of you not familiar with this gun, it is a rifle—an Army rifle. How I expected to "whip" out this 43-inch long weapon to defend myself is not quite clear to me even today.

I had been talking to myself for four days and really missing Dorci. Thus, on a whim, the idea of having a companion for the last two days appealed to me. Juan and I enjoyed the view of Port Orford. He had been walking south on 101, destination Mexico. That night we slept along the highway, Juan in his tent, clutching a large knife he carried for protection; and me with the 30-06 within arm's reach in the car.

The last day we drove the California coast heading for south of Los Angles. Big Sur was magnificent, probably the most spectacular view of my trip.

I had told Juan I'd drop him off in Dana Point, since that is where Angelo lived although I hadn't told Juan that. I had purposely been vague about my plans, unsure of Juan's intent. Trying to think like a CIA operative, I chose to stop at a shopping center. Then, remembering the tricks of James Fennimore Cooper's hero, the Deerslayer, I furtively back-tracked about five miles in the Datsun before heading to Angelo's house. My paranoia would keep me safe.

At Angelo's house, I headed directly to the shower after my five days on the road. Although I enjoyed visiting my brother's family, I only stayed a couple days. I missed Dorci too much and had to get back home.

I drove only 400-miles the first day, stopping in Chino Valley to see Dan and Lori Crawford. That evening, in his usual show of wisdom, Dan looked at me and said, "You miss Dorci, don't you?" At sunrise the next morning, I hopped into the 4-cylinder, smooth operating B 210 and drove the rest of the way to Wentzville, 1400-miles. I stopped for gas and bathrooms. Lori had fixed enough food for the 21-hour drive home.

I had had my "fix." The trip had been successful. I was happy to be home.

* * *

Mid-winter in 1984 I took another impulsive trip. Desperate for a break from the routine of teaching at Wright City, I phoned in sick for Friday classes. It was 1984. Beth (14), Matt (13), and I hopped in our Volkswagen pickup truck Thursday night. Dorci had packed everything, including food. We were going to drive from Missouri straight through to Keystone, CO, to ski two and a half days.

In the middle of Kansas, snow began falling. After a while it started to hypnotize me. With my eyes worn from the headlights hitting the falling flakes, I told Beth to take the wheel. For about fifteen minutes I'd close my eyes intermittently while she steered. I cautioned her that should she approach any cars or someone approach us from behind, she needed to alert me. Why? Don't think it's because I was worried about driving safety. Not me. My obsessed mind always conjured a different scenario.

Now remember: It's 2 a.m., in the middle of Kansas, in the middle of a snowstorm. Who might be lurking in six inches of snow on the interstate highway? Obviously, some sick-minded predator. In my mind, stopping was an invitation to some scumbag who was prowling around in that snowfall, waiting for stranded motorists like us—in the snowstorm—in the middle of Kansas—in the middle of the night. What better opportunity than that for such a lowlife. I'm no dummy! I'd read Truman Capote's In Cold Blood.

The family knows my "paranoia" about things like that. When Beth was about ten years old, Dorci and I went out for a few hours to visit the neighbor across the street. It was the first time we left the kids alone. Matt was nine and Bri, two. They knew where we were going and had the phone number.

When we returned home, all three children were huddled in a corner, fear on their faces. Instilled with an abundance of caution and warnings, they had become so afraid that they sought the safety of a bedroom corner. Now, I have to believe that they embellished my warnings. For my own sanity I believe that. I certainly had no intention of raising timid children.

And Dorci's viewpoint was always a good counterbalance to my neurotic concerns. She tended to go the other way, responsible but devoid of any paranoia. She scares me sometimes the way she can be oblivious to danger. I still find doors unlocked in the morning when I awake. In some cases the sliding door downstairs has been not only unlocked but open for a couple of days.

When I became a parent, I determined that as a family we needed to protect ourselves. I created a "code" that would act as a signal for danger. If anyone was in trouble, he would use the code. If anyone saw the code, he'd know that some family member needed help. I still don't feel it is safe to put the code in this book; but, believe me, my three children, to this day, know what the code is. And, they know I am still paranoid.

* * *

A couple of years ago, this came to laughable reality with Beth. Dorci wrote a little story about the events…

PREFACE

On Friday evening, John and Dorci went to the local college to see a performance of The Village People. (A neighbor gave them the tickets—John is too cheap to purchase them.) Also in the audience were friends, Sharon Wenner and her daughter Beth who was in town for the weekend. After the show John and Dorci visited with Sharon and Beth in the lobby for a few minutes.

Chapter 1

Saturday morning John starts thinking about taxes. (It's February and he's trying to get all the paperwork in order.) His friend Bill Wenner (husband to Sharon) has been giving him advice on how to handle taxes this year since Dorci has been working as a mystery shopper. John is in the kitchen at the table; Dorci is eating cereal at the table. He picks up the phone and dials a number. Now, reader, you have to know that John has always prided himself on his ability to memorize phone numbers. This is the conversation Dorci hears from John:

"Hello, Beth?" (some response on the other end)

"Is your dad there?" (response again)

"This is John Leara. Your dad has been helping me with my taxes, and I wanted to talk to him. Will he be home sometime today?" (response again)

"Would you have him call me?" (response again)

"Thanks. Bye"

Chapter 2

Within a few seconds of hanging up the phone, John gets this perplexed look on his face and says, "I think I just talked to Beth…"

For an instant Dorci thinks, "Well, yes—that's who you called!"

But John continues, saying, "Beth, our daughter."

Chapter 3

John picks up the phone again and dials.

"Beth? Did I just call you?"

Dorci picks up another phone so that she can hear the whole conversation.

"Yes, Dad, you did."

John asks, "Well, why didn't you say something?"

Beth responds, "Well, Dad, I thought you were playing one of your games."

John asks, "But why didn't you let me know it was you?"

"Because I thought you were trying to send me some secret message. You know how people will say 'collect call from John Leara' which really means, 'call John Leara after rejecting the collect call.' Dad, you know how you try to convey things on the sly. Don't you remember your code; the code you always told us meant you're in some trouble?"

"Oh, Beth," John says while bursting into uncontrolled laughter, "I taught you too well!"

Beth, John and Dorci are all laughing.

THE END

* * *

My wife frequently tells me, "John, your idiosyncrasies are what make you so lovable." By the same token, they are what make some people dislike me. There seems to be no middle ground. There have been women who thought me chauvinistic. Maybe they just misinterpret my laziness and reliance on Dorci. She and other female friends know that I am actually a great supporter of women and their causes. I'll tell Dorci, "Men are jerks—with all their physical abuse." I sympathize with females and the things they endure at the hands of men. By the same token, I can't stand those women who purport to represent women's rights. They have an ideological agenda that has little to do with helping women.

Dorci tells me, "You are without façade. People don't know how to react to that." I care little for fashion and know a golfer who is bothered by my lack of a belt. I pride myself in my untied shoe laces. Friends know I'll keep my jacket on in their home so that my shoulders and neck stay warm. At home, jackets hang on several doorknobs and chairs, even in summer months. I once had a favorite green sweater that after ten-year's wear, Dorci wanted me to cast off. When I was still wearing it ten years later, she took that sweater and burned it. (See picture in Chapter 8 with Paul Hendricks and Neil Miguel.)

Dorci used to put a new quotation at the top of the blackboard in her classroom each day. One of them cited Popeye's motto, "I yam what I yam." So, for the love or irritation of others, I have my secret code, my paranoia, my desire for change, my spontaneity, and, like the cartoon sailor, "I am what I am."

Occasionally, I reflect on my uncommon nature, its origins and influences...

CHAPTER 11

MY UNCOMMON NATURE, ITS ORIGINS
AND INFLUENCES

In 1919 Alex Leara, my father, immigrated to the United States from Korce, Albania. He was sixteen years old. His two older brothers had already been in the U.S. for several years, settling in St. Louis. They all worked for the International Shoe Co. The brothers lived together in an apartment. Each one sent money back home to their mother, a widow, to purchase land in Albania. Each planned to return there to marry and live. After a few years, they received a letter from their mother who wrote that all the money they had sent was gone and they should stop sending money. Apparently, other family members had squandered it. No land had been purchased.

Alex began accumulating his earnings. He had a plan: He would become a citizen of the United States; then he would find a wife in Albania and bring her back to the States where she would also become naturalized. After accomplishing the first, he returned to Albania by boat to do the second. The year was 1932 and he was twenty-nine. He met Alexandra Mustaka in his home village. She was ten years his junior and lived across the street from his mother's house. They married, spent six months visiting relatives in Albania, and then returned to America. My mom was pregnant.

My mother tells the story of her naiveté. On the boat to America, confronted by foods she had never seen before, she selected a banana. She asked Alex, in Romanian since she spoke no English, "How do I eat this?"

My dad could be a prankster when opportunity presented itself. "You just bite into it." Which is what my mother did.

"Ugh," she tells us. "It was awful!"

My dad, laughing so hard he barely got the words out, said, "Alexa, you have to peal it first." He pretended to be innocent of what he had done, but my mother knew differently.

My parents settled in St. Louis where there were many other Romanian families. My father's cousin got him a job as a chef. They lived with relatives until after my sister's birth. Then they moved into their own apartment. My dad worked two jobs, his second in a shoe factory, continuing to save money. Three years later my brother was born.

Dad's dream of owning his own business became a reality. He had saved money for years, even before meeting my mom, with this hope in mind. Before my birth, he and a cousin opened a restaurant with a bar, my dad putting up all the cash. For over a year, the business was successful. But when a new bar opened across the street from them, the competition was too much. After struggling for another year, the business failed. My dad lost all his money. The family began living from paycheck to paycheck.

By 1940 he had three children: Olga, then 7; Angelo, 4; and me, an infant. When he heard about a good paying job from relatives in Southbridge, Massachusetts, off we went. He was hired at American Optical.

With a family to support, he worked long hours so as to begin saving again for another business. He took the day shift and my mom worked the night shift. During those years in Southbridge, I was hopping on trains, swinging in trees and just having a good old time. As a youngster I was oblivious to any financial concerns of my parents. Although we lived in a little apartment, to me, it was a castle. My mom and dad showered their children with love, and we didn't need anything else.

By 1947 when the entrepreneurial bug bit him again, my dad had enough money to invest. My mother's sister and her family lived in Bridgeport, Connecticut, about one hundred miles south. A restaurant owner was looking for a partner with some cash. Dad decided to join him. We moved into half of a two family house owned by my aunt. She, her husband and four children lived in the other half. The restaurant demanded even more time from my father. He was the chef, a good one. I distinctly remember eating delicious food during that time, leftovers from the business.

A few years after we moved to Bridgeport while rushing to catch a bus, my dad suffered a heart attack. He was forty-seven. That did not deter him from continuing to put in long hours. However, all his hope and work was for naught. The restaurant in Bridgeport failed, and in 1949 we returned to St. Louis.

Dad's brothers and other relatives still lived there. In St. Louis, Dad again worked in a restaurant. After a year he bought a dry cleaning business near Grand and Olive. The business struggled, but my parents managed to save enough to buy a little house. Dad decided to change locations and bought a cleaners in what was supposed to be a better neighborhood. It would be the last business he owned.

Because my brother had enlisted in the Army, it fell on me at fourteen to help Dad when I could. Many Saturdays found me at the dry cleaners. After I turned fifteen and without a driver's license, I'd make deliveries throughout the city in a small van while Dad scrambled to get all of the orders ready for the afternoon rush. I remember taking clothes to a man named Guggenheim. I think he eventually became famous in Hollywood.

Saturday brought in the most cash as people tended to pick up their orders that day. Every Saturday afternoon on the way home, my father counted the dollars to tally the week's income. Fifty-five years later, my mind conjures distinct images of him and his mannerisms from 1956. "I'm in the van sitting next to Dad. I'm driving home. I glance over and see him lick his thumb so as to separate the paper bills. His expression is worn yet hopeful. His speech, with its lingering accent, sounds clearly in my ear. 'Well,' he says, 'it was a good day. We made $150.'" These memories resemble film clips running through the projector of my mind. And, always, he was working, working, working, six days a week.

Most Sundays, after attending church, my dad just shut down. But, there were a few summer Sundays when, with the encouragement from a distant cousin and the harassment of his kids, he took the family to Rockford Beach on the Big River. Dad piled us into the small van from the cleaners and headed west about an hour's drive. What a treat for the family! Not only would we swim, but Dad joined us in having fun.

In the 1970's this area became part of the state's conservation department; but in the 50's, it was private property. A land owner who bordered the river charged people to cross his bridge to the swimming

Alex Leara with his bride, Alexandra (1930's)

Alex and Alexandra (1953)

hole. A dock floated 40-feet from shore, above deep water held back by some sort of dam. I had taught myself to swim by the age of five at the beach in Massachusetts, imitating other kids, jumping off the peer into frigid ocean water. Rockford Beach had no lifeguard. What with the river's current; the murky, deep water that hid rocks and logs; dozens of kids jumping from the dock with others under it; this was a recipe for disaster. During my youth, I was unaware of any tragedies, but in later years I heard a report of someone hitting a rock and becoming paralyzed.

As for my dad, these days were unlike any others I recall with him. My teenage memory stored these unusual pictures for future reminiscence. Here, Dad had fun. Even though the dry cleaners consumed his life, he experienced some light moments at Rockford Beach. After 60 years, I still see him, along with his cousin, diving from the dock. "Pale" is inadequate to describe their complexion. "Pallid" or "pasty" might be more accurate. Their white skin was offset by the outlandishly colorful, baggy swim trunks they wore. They looked like foreigners. The image makes me chuckle even today. Their hands held awkwardly over their heads, elbows bent, they must have been trying to imitate someone they had seen before. They dove with their legs apart and knees crooked, all angles, ungainly and gauche. But, we were all having too much fun to be embarrassed—having fun with Dad—an unusual and rare experience.

Though an immigrant caught up in trying to succeed, my father was not narrow-minded when it came to his children participating in sports. He had enjoyed listening to baseball on the radio. When his children wanted to play ball in high school, he consented. Angelo had played football in high school. When I became a freshman and wanted to do the same, my parents willingly gave their permission. They seemed to think that my fascination with sports was somewhat extreme, but they wouldn't get between me and any dreams I had. Even though my games were scheduled on Saturdays, the day I helped at the store, Dad didn't hesitate to let me play.

But, he was no pushover. He did not put up with any bullshit. I remember doing something stupid one time—I don't remember what it was. Just something I shouldn't have done. In fact, I felt embarrassed that my dad discovered my escapade. I was no angel, but I desired his approval and respect. I felt proud to be his son and wanted him to reciprocate. Dad grabbed me and pinned me to the bed and said, "You cannot behave that way!" He impressed upon me that I was being an idiot, which I already knew. Dad's disappointment in me, my embarrassment and self-denigration at having failed him proved effective punishment.

Although I was lead running back for the high school team my senior year, my father did not attend any games. He was at the dry cleaners. I was kicking off, punting, returning kick-offs and punts and, of course, running the ball from the line of scrimmage. Sometimes I reflect on that era and wonder how many other fathers were unable to attend their sons' games in 1957. Weren't those the golden years? The Ozzie and Harriet years? One income often supported a family. But Alex Leara's family didn't quite fit that mold. I remember looking to the stands, hoping to see my dad. Instead, I always missed him.

One might think I felt "disappointed," but where my father is concerned, I hesitate to ever use that word. I loved and still love him deeply. How could I be disappointed with a father who worked sixty to seventy hours a week to give his family food and shelter? Sometimes, when my siblings and I would ruminate about Dad, we shed tears. Some ten years ago, my sister sent me a Christmas gift of old family snapshots she had found. Sitting there among the chaos of newly opened presents, with children and grandchildren around me, I started crying. Each of the photos showed my dad. I shed tears seeing that he obviously wasn't well, knowing that he was working his ass off and slowly dying. My tears paid tribute to his memory.

As much as I loved my Dad, I find it ironic that I became so enamored of sports. I think it is a sign of my being first generation American. My passion did not originate from my dad or other relatives. It commenced the day I first threw a ball. My fascination seems to be part of the fiber and allure of our nation: land of the free where each citizen has the chance to pursue a dream. As such, I was introduced to football and baseball and the pursuit of physical challenges. Hell, what was more challenging than jumping on and off trains at age six! Every sport and contest I played resulted from self-discovery. Today there are parents who employ mentors and professional trainers to support their child's hopes of becoming a professional athlete. Kids begin training before kindergarten. Who would have dreamed of such a scenario in the 50's?

I sometimes wonder where I would be today if I hadn't focused on football. My fascination with balls coupled with my natural skills and agility may have made the perfect combination for my becoming a professional golfer. Until my teen years, I was unaware of golf; and, of course, by then, my dreams centered on the NFL. "Golf is for sissies," I thought. "A real man has a helmet strapped on his head," declared my macho voice, little knowing that football would hasten the degeneration of my cervical spine.

My dad did, finally, see me play in a football game. He made one trip to Cape Girardeau my freshman year in college. A couple hours before the game, as the team exited a pre-game meeting, there stood Alex Leara. Attired as a typical 1958 gentlemen, he wore a fedora and a light topcoat. We spied each other. Dad yelled "John!" His voice was music to my ears.

I always held my dad in high regard. He had given me a happy life in this wonderful country. He possessed the heart, courage and ambition to come to the United States. I long knew that, otherwise, I might have been born in that wretched communist country—with a government that for forty years prohibited my mother from seeing her sister, brother, and other family, until 1972. These insights remind me of who I am, John Alex Leara. I am proud to have my father's name. I don't want to be anyone else. Dad will always be fearless in my eyes. He suffered immensely, but he never said a word to me about his concerns and pain; he wouldn't burden his children. When I think about how much I complain about my pain to others, especially to my children, I am embarrassed.

Income from the dry cleaners enabled Dad to feed the family and pay the mortgage during my high school years and freshman year of college. We didn't have money for extras, but Dad was saving a little. Unfortunately, life threw us a curve ball. For some reason, the insurance on the dry cleaners lapsed and trouble followed.

Customers paid to have their furs stored during the summer at the dry cleaners. Shortly after the insurance was cancelled, thieves broke into the building. They took all the furs. All of the savings and then some went to pay for the coats that were stolen. Dad could not overcome this setback. Although he managed to hang on to the cleaners, he now faced a deep financial hole. There seemed to be no light at the end of the tunnel.

Dad was too nice. I think that is why I've been such an ass most of my life. I have harbored a general resentment at having lost my dad. I saw my father, a good man, lose his money, and in some cases, his dignity. He never stopped trying, though. He worked and worked and looked older and older. The family always had enough food to eat, but at what price. At 74 I look healthier than my dad did at 49. My doctor recently told me I have the body of a sixty year old. (I throw this medical observation into conversations at every opportunity.) In the pictures I received at Christmas taken in 1952, Dad looks terminally ill.

Warren Buffet, when asked about his success at earning money, said, "I was just wired right at the right time." I think that is a very humble answer. I respect that. It makes me think, "I guess my dad was just not 'wired right' regarding business acumen." I don't know what he lacked. He exerted great effort, was sincere and honest. These are admirable strengths but not necessarily the key to success for an entrepreneur. My mother often expressed the opinion that, had he worked a typical 9-5 job, Dad would have been financially comfortable.

However, I know my dad was "wired right" as a father. My eyes lit up every time I saw him. I used to wonder whether my children loved me as much as I loved my father. They seldom ran up to me yelling, "Daddy, Daddy!" when I returned home after four days on the road selling dresses. I used to think, "What's the deal here? They don't get all excited like I did with my dad." I guess it was my personality! Or, maybe with the infusion of their mother's German heritage, my hot-blooded, emotional genes became too diluted with her cool, Aryan ones.

I enjoy vivid memories of my family from the time I was six. I've concluded that my father immigrated to the United States expecting to find the streets paved with gold. Really! My mother tells a story of a relative who arrived before my dad and mother came. This relative, shortly after departing from the ship, found a $5 dollar bill lying on a street in New York City. She told everyone back home that the rumor was true about America being a land of opportunity. She went so far as to throw it away thinking there'd be plenty more where that came from. (Reminds me of throwing back that twenty pound salmon in Alaska.) Dad did not hesitate to chase one dream after another to find a successful business. But, without good advice and a support system, his ambitions lacked foundation.

My father died in November 1958. The weekend I was to play the last football game of my college freshman year, he had planned to come down to Cape Girardeau to watch another game. I saw my siblings arrive without him; they said he didn't feel well and Mom had stayed with him. After the Saturday game, I went home with them. Dad was in the hospital. I visited him Sunday. We didn't know his prognosis nor how serious his condition was. My mother stayed at the hospital for the evening while we all went home. He died later that night. We never knew what killed him since my mother didn't allow an autopsy. I suspect he had cancer because he had looked unhealthy for five years.

My dad's death was my first experience with the loss of a loved one. I believe a person of Christian faith should accept death in a peaceful manner, feeling great sorrow and loss but possessing the confidence of salvation. But that is not the old country way. My mother started wailing. She traumatized me. Inside, I felt the void of losing Dad, yet there was no solace. My mother screamed and moaned for days on end. At eighteen I was horrified by her behavior. Was there something about death I didn't know? I felt so emotionally taut that if anyone approached me, I felt hostility, wanting to strike out. I desired solitude, to be left alone in peace to mourn.

Thoughts about the future blurred. I still had over three years of college study ahead and three more football seasons. I needed to pull myself together and get back into the routine of school. My brother and sister supported me in every way possible. My full scholarship to play football alleviated some of my financial worries. But at eighteen, I could not easily shed the pain of Dad's death.

Angelo and I have just recently revealed the fear we both experienced for some years after Dad's death. The anxiety of financial uncertainty burdened us—the basic needs of food and shelter! Our mother was broke. Dad left debts. Angelo had married just two months previously and the struggling cleaners fell to him. Within a year it closed. Our outlook was dismal. There was no one to fall back on. The family seemed broken with Dad gone. With him went any security we had felt.

Three years later, a couple of months before my graduation, Angelo visited me in Cape. We went out with some of the football players I still hung around with, had a few beers. Then Angelo and I went back to my apartment in town. I don't remember how we came to mention Dad, but I started crying. My emotions were tearing me apart. I hated the world right then because Dad died so early. After four years of banging into other players on the football field, I still felt pent-up rage and hostility. In anger and sorrow I slammed my forearm through the wall of the living room. My father had wasted away, toiling year after year, only to die broke and in debt. No doubt, I had some demons and they would show up from time to time.

My father's desire to follow a dream definitely seeped into his children.

In fact, Angelo represents the American Dream that Dad never found. Although he dropped out of high school before his senior year, his is a success story. After Dad's cleaners failed, Angelo went into sales but never gave up on the idea of owning his own business. By age thirty, he managed to open his own store, ironically a dry cleaners. After struggling for four years he went back to selling. In the company he joined, no one could keep up with his volume. Though successful for eight years in sales, he again opened his own company, this time manufacturing dresses. When the interest rates went from 6% to 20%, he liquidated and returned to sales. But he wasn't yet ready to forsake his dream and once more began a business mixing and selling chemicals and cleaners manufactured out of his garage. The business grew, expanded, and grew some more. He currently owns Alexis Oil which, among other things, is a distributor for a major oil company. He employs his three children and thirty other people, retaining them even during recessions. Angelo; his wife, Denise; his children, Mark, Dan and Diana have benefitted the American society immensely because of their success. Just as our dad was committed to family and God, so too is Angelo. So, although Dad wasn't able to attain his goal, I know he'd be proud of his son who did achieve the American Dream.

Olga followed a path similar to Dad's with dreams of owning a business. The results were akin to his. After her divorce, she toiled as a single parent raising two children, Kevin and Cheryl. With zero support from her former husband, she worked to feed, clothe and house her family. With a partner, she opened a jewelry-gift store which actually survived for ten years but consumed all of their savings. She returned to working at a 9 to 5 job for some years, and then once again opened another business. She started a child care center which, in my mind, was successful, for it managed to pay the bills without incurring debt. However, with too many of my father's traits, she let big dreams get the better of her. Throughout her life she was susceptible to the idea of "striking it rich." She decided to expand, leasing a huge building. It failed within a couple years, leaving a massive debt and tax problems. She returned to the smaller daycare that operated for years until a drunk plowed into the building one weekend. Her hope for a big settlement resulted in no settlement at all. Like my dad, I don't think Olga was wired right when it came to business sense. Like Dad, she worked six days a week and poured herself into her work. She lived to 75 but, also like Dad, died within a few days of entering the hospital. The debt she left her daughter could have been avoided with better decisions. She dreamed of huge success but was pummeled by life's unfairness.

As for me, Dad certainly seeped into my persona. How else do I explain leaving a good-paying teaching position in Belleville, where I had established a pole vaulting tradition in just five years, to "possibly" become a head football coach earning less money? That decision involved selling a house, traveling 1500 miles, moving my pregnant wife and toddler. It's in the genes. I know men who took teaching jobs right out of college and stayed at the same school district for thirty years. Financially rewarding, yes. But I couldn't do it. My decisions were to bite me in the ass on several occasions, but I was more fortunate than my father. I didn't speak broken English; I wasn't uneducated. For the most part, jobs in teaching and coaching were somewhat plentiful and easy to acquire. Until the age of forty.

After I turned forty, despite my accomplishments in coaching and teaching (more so coaching), personnel directors at some of the nicer school districts gave me strange looks whenever I applied for a job. It's easy to see why. Looking at my resume, one might reasonably conclude that hiring someone who moved about from state to state and in and out of education could be risky. Maybe they were troubled by my four-years as a dress salesman. That hiatus was necessary after the two life-changing, traumatic years at Sells, Arizona, where I surely thought I was dying. I had taught at five different school districts over the course of seventeen years. One year I built homes. In spite of this resume, Wright City hired me, and there I concluded my teaching career.

With every position that I sought, I pretty much showed up and said, "Here I am. These are my qualifications and accomplishments." I wasn't hired because I knew someone in the district. The only time I knew someone in a district where I wanted to teach occurred at my wife's school. She was gaining a reputation as an outstanding teacher. By 1994 she was awarded Teacher of the Year. But, her school never offered me a position.

Happily, my marriage stayed constant, forty-five years and counting. Dorci has been told many times that she puts up with a lot, referring to me. Maybe it's because of some of those demons? I guess I am luckier than other guys. Our genes seem to have meshed well together because our three children all are smarter than their parents. That's "smarter," not wiser. They can read a book in two or three evenings, whereas I require two or three weeks. They also did extremely well on ACT's and SAT's. They were straight A students, valedictorian of their respective high school classes. I failed a history class in high school. Ugh! I did get some B's in algebra and English. And now I love history. Can't get enough on the History Channel. Ironic, isn't it?

Being the child of immigrants made me sensitive to exclusion. Rejection is hard to live with. My mentality developed various ways to respond. As a teacher I had empathy for lonely students, in a protective sense. When I witnessed bullies who were arrogant and mean-spirited, treating shy students rudely, I made a point to step in and stop it. Had we been out of school, I would have preferred to knock their teeth out or break their noses. I know of one selfish, arrogant student who did get his face smashed by another student; yet it did not change him a bit. He remained a jerk! So much for responding violently. Sometimes standing up to bullies works, but I'm not sure anymore with what I witness in the news. No doubt bullies need to be dealt with rather than ignored. I have long wanted to respond violently to people or situations that cause the suffering of innocents, but I have never acted on my feelings.

As a coach I used exclusion as a motivator. With the boys in Sells, I, the immigrants' son, aligned myself with the Papago boys. Although we shared no heritage, I empathized with their situation. Together we fought the "white" boys. We, the underdogs, the minority, would show our capability and strength, earn respect and achieve victory.

Through my years in elementary school, I struggled with the fact that my parents spoke broken English. Hell, my mother at 97 maintained a strong accent and still spoke better Romanian than English. She never re-married after Dad's death in 1958 when she was 44. Maybe she took to heart what Angelo and I told her in our grief: We did not want anyone to replace our father. (We were very selfish.) Also, she never learned how to drive.

For many years she lived with one of her children. She always had a couple of children that she took in to babysit and sold crochet items to make money. For a few years she became legendary in the Wentzville School District as "Grandma Leara," caring for various children of the teachers. Her chicken noodle soup and peta were famous. Then, in the early 90's, I thought she'd be best on her own in a condo. For some fifteen years she was pretty much self-sufficient.

I take after my mother in many ways. Our major topic of conversation—now you have to realize I was 71 and she was 97—was constipation. Had been for years! Also, with regard to dollars, she and I verged on being miserly. We could stretch a dollar farther than 98% of society. When she lived in her condo, she received $550 in social security and $200 from Angelo. She paid $400 rent, paid for her food, which I bought every week, and paid all her utilities. Not once did she ask for any extra financial help; in fact, she saved a tidy sum. However, for the last three years of her life, she lived in assisted living for which Angelo paid three-fourths.

My mother had maintained a strong faith throughout her life. She loved being the center of attention, although, with her failing senses, she struggled to participate in social situations. With Dorci's help, she wrote "Her Story," about her life's experiences. She sent an afghan to President Bush and proudly framed the form letter that thanked her. She had strong opinions and willingly expressed them. Like many mothers, she continued to tell her children how to live.

My parents were immigrants, but I am proud of what they did and grateful for the opportunities their daring gave me. For a long time I felt different from other kids, like I was second class. But, I realized that I needed to get over that feeling. I think that is what being an American is all about—getting over any feelings of being different—not necessarily "fitting in" but accepting one's self and having confidence in one's identity. I think my father's passion to succeed in business, his devotion and drive, were transformed in me into a pursuit of sports, a fascination with any kind of competition or challenge. And, my love of balls became the best opportunity for me to feel truly American.

CHAPTER 12

SWINGING A ~~BAT,~~ ~~CLUB~~, HAMMER!

In early 1974 with Sells, Arizona, in our rearview mirror, we were back in St. Louis. Angelo had been working as a salesman for Alfred Werber and convinced me that I could earn good money doing the same. I became a manufacturer's representative, a fancy term meaning traveling salesman. All of my investments had crashed, and Dorci and I were starting over financially. During my five-month training period, we lived with my sister in St. Louis. Olga had generously offered her basement to us. I was on the road with Angelo traveling his territory of Missouri and Iowa. Dorci, with Beth and Matt, made do among stacked furniture and unpacked boxes.

After my training, Angelo was moved to California, and I inherited his territory. Thus I began traveling to dress shops in Missouri and Iowa. Yes, you read right, "Dress Shops." I was selling ladies' ready-to-wear. I'd gone from the gridiron to the ironing board! Now how in the hell did that happen?

Angelo had "salesman" in his blood. Although he, like our dad, dreamed of owning his own business and eventually would do so, very successfully I might add, before that was to happen, he was in sales. Alfred Werber, a sister company to Bridal Originals, created expensive ladies' clothing, sold in better department stores and exclusive dress shops. Angelo had become very successful in this company. He knew my emotional and physical situation and convinced me that I should get out of education. This new profession would pay me more than I had ever previously earned.

Thus, in 1974 at age 33, I went on the road selling. That first year I made an average of $2000 a month. (My annual salary at Sells had been about $8000.) Out of my earnings I paid for motels, food and auto expenses, driving roughly 40,000 to 50,000 miles per year. Werber had four seasons, or lines, and I established a route of travel that I repeated four times a year. Did you know that Motel 6 originally cost $6 per night? I'd stay there or in other cheap motels. Being a salesman enabled me to actually live as frugally as possible.

My "on-the-road" stories began to accumulate. A story about an overnight stay in Sioux City, Iowa, included the motel manager and food poisoning. One of the worst things about travelling was having to eat fast food—that, and developing hemorrhoids from sitting in a car for hours each day. On this particular trip, after eating at Kentucky Fried Chicken, I fell ill in my motel room. The manager took me to a hospital emergency room. A nurse took my temperature: 93. She called the doctor and he took it again. Still 93. After asking me about my dinner, he concluded that I probably had food poisoning from the coleslaw. Needless to say, I removed KFC from my choice of eating establishments.

Having suffered from a spectrum of respiratory problems during the two years in Arizona, I continued to experience flair ups from my chronic bronchitis. One week when I was too ill to travel, Dorci went out in my stead. She traveled to southern Missouri, to several of my favorite customers. She did a good job with her amiable personality and brought in a large order.

The most distasteful aspect of this job was being away from Dorci, Beth and Matt. I once again experienced "yearning," yearning for home and family. The episode with the food poisoning especially depressed me since I had been 300-miles from the comfort of home. There were very few times I left the house on a Monday morning that I didn't lament my job. But, earning good money, a relatively new phenomena for me, kept me out on the road.

After my training, we had moved to Wentzville in the spring because of its location in the highway system. Calling itself "The Crossroads of the Nation," Wentzville was a small, rural town about thirty miles west of St. Louis, population 5,000. Interstate 70 running east/west and Highway

40/61 (now I-64) running north/south made for efficient travel to destinations in my territory of Missouri and Iowa. I could live in Wentzville with its proximity to the factory without having to confront the traffic problems of city life. Initially we rented a small apartment.

The $2000 per month more than doubled my teaching salary. I felt wealthy! With our savings growing, I thought, "What the hell. Let's buy some land." Ready to settle in one place for a while and with two children approaching school age, I determined that land would keep me grounded—pun intended. With the aid of a local realtor in August, we found 56-acres just out of the town on Jackson Road. The plot came from a larger parcel a farmer was dividing and selling since none of his three sons wanted to continue working the land.

Two months after purchasing the acreage, I convinced Dorci we could afford to build a home on the land. We were anxious to get out of the apartment. She reluctantly acquiesced, with both financial concerns and the knowledge that I was not "handy." For, when I said "build a home," I meant "we would build it—that is, hire one man and work with him."

Now, Dorci had never seen a hammer in my hand, and she came from a family whose grandfather, father and five brothers were all "more-than-just-handy." One or the other could fix anything and everything, build furniture, repair car engines, build tool and die machines, repair or construct electronic equipment, and so on. Dorci was "handier" than I and usually fixed things around the house. I'm sure she thought, "What in the world is he getting us into now?"

My attitude and enthusiasm overwhelmed her. I had her believing we could achieve anything after the earth-shaking success in Sells. Sells—the place where I had almost died from self-inflicted stress with a large dose of valley fever and infection. I'm sure she envisioned many a purple thumb on my part.

At the suggestion of a friend at our local bank, we sought financing for this venture at St. Charles Savings and Loan in St. Charles, MO. Without an appointment, I simply appeared at the savings and loan and asked to see the president. Walking into his office I said, "Judge Bruere, my name is John Leara, and I'd like to build a house. I need to borrow some money from you." After ten to fifteen minutes of exchanging information, I handed him house plans. These "house plans" were drawn by Dorci on an 8 ½ x 11 inch piece of graph paper. She had made a representation of the floor plan, no elevations, no electrical or plumbing layouts, no structural specs. It was merely a pencil-drawn sketch of the home's layout.

Then the clincher came when I said, "We are going to build it ourselves." I didn't offer details about my lack of experience with a hammer.

We liked each other, Judge Bruere and I. I suspect my no-nonsense approach appealed to this man who presided over his own financial institution. He was a legend in his own time. Although I actually interacted with Judge Bruere on only a few occasions, those times became once-in-a-lifetime memories.

I showed him our bank accounts revealing my frugality. Every month since I'd started working for Alfred Werber, much more came in than went out. When I alone worked as a teacher in 1971 and 1972, we had saved about $2500 each year. Dorci knew how to shop and cook on a tight budget. She always had a vegetable garden.

These days I think she lives by a different code. Although she claims differently, she has more than made up for any spending shortages in the '70's. I think she's taking advantage of the fact that I'm five years older and getting senile. (Only kidding.)

So, with Judge Bruere agreeing to give us a construction loan to be followed by a permanent loan once the house was completed, we began a new adventure. We hired one carpenter, a man 65-years old, Melvin McMullen, who came highly recommended by a farmer down the road from our property. We arranged for all the sub-contractors. Excavation started in November; and by Thanksgiving weekend, the footings and foundation were finished. Next came roughed-in plumbing followed by pouring the basement floor.

Our carpentry crew consisted of Melvin; his 20-year old son, Jeff; Dorci and me. We rough-framed that bugger in no time with mild December weather aiding our endeavors. Mel delegated work with the best of them. He and Jeff took the more difficult tasks. Dorci and I took on the simpler ones. Dorci wielded a mean 20 ounce hammer, pounding in 16 penny nails at a rate that impressed Melvin who raved about her abilities. Me, I learned to swing a hammer, too; and we were evenly matched. Purple thumbs occurred infrequently.

Since the time between Thanksgiving and Christmas is slow for travelling salesmen, I looked for a break from sales and the pressure of house-building. We decided to take a ski trip to Colorado where we would meet with Angelo's family who drove from California. Unfortunately, while skiing with one of my nephews, I fell and suffered a slight concussion. I returned home unable to do any work on the house. Dorci likes to tell the story of how she and Melvin finished the roof in a snow storm. As I lay at home recuperating, they finished nailing down the shingles as snow began falling. No wonder she impressed Melvin!

By February we were living in the house, even though the floors were not completed—those were the days of two layers of subfloor and only one had been laid. Nor were the walls or ceiling painted. Running water was available only in the one bathroom since there were no kitchen cabinets, no sink. With me back on the road, Dorci, while caring for two toddlers, proceeded to do a lot of work herself. She finished putting down the second layer of flooring, no easy task since it required cutting particle board and nailing it down. People couldn't occupy a house in that state of incompletion today with increased bureaucratic regulations. We definitely were roughing it; but this was a labor of love, and we were young enough to forego comfort for "adventure." My energy levels were soaring. The high resembled what I felt when playing college football.

We lived in this home for five years. Slowly we had finished the downstairs with a bathroom, bedroom, recreation room, large laundry area and a cold storage room for Dorci's garden produce. We had a wood burning stove put in the lower level right by the open stairwell which enabled its warmth to rise upstairs. Around this stove Dorci built the hearth and lined the corner walls after a bricklayer had said, "Women don't work with mortar and bricks." In 1979 we sold this house with six acres.

We moved into town after buying a "shell" from a developer on a city lot. We finished the interior ourselves and lived there for just one year.

In 1981 we built our third house on another city lot. It was a three-bedroom, two-story on a corner lot in a new subdivision. As before, Dorci drew the plans. I decided to tackle this construction on my own since I was between teaching jobs. Dorci worked full time teaching, and the kids were too young to help. Fortunately, a carpenter friend was building a house across the street. Whenever I felt uncertain or had a question, I yelled over to him, "Gary, how do I…?" Being a congenial fellow, he willingly directed me with a return yell. To this day Dorci proudly states that I built that one without her help. I did hire a young fellow, also unemployed, to aid with some of the tasks that required two men. But mostly, I worked there, day after day, enjoying the fruits of physical labor. We lived in this home about five years and then returned to our land on Jackson Road.

We built three more homes in the Wentzville area. We lived in two of them. While we were constructing the fourth one, the interesting lines of the roof caught the eyes of a passing couple. They stopped and inquired about its purchase. We negotiated a contract and the house was sold before we finished building it.

Dorci had designed the elevation and floor plan from a house she found in a book from the library. It was an actual residence in a town in Massachusetts with the street address printed in the caption under the photograph. I phoned the town's local post office and convinced them to give me the owner's name so that I could call them. During the course of my phone conversation with the home owners, I invited myself to visit in person. I asked if we could spend no more than two hours measuring rooms and angles. They said, "Come ahead."

Dorci and I drove straight through from Missouri to Massachusetts, tape measure, pen, paper and camera in hand. The folks served us lunch. They were a delightful couple, curious to meet me, impressed by my outlandish quest. Within a few hours the same highways that saw us heading east now passed by in the other direction. We made one stop on the return trip to see Dorci's father in Richmond, Indiana. Once back in Wentzville, Dorci started drawing up the plans. She had, by now, taught herself how to create elevations. She could produce a set of drawings with electrical and plumbing layouts. Truss companies did their own drawings from our roof design.

Andy Burt came to our rescue with this fourth house. I had taught him in senior English at Wright City in the early 80's. He was very intelligent; his IQ probably registered among the top ten percent of all students I ever encountered in my classes. However, he had no interest in formal English. He could mimic Walter Brennan of "The Real McCoys" TV show at any moment. In the spring of his senior year, Andy moaned when I announced to the class that we would study a unit of advanced grammar. "Whatta we gotta study that for?" he asked with only a trace of actual challenge in his tone. Andy was always good-humored.

"This IS English, Andy. Grammar is part of the curriculum," I answered.

"Yeah, well, we all speak English. Why do we gotta study grammar for?" he quipped. "We ain't never gonna use it no more." His response purposely defied rules of proper English.

"Well, Andy, like it or not, the test will count heavily towards your quarter grade." This challenged him, for he did take pride in his grades.

Andy listened carefully every day. I relished those ten days of nothing but grammar, grammar, grammar. My love affair with grammar had begun in sixth grade when my teacher bragged about me in front of the whole class. In college my football buddies had come to me for help in their English courses. Now, here sat Andy in my class absorbing the lessons. He easily aced the test with an almost perfect score. He knew his grammar but found little use for it in his life out of school.

After high school Andy went into an apprenticeship to become a carpenter. He worked in the union for some years until he decided to go out on his own. He became one of my heroes. He utilized his brain and talents and created a successful carpentry business. For a while he employed his younger brother and father when he built homes.

In 1986 when we began our fourth house, I called on him. He was still employed by the union and could only help us after his regular hours. His great mind, his admirable work ethic and his superior craftsmanship revealed themselves to anyone who worked with him. After this house, he helped on houses number five and six.

We took our cabinet designs for the fourth and fifth homes to an Amish family in Bowling Green, Missouri, some fifty miles north. We had seen their work in a friend's new home and made the drive to their workshop to discuss an agreement. The Eicher brothers powered their machinery with a diesel tractor engine since they did not use standard electricity. We knew there were some disadvantages for us in this arrangement. The Eicher brothers did not have telephones; thus we had to drive there if we wanted to discuss something. They did not deliver since they didn't drive cars or trucks; we had to pick up the cabinets ourselves. But we admired their craftsmanship and came to respect the families we met.

Because the fourth house was under contract, we were on a schedule. The weekend we arranged to pick up the solid oak cabinets, our plans went awry. In addition to using our van, we had borrowed a small truck. This required two drivers but neither Dorci nor Beth was available that weekend; and a friend had to cancel at the last minute. That left Matt. At fourteen he did not have a license. Contrary to many other kids who lived out in the country, Matt had no experience driving, other than our riding lawn mower. However, we were confident that he could manage our van, with me in the lead in the truck. The one thing I emphasized to him, "Avoid a head-on collision!" Other than occasionally riding with the right tires on the shoulder of the state highway, Matt drove like an old-hand. Reminds me of making deliveries for my dad's dry cleaners in St. Louis at age fifteen.

Having sold, in the spring of '86, the two-story that I had built, we rented a place to live. During that summer we were completing the fourth house for someone else. That fall we started drawing plans for our fifth house, having found another one to duplicate. Fortunately, the house we copied was in a neighboring town, not halfway across the country on the East Coast. The foundation was poured in the fall; and when the weather allowed, more concrete work and drain tile were completed in the spring.

By Memorial Day in 1987 work began in earnest on our fifth house. It was the last one we built on the original 56-acres we had purchased in 1974. Two homes had been built in the city limits of Wentzville. Our sixth house was also "in town," on a lot bordering a golf course. The fifth house would be our home for fifteen years, longer than any other house we lived in to date. Building this one turned into a real family affair. Beth had turned seventeen; Matt would be sixteen in October. Briana at ten did a lot of cleanup work, the least attractive of all the jobs. But, many of the door headers have nails pounded in by her.

With school out for the summer, the whole family went to work. The house would be finished before school started in August. Matt hammered the most nails. Dorci parsed out the most instructions. Andy helped immensely after putting in eight hours at his day job. We worked until dark or later every day. At 47 I found the work more challenging than it had been previously. This home proved to be very comfortable and more attractive than our others.

We planted over 200 trees on the three-acre parcel immediately surrounding the house. In 2009 when Dorci and I drove by, some of them rose over 40-feet. There are White Pine, Pin Oaks, willows, Mountain Ash, cottonwood and a variety of maples. The trees came from nurseries and wooded areas where we dug them out ourselves. The house had great passive solar heat from the two levels full of windows facing south. Many a winter's afternoon found me or Dorci napping in the sun on the living room floor. These southern windows looked out on the rest of the 47 acres of hay, a creek bed and wooded area.

While living in this house, we gradually sold off the rest of the acreage. A young man and his family bought twenty acres from the creek bed to the back property line, all of the wooded area. He put in a road and built a home with a swimming pool. When we decided to sell our fifth home with three acres, we asked if he wanted to buy the approximately 24 remaining acres. He did.

Reflecting on the purchase of the original 56-acres in 1974, I easily see how it set us on a life-style path. We became rooted in Wentzville. Our three children went through the school system from kindergarten to twelfth grade. Dorci taught for over twenty years at Wentzville High School and retired from there. Matt hunted and fished on our land. He'd be gone for hours, roaming far beyond our acres. Riding lawn mowers, large summer gardens, home canning, unpasteurized milk from neighboring farmers with its homemade butter and ice cream, these were part of our everyday life. Dorci and the kids picked gallons of blackberries in the summer on our land. For a few years I owned a tractor and played at being a farmer. We bailed hay. I cut cedar trees and sold fence posts. We built a low-water bridge over the creek. We raised a few head of cattle.

In fact, the 56-acres became a haven for me in 1993-94 when I was 53. After more than a decade of teaching at Wright City High School, I had slowly become consumed with frustration and disenchantment. Changes in administration around 1990 had made matters worse. A thought inspired me: "Maybe if I take a year off, I can come back renewed and teach until I'm 60." Some schools allow for a year's leave with pay if the teacher takes classes or in some way enhances his credentials. I wanted none of that. I just had to get away and find peace of mind. And so, the school board granted me a leave without pay for one year.

That winter had many sunny days with temperatures in the forties and fifties. The weather was perfect for being out of doors. I spent many hours clearing the back 20-acres. With my tractor and chain saw I cut trees and shrubs, working incessantly throughout the season. There were hundreds upon hundreds of useless, scrubby trees, some with inch-long needles sticking out in every square foot.

Because we lived outside the city limits, I burned many piles of brush. Cedar makes one hot fire--so hot my face seemed to burn although I stood fifteen feet away. I sometimes thought I had become a pyromaniac. My adrenaline surged, especially when it seemed the fires might rage out of control. They never did. I felt 25 again.

One weekend afternoon with Dorci helping me, I got the saw wedged in a tree. I struggled with the thing for a long time, long enough that I neared exhaustion. I cussed at myself. Finally, we managed to free it. Dorci saw how aggravated I was with myself for allowing the saw to become trapped. In her usual manner she tried to assuage me. In fact, she became somewhat impish and suggested we make love. This was not unusual for my wife, experiencing a surge of affection and love for me when I got down on myself.

It was a glorious day. The sun shone. The temperature hovered around sixty. We were hidden in a semi-wild spot. We found an area on the ground with few bumps and no rocks. We didn't have the beautiful ocean that Burt Lancaster and Debra Kerr had in From Here to Eternity; but, then, I had never thought rushing salty, sandy water was the best setting for lovemaking. We lay in grass, with birds calling and trees filtering the sunlight—although we weren't paying much attention to all that. I think our spontaneity took second to none.

We still laugh when we talk about it. We chuckle about that lovemaking in the woods and several other times when Dorci got a passionate hair. Like the time after seeing a movie at the mall and we moved our car to a dark corner of the parking lot. And the time we were swimming in the clear waters of Norfork Lake in the Ozarks. I was scuba diving; and she, treading water at the surface, discarded her top. Seeing her lovely breasts, I forgot the caution about ascending too fast. With my flippers propelling me quickly, I soon reached the surface. The lure of breasts, it seemed, from my thirteenth birthday when I tried to touch them and got smacked, to that day on the lake, continued to get me in trouble—in this case, with possibly fatal results.

From September to May, I mostly worked by myself. Not once did I feel lonely. My mind actively made calculations so that the larger trees fell in the right place without danger to me and without getting hung up on others. The solitude and physical labor gave me much comfort. My mind wandered and traveled in so many different directions without interruption. Every once in a while I just sat down, surrounded by the tall, peaceful trees, and let my eyes wander and ears listen. This portion of the 20-acres had beautiful 70-foot to 100-foot trees. They stood farthest from the creek that divided our land in the thickest woods, separating the southern section from the alfalfa field on the north.

Though I tried to remain alert to my task, the chain saw got the better of me one time. On this particular day, Dorci was once again helping. We were cutting up logs into firewood. Some were lengthy and lay at awkward angles. I'd cut. Dorci would remove the smaller piece. I cut. Dorci tossed. I cut and cut. Dorci yelled, "John, stop!" Somehow, as I cut into the log, I also cut into my knee that I was using to prop up the wood. Not once but twice. I didn't even feel the saw. Dorci saw the blood coming from the knee of my jeans and the slice through the fabric. She drove me in to the doctor who laughed as he stitched me up. My two scars are both two inches long, a half inch apart, running parallel to each other. That was my only mishap—except for another time we cut firewood and I somehow managed to hit Dorci in the face with a piece of wood. She had a good story to tell in explaining to her fellow teachers how her husband gave her a black eye.

All too soon my leave of absence came to an end and I stood in the classroom again. How quickly the frustration and disillusionment returned. I could not accept the values, or lack of them, and behavior of the current generation of high school students. The administration gave me no support. The popular concept of education stood much at odds with mine. By Christmas I had made up my mind to retire. Dorci encouraged me. All she had to do was look at my physical state, my drawn face, my mental lethargy and spiritual void.

I calculated what was necessary for me to leave as soon as possible. The Missouri Public Retirement System required a minimum of 25-years of service in order to collect retirement funds. They had crafted a formula whereby a teacher could earn credits by paying for time spent in military service and years worked in private or out of state schools. Those credits would then be applied towards years of teaching in the Missouri system. I probably studied my computations a dozen times. Working with the state system, I determined how much credit I could "buy" and sent in the money. The state and I had agreed that on March 10, 1995, I would have exactly 25-years of service. That is the date I wrote into my letter of resignation from the Wright City School District.

The district was not pleased with my request. First of all, they had given me a leave the previous year under the assumption I'd be teaching there for several more years. I had not deceived them. I had fully hoped and intended to teach another five years. But I couldn't do it. Secondly, leaving mid-semester in March did not sit well with the superintendent. But, when Dorci sees pictures of me during this era, she says I looked like I was dying. I needed to leave ASAP. I also believed the students would be better off without me. And, maybe I'd add a few years to my life.

Dorci and I had occasionally talked about selling our land. We had contemplated leaving the state, finding a more amenable climate, once she retired. Since my retirement in 1995, I had been sort of waiting for her. Although she enjoyed her job and could teach many more years, I encouraged her to retire after 25-years as I had done. So, her career ended in June 2000. We began talking more about leaving our country-style life. We both wanted some sort of change. I was especially restless after five years of retirement. The acreage lay three miles out of town which seemed like three miles too far going and coming. It wasn't a decision reached easily, but after two years, we made the move into town, deciding to build another house in Wentzville. I relished the idea of throwing myself into the project.

By this time when we were ready to build the sixth and last home in Wentzville in 2002, Andy Burt had his own construction business and had built several homes, for himself, family members and as a contractor for other people. For our home, Andy headed a crew of four: his brother, his father, Dorci and me. Dorci and I collaborated on the plans for a 3500-square foot atrium ranch to be built on a new golf course.

Although Andy was the boss, he kept us laughing. Not only is he smart; he is naturally very humorous. As I mentioned before, he could break into his imitation of Walter Brennan at will. When I began to stress over something, as frequently happened, he'd say, "John, it ain't no piano!" Another time when his dad couldn't locate a tool, in his light-hearted tone he said, "Dad, it's right there by your dick!"

Andy's adages have served Dorci well. Occasionally, when my obsession over accuracy or details gets out of hand, she gladly reiterates his wisdom. "John, it ain't no piano!" During other times of worry, she reminds me of several maxims another friend from our past used to quote. One from Max Ehrmann's "Desiderata" says "…no doubt the universe is unfolding as it should." And another which refers to the idea that most details and worries of today will little matter in one hundred years.

One day Andy's attention to detail got the better of me. He and his brother, Curtis, moved slowly around the perimeter of the subfloor using a laser transit as a measuring device. Every three feet he paused and took a reading. He wanted to make sure the floor was level. He would say "Plus a quarter" or "Minus an eighth" and that was written on the floor. Later, appropriate adjustments would be made. For now, they were just making calculations. It was time consuming. In my mind, I tallied the hourly wages, the increasing total ringing in my head like the sound of a cash register.

Finally I said, "This is one hell of a job you have, Andy." Knowing me as well as he did, Andy just brushed me off with one of his quips, probably with a reference to my being a tightwad.

One day when the exterior walls were being raised, Andy had climbed to the apex of the rear vaulted wall. He sat perched on the top plate about sixteen feet above the floor. It was mid-afternoon and the summer sun beat down. Andy sat waiting. The temperature and humidity had us all perspiring. He waited for his brother and dad to complete some task below. Rather than lose his patience as he sat there, he called down to them, saying, "Hey, guys! It's hotter up here closer to the sun. Hurry it up!" We all laughed... and hurried.

This house had a plethora of windows; seventeen in the atrium stairwell alone. I figured it would take a couple of days to install them all since more than half were second story or even higher in the vaulted area. When I mentioned this to Andy, he and his brother and dad said, "Hell, no. We'll get all the windows installed in one day." I didn't believe them. Andy responded, "Let's make a wager. How about a steak dinner?" Since I frequently was pushing them to go faster, I willingly agreed. Even though a week later on a Friday night I paid the bill for several steak dinners at Outback, I had fun and, as usual around Andy, laughed a lot.

For that home, Andy built and installed all the cabinets. Dorci had drawn up a plan for her "dream" kitchen, knowing Andy's skill. It combined oak and beadboard. She had Andy construct a butcher block top for the peninsula that was seven feet by three and a half feet. It was so heavy that Andy and Curtis had to carry it into the house in two pieces. He built a bar for the family room and an in-wall entertainment center. He designed, built and installed a unique staircase. Andy told us that building staircases was his first love.

For Dorci and me this house brought more stress and disagreement

Our first house on Jackson Road in Wentzville

Spring - Beth helps John wash the car, Matt rides his bike

Our last house - John in trusses and Dorci sawing

than any previous one. It had been fifteen years since we had completed our fifth home. I guess we were both getting old, cranky and more set in our ways. We argued over where to put a particular window. We argued over where the carpet should end and the wood floor begin. If I said "right," she said "left." I had thought building at age 47 a challenge; but now I was 62 and the work proved more taxing to my body. In addition, bureaucratic regulations caused us some nightmares. Building our first house in 1974 had been, to use a trite expression, "a piece of cake" compared to the regulations and hoops we faced in 2002. I saw it all as, excuse my French, "bullshit."

Dorci and I sort of agreed that this would be the house we wouldn't leave unless it was "feet first." Building another home seemed to be out of the question for two reasons. I didn't think my body was physically up to it and emotionally there had been too much stress and disagreement. Then, within eighteen months of our moving into the home on the golf course, life threw us one of its ironies. On a visit to Florida for our granddaughter's christening, Beth asked us, "Are you ever going to move to Florida?" She had been living in Florida since 1999 and now had two children.

Although we had considered moving there many times years ago, we told her, "No, we don't want to live in Florida."

"Well," she responded, "we don't want to move to Missouri. However, we want our children to grow up near their grandparents. Is there a place we can mutually agree to?"

That's how we ended up back in Arizona. We had long visited Dan and Lori Crawford whom we had befriended in Sells. They had moved from Sells to Chino Valley just north of Prescott. We knew of Prescott's mild four seasons and beautiful scenery. So, in 2004 it became home to us and to our daughter's family.

CHAPTER 13

THE GENETIC CONNECTION

Can a fascination with balls be inherited? Did I pass on to our children the desire to do crazy? Or, my impulsive, restless nature? Is there such a gene? All three children were involved in sports in their youth; but, more than that, they exhibited a love for the physical in other ways.

Beth: Our First-Born

Beth has long been a dare devil. When she was two, I used to ride her on the front of my motorcycle in New Mexico. She'd sit on the gas tank on my 400 Suzuki dirt bike, and we'd ride up and down small hills, some of them pretty steep. No fear from her! At four she said she wanted to learn how to swim; and I told her, "You have to go underwater like this." I descended a couple feet. She followed suit, undaunted. She was swimming that day. At ten she wanted to jump from the highest platform at the Clayton pool in St. Louis, 10-meters (33-feet). When she approached the stairs to begin her ascent, a lifeguard stopped her, saying she was too young. Here was a child who seemed to have inherited my reckless behavior.

She began playing softball in the children's leagues; but when she entered high school, she focused on soccer. At fullback, she was an integral part of her team. Her skills and persistence allowed her to successfully forestall opposing scorers. Covering a forward can be a thankless job, but her dedication made her an outstanding defensive player. I loved watching her aggression and strength. Opponents had no easy path to the goal.

The highlight of Beth's high school soccer occurred her junior year when the team advanced in playoffs to the state semifinals where they eventually placed fourth. In their final game, the tension and excitement pumped through the players and fans. At fullback Beth defended against the opposing team's top scorer. Tenacious as ever, she stayed on top of the forward, looking like her shadow. That position seemed to be the perfect spot for her. Unfortunately, Wentzville lost but by only one goal.

When we discussed her high school days, Beth told me, "Sports gave me another way to excel—beyond academics. I enjoyed being aggressive and competitive. Those qualities were encouraged when I played." Beth took seriously her role on any team in any game. Her face and play showed effort and determination. Her attitude reminded me of myself except that she relished the bonding that occurred among her teammates while I frequently antagonized my fellow players.

Back in 1956 when I attended high school, I saw girls as cheerleaders and not much else athletically. I was as oblivious to their abilities as was the rest of the nation. Then the country woke up, and women's sports grew in popularity. However, I remained oblivious. I naturally gravitated towards helping Matt and didn't appreciate Beth's talents. Aware of this she says, "I felt like I was competing with Matt. I always tried harder." Meanwhile, her dad didn't wake up in time to help as she developed her soccer skills. I should have but didn't.

Being oblivious is something my wife often accuses me of. I can take the same route to and from the golf course or gas station for years; yet when Dorci says something about a place located on that route, a house or business, I have no idea what she's talking about or where it is. My usual comeback has something to do with "priorities"; it's just not important. I have to admit, I'm not very observant unless something is sports-related.

However, I didn't remain oblivious towards women's athletic prowess forever. Ironically, today, when I'm on the golf course, I picture Karrie Webb's tee shot when I swing my driver. I watched her practice before an LPGA tournament in St. Louis one summer. Her swing was effortless and fluid, and the ball exploded off the face of her club. I use her name as a mantra, "Karrie Webb, Karrie Webb." My buddies ask me what I'm mumbling. My hope is that by visualizing her performance, I'll be able to emulate her success.

When Beth attended Rice University, she continued to find all sorts of opportunities to compete physically. She played powder-puff football, softball, volleyball and ultimate Frisbee. The most important and popular social event at Rice was the annual Beer Bike competition, bigger even than homecoming. Beth was a star each of her four years, classified as "iron woman" because she not only sprinted on a bike for two-thirds of a mile but also chugged the beer—warm, flat beer in a special chugging can.

She played club soccer for four years and invited me to New Orleans to watch her team in an invitational tournament. That was in 1993 when I took my leave of absence from teaching. The high school environment at Wright City, with its lack of respect and discipline, clashed with my nature; and I had to get the hell away for a while. During the years from 1964 with my first teaching job to 1993, the country had changed, students had changed, parents had changed and the schools had changed. I hadn't adapted to those changes. With the superintendent and principal suggesting or demanding I pass students or ignore basic rules and principles I held dear, I felt my life and person were being violated. I needed a hiatus. So, with the radio carrying the Clarence Thomas hearings, I made the drive to New Orleans to watch Beth play against Tulane.

Her teammates exhibited behavior which would inspire the most cynical of us. They were really neat young women. Full of smiles, they enjoyed the competition and challenge of club soccer. They were intelligent (Rice University wouldn't have anything less), well-mannered and self-confident. If you have ever seen the students Jay Leno interviews, think total opposite. I can guarantee you, the girls I watched compete that weekend could point to Chicago on a map in a split second and probably give you stats on the state of Illinois' economy, history, and political influence. In other words, they knew more than who was the latest contestant voted off of "American Idol."

After graduation, to establish residency in Texas, Beth worked for two years in Houston before starting medical school. During that time she continued playing soccer in a city league, on both a girls' team and a co-ed team. During med-school she played inter-mural and city league softball. She definitely seems to have inherited this passion for participating in sports, for exertion, and competition.

Throughout the summers of her adolescent, teen and college years, Beth's dare-devil spirit was ever present. She nonchalantly followed me when I jumped from the 40-foot rock cliffs at Johnson Shut-Ins in southern Missouri, a place now closed to jumping after several deaths occurred. One summer we joined my nephew Mark and family in Cottonwood Cove along the Lake Mead National Recreation Area. We took to jumping off escarpments that were 10 to 20-feet and higher. To my chagrin, at one point, Beth kept climbing until she reached what looked to me to be about 60-feet. As she appeared to prepare for a jump, nausea overcame me and I was petrified! I yelled up to her, pleading that she descend to a lower level. She did, eventually, but I had to talk her down from the 60-feet. (Memories of the tragedy in Acapulco screamed at me to avoid misfortune that day.) Instead, she jumped from about 45-feet.

Beth seems always ready for physical challenges and continues such behavior as an adult. She decided to run her first marathon in 1998 at age 28. In addition to the physical challenges required of her for that marathon, it was in San Diego, California, on the day before she was to start her residency in St. Petersburg, Florida. She had to hop on a plane and fly cross country after completing the race! In 2007 she ran the Marine Corps Marathon in Washington, D.C. And in 2008 she did a half marathon in Phoenix.

Being a family practice doctor, wife and mother of three hasn't stopped her from pursuing physical activity. Her medical office formed a team in the summer, adult, co-ed softball leagues, the "Fun-gi"; and she was one of the strong players. In one game, a guy on the opposing team tried to intimidate her as she covered second base. He ran at her full-force. He didn't know this was John Leara's daughter who would not flinch. He knocked her over, but not before she had tagged him out. That made the third out for the inning. To the cheers of "You go, girl" from her teammates, a bruised-but-satisfied Beth jogged to the dugout.

With her sports background, she has taken on coaching her children. In 1997 she married Steve Luce, an occupational therapist, and they have three children. The softball and soccer seasons find her on the field mentoring the girls on her daughter's teams. Her daughter, Isabella, by the way, shows signs of following in her mother's footsteps. In one soccer game after Bella had made four goals and the score stood 4-0, Beth told her to pass the ball off to her teammates, none of whom scores like she does. Her youngest, Jackson, loved to play with balls as soon as his fist was large enough to grasp one. Before he could walk, when he was crawling around the grass at his older brother's soccer games, he'd be bumping a soccer ball with his fists and clambering after it. As for Nicholas, the oldest, he enjoys sampling all forms of physical activity and hasn't yet decided on any preference. However, when it comes to reading, he has been devouring books since he was three.

Her love of the outdoors has not waned. Living just 90-miles from Flagstaff, she has introduced her children to snow skiing. The family also camps. She and her husband purchased a 29–foot trailer. They average four trips a year around Arizona over long weekends with a circle of friends. Swimming in lakes and rivers, hiking, fishing, four-wheeling, and other activities fill their days. At one spot a rope hangs from a tree for the kids to swing from and drop into the water. Brings to mind camping with my pole vaulters and the rope we swung on.

Beth recently participated in a "Warrior Dash," a competition of 3.4-miles with various obstacles. I watched one of her training sessions which included getting over a 6-foot wall, running through tires, and climbing a 12-foot cargo net. Actually, I think she's a bit too crazy, risking injury. Acting "fatherly" I asked her, "And you're doing this because…?"

"Yes, just because," she quickly interrupted.

I could probably have correctly added, "…because you're my daughter and you have 'crazy' in you."

Since her graduation from college and medical school, I have a new connection to Beth: medicine. Had I been a better reader with a dash more (or maybe a cup more) of IQ points, I would have enjoyed being a doctor, which seems somewhat akin to coaching. I could see myself "coaching" patients into taking better care of themselves. I continually converse with Beth about necks, shoulders, infections, stomach problems, skin, and such. Whatever my current ailment, I'll ask her about it. Sometimes I tease her. "I know more about necks and shoulders than you do."

She just says, "Well, you should, Dad. You've been studying neck problems for 30-some years!" And, when she tires of my questions, I'll sometimes consult Matt, who, as a veterinarian, can also give me medical advice. However, neither one will agree to cut the cystic lump from the side of my nose, even when I remind them of the money I contributed to their education.

Beth, Bri and John at Norfolk

Three valedictorians

Our "rain gear" for the Taum Sauk Trail (1992)

Glacier National Park (1994)

Matt: The Middle Child

When Matt turned three, I took him to Tower Tee in St. Louis, a practice driving range, where he knocked the hell out of golf balls, left-handed, his natural side. He had almost perfect form. For those of you who have seen the movie <u>The Natural</u>, Matt was like the character played by Robert Redford. He could do anything with a ball, and do it well: dribble a basketball, throw a baseball, hit a baseball, hit a golf ball with a driver or an iron. He was catching fly balls at age five. A friend cut a left-handed iron in half, and Matt hit golf balls around the yard (we had two acres of grass) at ages four and five.

Unfortunately, when tee-ball started, golf was put on the back burner. All the other kids played tee-ball and Matt joined them. From age six through age sixteen, he concentrated on playing baseball and soccer. And, as it turned out, soccer brought us together, finally, as coach and player.

In 1977 Matt entered the St. Charles County Catholic Soccer league. He was in second grade. I volunteered to coach the team that year and then stayed with them for the next seven. When the boys first assembled, their attention span of about 30-seconds took me by surprise, although it shouldn't have. They were only seven years old. They also lacked skills. Matt's teammates couldn't come close to controlling the ball with their feet. Although their abilities were to improve, gradually, their attention span would be my nemesis for the next few years.

Being familiar with the drive and dedication of fourteen, fifteen, sixteen and seventeen-year-olds in my coaching past, working with these six, seven and eight year olds totally challenged me. For the first three years, the boys showed a real discontent with my intensity. I had to make sure I didn't talk too long when instructing them. During a game, if they weren't on the field, they showed little interest in the game. Hell, sometimes even on the field they didn't pay attention to the game's progress. However, the boys managed to play respectable soccer; and, over the years, they seemed to learn important skills: like centering the ball after taking it down the sideline.

We had every manner of athlete on our team over the course of those years. The boys were Catholic and non-Catholic. Some lived in very nice homes and some in broken-down housing. There were Sunday-school, alter-boy types mixed with boys who would cuss and spit. The naïve with the street-wise. Some of them were a real pain in the ass; but in this league, I was required to work with whoever came out; and, much as I disliked doing so, I had to play every boy. What mattered most to me was their attitude and desire.

One of the toughest boys was also the smallest. He was street-wise but had a lot of heart and wanted to play. He'd control the ball some 40-yards down the side line, tiring himself to the point that an opponent could take it away. I'd bench him and tell him for the umpteenth time, "If you don't center the ball before someone takes it away, you're coming back out!" He wanted to do the right thing, even though he was always snarling and looking at me out of the corner of his eye. Of course, one of his eyes was askew to begin with—maybe that's why I got the sideway glance. I would talk to him one-on-one. He knew I respected him and cared about him. I never saw his parents attend a game.

Then there was the kid whose parents were at every game, a spoiled boy from an upscale neighborhood. He was a trouble-maker. There were occasions I made him run laps just to try to get him to quit. He had an undeserved "prima-donna" attitude and denigrated other players. During our seventh grade season on picture day, he got his comeuppance. With my back to the boys while talking to the photographer, I heard a grunt and then painful coughing. I saw the "prima-donna" doubled over. Another boy who had a slight stutter stood next to him. This other boy, a sort of "gentle giant," was a dependable but sometimes clumsy player. The trouble-maker frequently mimicked his stutter. On picture day it happened one too many times, and the "gentle" boy delivered a blow to the bully's solar plexus. I had to laugh. "Well, he got what he deserved," I said. And secretly I thought, "Good for you, Danny." (not his real name)

Having spent thousands of hours around high school kids, I was used to certain facts. 1) Kids pick on other kids. 2) Often, nobody helps the underdog. 3) Addressing bullying quickly can resolve the problem. I made sure the conflict ended there; justice seemed to have been served.

Another boy, Neil Feldewerth, who would later play baseball with Matt, was slow as molasses but big and smart. He knew what to do and when to do it. His steady influence held the back field together. An opponent might challenge him, but Neil didn't make mistakes.

One kid was lightning fast and good with his right foot. However, his left was useless. He'd swipe at the ball with his left and totally miss it. Another boy, a somewhat awkward player, could never head the ball. If he looked up, he'd get dizzy.

But even with all these differences in personalities and skill levels, the team seemed to improve a bit each year. The boys, for the most part, congealed as a group with the occasional influx of new players. My reputation and the team's success became known. One boy who attended an elite Catholic high school in St. Louis County but lived some 20-miles west of Wentzville signed on. His father liked what we were doing and often expressed his frustration with what he called the "Mickey Mouse" regulations of the league. His son was brilliant; I'm talking intelligence. He was small but never made mistakes on the field.

Matt played center halfback where he excelled and could distribute the ball. He settled it quickly then passed it off. Or he'd dribble the ball until someone was open. He was not greedy like a lot of the other boys who wanted to keep the ball. I would remark to Dorci, "I wish he were more aggressive." But, maybe I just wasn't playing him in the right position. That is the conclusion I drew after what happened in our very last game of our last year in the Catholic League.

By the time eighth grade rolled around, our team was a juggernaut. Darryl Kersting had been on the front line all year. He had been on the team as long as Matt. He went on to play high school and college soccer, the later on scholarship. He had great speed and seemed to relish collisions. I loved watching him collide because he most often came out ahead. On the front line, he lacked a "supporting cast." Note: I didn't encourage collisions.

During the seven years of coaching Matt's team, I had kept him off the front line where the forwards played. I didn't want to be accused of nepotism, didn't want Matt put on the spot as "coach's son." But when we entered the championship game in the eighth grade, I put him on the line with Darryl.

In that game, Matt and Darryl went berserk, feeding off each other. They went on a scoring binge. We had been a good team during our past years, but something inspired us during the eighth grade season. My guess regarding this game is that the boys were just thoroughly psyched. This last game determined the championship of the league. The team exploded with enthusiasm to prove their power and dominance. "Nepotism be damned.

This game would be ours."

Darryl and Matt played faster than I had ever before seen either of them. I knew Darryl had speed, but Matt surprised me. He played like a voracious shark in a feeding frenzy. Anytime the ball got within 35-yards of the opponents' goal, he was on it, an opportunist looking for the opening to score. Any opening meant a shot on goal. Or else, he'd pass the ball to a teammate who had a better chance.

When we scored our sixth goal at the beginning of the second half, unbeknownst to me, the other coach became belligerent. Mesmerized by Darryl and Matt's play, I watched intently, enjoying their performance. I felt we were just getting warmed up. The other coach's frustration and sense of powerlessness overwhelmed him. He reminded me of myself in Sells, AZ. Because of his shouting and distemper, the referee stopped the game. Our opponent forfeited the game at 6-0, and we became the league champions.

To the best of my memory, that was the only time Matt played forward in the Catholic League or in high school soccer. He shocked me by his aggressive play that day. Normally, he demonstrated a cerebral game, not aggressive and body smashing. In that short game, he ran straight for the goal regardless of what lay in front of him. He had great moves, but his single-mindedness overpowered everything else.

Matt played soccer for two years in high school, his skills and intelligence serving him well. He was the sweeper, unselfish, generous to a fault, always passing the ball to an open man. In one game, however, he held on to the ball all the way down field and then, just before the goal, he passed off to another player who put it in the net. He reminded me of a football running back going against the grain, the way he could weave in and out of opponents.

In his freshman and sophomore high school years, he suffered several injuries. During a practice session he dislocated his knee after landing awkwardly while performing drills. It required surgical repair. Then he dislocated the other knee in a baseball game but didn't need surgery. In another baseball game that he pitched, a line drive hit him in the eye. With these injuries in mind, he made the decision to concentrate on one sport for his junior and senior years: baseball.

When Matt was twelve, I taught him how to throw the split finger fast ball as described by Bruce Sutter. Sutter was considered the best relief pitcher in baseball when he played for the Cardinals in 1982 when they won the World Series. To a batter, the split finger looks like a fast ball but drops and "dances," losing its velocity and moving left or right at the plate. If Matt got two strikes on a batter, his split finger made the batter look like he was swatting flies for the third strike. I sat behind home plate to witness this in one game during Legion ball. With the count at 2 and 2, a tall stocky batter swung and missed. The guy turned around and asked the catcher, "What was that?"

Matt didn't begin to bulk up and mature physically until his junior year in high school. Before then he was a bit "scrawny." But his size belied his effectiveness as a pitcher. At one summer Legion game, Dorci and I actually commented before the game began about how hefty and mature the opponents looked; after all, they were mostly two years older. The boys he struck out seemed to dwarf him. Matt threw strikes and nibbled at the corners of the strike zone and his team won.

Matt could throw strikes almost at will. He could adjust his pitches to the situation. After one game in which he struck out eighteen opponents in eight innings, he told me, "Dad, they kept swinging at my high fast ball. So, I kept feeding it to them, inching it up higher and higher…as long as they kept striking out."

Many parents and coaches are unable to objectively judge the athletic skills of their youngsters. However, when I looked at Matt, I knew objectively that the word "winner" best evaluated his athletic prowess. But, because he was neither self-aggrandizing nor flamboyant in behavior, some of his coaches didn't see his potential. Having played and coached many sports, I knew that Matt had tangible and intangible talent. One tangible was his ability to throw strikes or use his split finger fastball to blow away a batter. An intangible was his calm. Over and over again when a strong opponent had the bases loaded, Matt could calmly strike out the batter to get the third out.

My point is that parents and coaches frequently fall short of analyzing and handling their children and athletes. Once Matt entered high school, I no longer instructed him so as not to contradict whatever his coaches were teaching him. However, that did not keep me from laughter and disbelief watching how they handled him.

On one occasion his freshman year, Matt came up to bat with a runner on third base. His coach called for a "suicide squeeze." Now, the purpose of this play is to bring the runner home. It is assumed the batter will be thrown out. The play is used when a team is desperate to score a run. It is used when there are no outs or only one out because a run that comes in when the third out is made does not count. The player on third is supposed to take off as the pitcher's arm is coming forward to make the throw to the catcher. So, he's running before the ball leaves the pitcher's hand. It is imperative for the batter to get the bat on the ball no matter what, to hit it softly. No pop ups, which, if caught, would result in a double play. It is assumed the bunted ball will be weak and the batter will be thrown out; but the runner will be able to score.

So on this occasion, Matt's coach gave him and the third base runner the signal for the suicide squeeze. The problem was, there were two outs. The call was ludicrous. The coach was telling Matt to make the third out which would mean the run would not count!

Matt felt the quandary. Being the non-shit disturber that he was, he calmly went over to the coach and said, "Coach, there were two outs." The coach just looked at him. Matt tried to explain nicely that he should change the call. To no avail.

So, what did Mr. Calm do? He synchronized his 145 IQ with his batting skills and pushed a bunt past the pitcher. Then he ran like hell for first while the other runner easily crossed home plate. Matt barely beat the throw to first and stood safely on base with an infield hit. And you know what? The coach actually thought he had made the correct call. Matt and I had a good laugh afterwards.

And, speaking of laughs, when Matt was a sophomore on the varsity squad, he got to know Larry Michaels, a senior on the baseball team. Larry played short stop. A couple years later when Matt and Larry were in a summer league together, Larry told him, "I had trouble in that position because I had too much time to think." Thinking was not something he liked to do. When Larry played on the summer team at third base, "the hot corner," he impressed Matt with his skill. At third base, he could just react. Anyway, Larry had a reputation in high school as a prankster and jokester. Dorci had him in English III, and she would occasionally tell us tales of his antics in her class.

One of the social studies teachers at Wentzville High School had a similar reputation for playing practical jokes. One day Dorci received a note from this teacher, "If Larry Michaels asks you about tennis, play along."

When Larry came to class, he said, with a gleam in his eye and a bit of a smirk on his face, "Hey, Mrs. Leara, is it true you played tennis in the Olympics?"

"Who, told you that?" she asked.

"Yeah, Mr. Allen. He said you were on the tennis team in the '68 Olympics."

"Well, he wasn't supposed to say anything about that. And actually, it's not true. It was the Pan-American Games. Tennis wasn't a category in the Olympics." Obviously Dorci didn't know what she was talking about since tennis was, indeed, an Olympic event. But she spoke with authority and Larry didn't know any different.

"So, did you win a medal?" Larry's eyes were open wide.

"Yes, I got third place," Dorci told him as straight faced as could be. "And I would rather you not spread this story. I try to keep my athletics separate from my teaching." Larry's face showed a new respect. She found out from the social studies teacher that Larry had made a slightly disparaging remark about her athletic ability and the teacher thought this little story would serve him right.

Dorci contacted Beth and Matt before Larry did and let them in on the joke. She also informed Joe Allen about her version of the story. Larry, told not to say anymore, managed to spread the story. And spread it did over the next year and a half. Months later Beth and Matt would occasionally be asked by someone, "So, did your mom really play tennis in the Pan-Am Games?" Or a student at Wright City would come up to me and ask, "Mr. Leara, did your wife win a medal at the Olympics?" The story details varied each time, but the whole family played along.

Wondering how long this would go on, Dorci came up with an idea for disclosing the truth. We felt confident that Beth would deliver the valedictory address at graduation. Dorci suggested she begin her speech addressing Larry among the graduating seniors and letting the truth be told. That is just what she did.

"Before I begin my speech tonight, I have a message for Larry Michaels. Larry, you have been the victim of another of Mr. Allen's practical jokes. My mother has never played tennis in the Olympics, the Pan American Games or any other international competition." Many in the audience were laughing, Larry most of all.

In high school baseball, Matt's pitching his senior year helped propel the team to the district championship, the first time for Wentzville. They advanced to sectionals and lost there 2-1 to Columbia Hickman who went on to win the state title.

Matt was a power hitter who also hit for average. That meant that he consistently got to first base with a hit, thus earning a respectable batting average of .350; and he frequently lined doubles to the wall and smacked home runs. In one Legion game, I was sitting in the stands, and Matt was on deck warming up. I took a bill out of my wallet and held it up for him to see. "If you hit a home run, it's yours." Matt thought it was $5.

With two strikes on him, he thought, "Just make contact. You don't want to strike out. Who cares about the money?" He swung and hit a home run. A teammate's dad sitting next to me went wild; he couldn't believe it. When Matt returned to the dugout, I told him he'd just made $50!

In another Legion game in Matt's senior year, the team was down by one run going into the bottom of the ninth. Matt was the lead-off batter followed by Donnie Joliff and Mike Stude. Matt said to Joliff, ""Hey, why don't we go back to back?" meaning both of them would hit home runs.

Donnie responded, "Yeah, sounds good."

Mike chimed in, "How about back to back to back?" Of course that would not have been possible because if Donnie and Matt hit home runs, the game would be over. Matt led off, hit a home run, tied the game. Joliff came up and hit a home run to end it!

Matt's senior year in American Legion Baseball his team won the state championship with a record of 19-1 in conference play (and a final, record of 40-8), the one loss that year occurring the night several seniors attended the high school awards banquet. He and Joliff were the heart and soul of that team. Neil Feldewerth (from soccer days) and his younger brother Brad contributed mightily, both very talented. Brad, only fifteen years old, stood 6'4" tall and threw a powerful fastball. As catcher Neil took a beating defending home plate and blocking pitches that landed in the dirt. He and the pitchers were in sync in determining pitches to strike out batters. Neil had a rifle for an arm and could easily throw players out who tried to steal second base.

The regional competition was held in Williston, North Dakota, about 45-miles south of the Canadian border. Quite a few parents and fans drove up to watch the team play. One faithful fan was missing: Rick Boedeker. He not only attended most Legion games; he would announce the play by play on the home field in Wentzville. Everybody knew Rick. One evening while sitting around the Williston motel swimming pool, Dave Dickherber, father to the second baseman Davie Dickherber, related a story that occurred in his youth.

Some 30-years in the past, Dave and Rick were sitting in their Catholic grade school class. Rick, as usual, was pushing the teacher's limits. The nun had told him, "Rick, you are flirting with a trip to the principal's office." She continued with the lesson, and Rick kept interrupting by raising his hand to ask questions. This went on for a little too long and the exasperated nun said, "Rick, if you raise your hand one more time, you're going to the office!" A few minutes passed. Dave kept an eye on Rick; something was churning in his head. Soon enough, Rick leaned back in his desk and raised his foot as high as he could to the ceiling. Dave demonstrated with his own foot sticking up from his lounge chair. The nun's face turned red. "That's it! Go to the office!" Poolside, we were cracking up with laughter, holding our sides in pain.

In North Dakota Matt pitched the first game which they won 6-0. Losing the second game, the team went into the losers' bracket and won the next two games. But Matt dislocated his shoulder in the fourth game and couldn't pitch the next. The team lost the final game 2-1.

Matt finished Legion ball with a perfect 12-0 record with a 1.03 ERA, which Matt disputes to this day. He thinks his ERA should have been half that had the scorekeeper tallied the errors correctly. He had 125 strikeouts to 25 walks. His best fast ball clocked out at 82-mph. A scout at an Atlanta Braves' tryout camp told him that his speed was 5-mph too slow for a lefty in the major leagues.

Matt has great hands. He juggles three balls better than I, and I'm sure his coordination propelled him to the successes he had in soccer and baseball. At Kirksville where he attended college (now Truman State University), Matt won thirteen games as a pitcher during his four seasons, a record that still exists today. Thirteen wins doesn't sound like many (and it isn't); but if you were to see the teams that Truman State puts on the field, you would be impressed by that number. They perennially lost more games than they won.

Thankfully Matt did not play football. He suffered enough injuries in the sports he did play. He injured his right knee in soccer, requiring surgery; hurt his left knee while getting a base hit, just swinging the bat; and dislocated his right shoulder while sliding back to first base during a pick-off move by the opposing pitcher in Williston. His face turned an ashen shade of green while waiting for the orthopedic surgeon to show up in ER. No one wanted to touch him, the dislocation was so bad. His damaged shoulder had to be surgically repaired twice. Also gruesome to see was the line-drive that hit him in the eye when he was fifteen. Had he played football, I can't imagine the additional injuries he might have sustained. As a father he'd be limping around and unable to lift his daughters over his head.

Matt's two daughters, Sydni and Alexa, have yet to show any leaning towards sports. But since they are only 8 and 5 respectively, they're still pretty young. I keep hoping that one of my granddaughters or grandsons will develop a passion for golf. Whether Matt's girls get involved in athletics or not, they will surely be excellent students, having learned sign language before they spoke in sentences and consuming books like candy.

Like his two sisters, Matt enjoys skiing. Like his dad, he gets a bit crazy. He suffered a very frightening accident in 2000. He loves watching "extreme sports" on TV. After what happened this one time, he says, "I should stick to watching instead of doing." Dorci and I had driven to Colorado to visit Matt and his girlfriend, Kristin Kunimoto, who became his wife. She had recently joined the veterinarians at the clinic where Matt worked. Beth was also on this trip attending a medical clinic at Copper Mountain. Maybe Matt was trying to impress Kristin; I don't know. (Remember me on the horizontal bar thinking I'd impress Dorci?)

When we rode the lift up the mountain for the last run of the day, Matt pointed out the Terrain Park. There were fantastic looking jumps, one beautiful mound after another. A skier could go airborne so-o-o easily. Beth, Kristin, and I decided not to try the jumps, but Matt asked a couple of Beth's doctor friends to join him.

They hit the first jump at a moderate pace and became airborne. Matt's endorphin rush propelled him to try harder, to get more air. On the next jump he gained more speed. He recalled to me, "As soon as I left the ramp, I knew I was screwed! From take-off my feet were up, even with my head. I just thought, 'Curl up in a loose ball and absorb the impact when you land.' Believe it or not, I can remember these thoughts racing through my mind like it was yesterday!"

As I stood there a witness to Matt's jump, I saw that he was much higher than he had been the first time. Losing equilibrium, he leaned back too far. My heart sank. I saw disaster. He couldn't make any correction to regain a semblance of control. I can still envision him helpless, up in the air, too high off the ground.

At some point Matt's instincts compelled him to try to brace his fall, and he put out his hand. He landed flat on his back and didn't move. Sick at heart, having seen it all, we skied to where he lay, expecting the worst. We breathed a sigh of relief when he spoke to us and moved his limbs. Amazingly, within five minutes the ski patrol arrived on a bobsled and strapped him to it. At the bottom of the slope, an ambulance took him to the hospital emergency room.

After careful examination of X-rays, the doctor found a compression fracture in his vertebra. Also, his left wrist was shattered. Since Matt performed veterinary surgeries, the doctor took special care to repair his wrist using a metal plate and multiple screws. Matt wore a white, plastic body support for six weeks to help mend his broken back. He looked like a storm trooper from Star Wars.

As serious as his injuries were, he seems to have successfully recovered. He has joined the ranks of millions who suffer from lower back pain, especially during the hours he spends standing during operations. His wrist doesn't seem to be a problem at all. We all thank God that he wasn't more seriously hurt after that fall.

Was it testosterone at work on those Colorado slopes? Or, was it the "crazy" he inherited from his Dad?

Briana: The Youngest

Briana, as the youngest, seems to be the least connected to a love for balls; yet she has a "go-getter" sense of adventure. At age four, independent of us, she frequently walked down to the neighbors' house to play with their dog. Dorci and I hadn't met them, yet let her go—pretty irresponsible of us.

I suspect my age at her birth (38) factored into her lack of interest in organized sports. When I attended her kindergarten open house, one of the many proud parents anxious to hear about his child's new experience, I was struck by the youth of my contemporaries. In fact, I felt like they were not my contemporaries. They appeared to be just slightly removed from my high school students. "Oh," one of them said. "Are you here for your grandchild?" Dorci and I looked around the classroom trying to find a man who looked older than I. She seemed to sense my disquietude. I was only 44, but among 20-ish parents, I seemed to be teetering on senility.

"Over there," Dorci said, pointing to a graying man with a worn complexion, glad to have found a man with more seniority. "That guy looks older than you." Later, when we realized we knew him through mutual friends, we discovered that, no, he was actually a few years younger than I. No wonder Briana didn't take to sports as aggressively as I'd hoped. Although being in my early forties hardly consigned me to walkers and diapers, my body suffered from miscellaneous ailments that resulted in less physical interaction with her. She missed out on lots of rough-housing and sports associated with play. My neck and back hurt too much to flip her in my arms or run around the yard.

Briana, as do all children, demonstrated qualities unique to herself, but which seemed so far removed from her paternal heritage that I sometimes asked, "Is this girl really my daughter?" Which leads me to tell two stories, one used as genetic proof she's my daughter, the other demonstrating how different she is.

I have preauricular skin pits at both ears. They look like little needle holes and are barely noticeable unless I point them out to others. Someone once told me they were the evolutionary remnants of gills from the fetal "fish" stage. Apparently that's hogwash, but these pits are hereditary. Briana and Beth both inherited them – for me, proof that, as unusual as Briana may seem, she is, indeed, my daughter. Not that I really need such proof – it's just a standing family joke and opportunity to show off our "gills."

The second story, showing how different from me Briana can be, occurred when she was in first grade. As her parents, we well knew what a perfectionist and how finicky she already had become by that age. Like pants... Yes, the clothing she wore over her legs. They had to fit her just right, and shopping for them involved her assuming every possible position that she might find herself in while wearing the pants to make sure they didn't "bother" her. Sitting in a chair (not easily found in the clothing section at Wal-Mart), crossing her legs in a chair, sitting on the floor, crossing her legs while sitting on the floor, bending over, walking, running, squatting. She found stances her mother didn't know existed. Dorci had long given up on hand-made clothing which Beth had so often worn. So, too, did her Aunt Denise and Cousins Diana and Cheryl give up on taking Briana shopping as she would spend an inordinate amount of time selecting an item, evaluating all its merits and uses.

This quest for perfection came to a head after Briana saw her initial report card in first grade. All her marks on this report were "O+'s"; that is, outstanding with a plus after it. All, that is, except "time on task" which was just an "O."

Briana saw that and said, "What is that one, Mommy? What does 'time on task' mean?"

Dorci read the teacher-written comments to Briana. She had to explain the part that said, "Briana wants everything to be perfect and is unable to reach perfection in the allotted time." You can bet that on the next grade card "time on task" had become an "O+"! How Briana managed to squeeze perfection into the allotted time remains a mystery.

Come to think of it, this tenacity to achieve a goal is actually not unlike me. I can spend hours, literally hours, practicing putting a golf ball or chipping onto the green. When I encourage my friends to practice with me, none have been interested in such devotion.

In other ways Briana lives up to the appellation of being a "John Leara offspring." She played volleyball in high school and enjoyed the sweat and effort and camaraderie of the game. Although she never demonstrated the same drive that Beth and Matt had in organized sport, she reveals her paternal influences in other ways. In fact, family stories about Bri usually center on her capacity to "take the road less travelled." A favorite tale occurred on one of our many family summer trips.

Since both Dorci and I taught, the family could all load up our van and head out for a month on the road. With my brother's family in California, we often drove west, plotting various itineraries and routes from one summer to the next. We drove through Texas one summer, North Dakota another, and all of the states in between at other times. On one such trip, as we headed south along the Pacific Coast and Dorci, Beth, Matt and I couldn't stop "ooh-ing" and "aah-ing" over the breath-taking views, Briana (about 7-years old) refused to take her nose out of a book she was reading.

Like me, she can be impulsive, as, for example, when she phoned to tell us she and her husband, Rich, "…are leaving for Argentina in sixteen days. It's really a challenge to arrange everything in just two short weeks!" Their vacation would begin in southern Chili, the starting point for a three-day hike (the first day covering 19-miles) through Torres del Paine. Memories of another hike with her in Missouri came to mind, another "Briana story." This time she was 14-years old. The whole family joined my good friend Harry Toll who was always inviting me to do this or go there—another impulsive guy who loves physical activity. This time we were going to walk some 13-miles along the Taum Sauk Trail in southern Missouri. For most of this trek, Briana moaned about her feet hurting or being too tired.

"And now she's actually planning a vacation to Argentina and voluntarily hiking for three days!" I thought.

Don't get me wrong. Briana has not shied away from adventure or daring deeds. Like jumping from rocks into water. Imagine doing so without being able to see! Of my three children, Briana's sight is the worst. The eyeglasses she wore as a child looked like thick magnifying lenses. By the time she was fourteen, her sight had deteriorated to 20-700, and we decided she needed to get contacts which would halt the decline of her vision. One summer we were at Lake Powell, jumping from rocks into the water and Briana wanted to join the fun. She didn't have her contacts in because she was swimming. One of us treaded water below making splashes so that she could get some idea of where to propel her body.

She continues to be physically active, even with her long hours at work. Sometimes I'll phone her at 9 p.m. her time, and she is just leaving her office. Living in Brooklyn and working in Manhattan she does a lot of walking. She plays in a volleyball league, enjoys "spinning" (stationary bike-riding) and "boot-camp" at the gym and has tried kick-boxing. She makes a concerted effort to be physically fit.

One of the many things that fascinates me about Briana is her grasp of finance and computer-driven technology. Although she graduated with a degree in Chemical Engineering, her career has led her into finance and computers. Currently, her official designation is "Project Manager of Accounting Software Implementation." That title took me about six months to memorize. I actually wrote it down and carried a little "cheat sheet" in my wallet to be able to recite her position when talking about her job with our friends. Not only could my mind not remember this title nor understand its implications, the words tangled my tongue. Because of her job and interests, we easily talk about mortgages, investments, retirement plans, etc. She blew me away once when she had interest calculated to the day after borrowing some cash from us for a down payment on her home.

A spread sheet showed up on our computer, everything spelled out in detail. I phoned her a short time ago and asked her something like, "If we pay $75,000 into our mortgage today, how much will we owe on the house in three years?" She had the answer in minutes.

Each of our children has an aptitude for math and science, something which most certainly did not come from me. My interest in numbers evolved much later in life. In high school they excelled in all subjects, so much so that each became valedictorian of his/her respective class. Dorci and I attribute this achievement more to the children's tenacity than to any expectations or requirements we put upon them. For Beth, when she was in eighth grade and attended her Cousin Diana's graduation ceremony, she resolved to become the valedictorian of her class. For Matt, graduating two years later, the path to being number one seemed as natural to him as his athletic talents. And then came Briana, at the same school seven years behind her brother. Unbeknownst to us (and out of character for her), she had resolved to follow in her siblings' footsteps.

In retrospect, she and I both agree that she could easily have forgone the honor of valedictorian and graduated from high school in three years. She was ready for college, somewhat bored with high school. Although well-liked and active, during her senior year she seemed merely to be biding her time.

Briana enjoys snow skiing. She and Rich will take long weekend trips with friends, renting a condo, enjoying not only the skiing but also the warm fires and warming wine. I'm glad she likes to ski because it is physically demanding, so much so that Dorci gave up on it long ago. A couple winters ago I drove up to Flagstaff after a snow storm to ski at age 69. After one hour and one hard fall, I turned in my rentals and drove home. The thrill succumbed to my aches and pains. No more skiing for me.

How different would our life have been without this third child? That is the kind of question that boggles my mind and stirs the imagination. In 1977 Dorci and I were living happily with two children, not the number we had agreed upon when we had first met and envisioned a family with four or five or six kids. When I asked Dorci that year if she wanted another child, she responded, "Absolutely." For me, this decision became a leap of faith. I had talked to my high school friend Mike O'Reilly whose fourth child had just been born. "Mike, what's it like having another child at your age?"

Mike, at age 37 responded, "Hey, John, it's wonderful!"

"Leap of faith" is so appropriate. I'd had many teaching jobs, worked in sales, built homes, moved from Illinois to New Mexico to Arizona and back to Missouri. Dorci had been teaching full time for three years. My income teaching at a private school was minimal. Add to that my paranoia. Yes, "leap of faith" is most accurate. Just as God had brought Dorci and me together nine years earlier when we met in a St. Louis bar, now He gave me the confidence to trust in this decision; and on December 26, 1978, Briana was born. How appropriate that her birth date is the day following the birth of Jesus.

CHAPTER 14

THE SMALLEST OF BALLS

I arrive now at the second to last chapter of my story which, appropriately, concerns the sport that continues to challenge me into my "golden years," although why they are called "the golden years" is beyond me. (My research offered two suggestions as to the origin of the phrase: A financial firm's advertising campaign or a reference to those old enough to have celebrated 50 years of marriage, i.e. the "Golden Wedding Anniversary.") "Golden"? I'm not convinced. My friends and I agree that growing old is not for the faint of heart. What with all our aches, pains, and surgeries, I think the only thing "golden" about this time is the money involved in keeping us upright and active.

Since I retired, the focus of my fascination turned to the smallest of balls, the golf ball and the game of golf. It's one game that can be played well into old age, as long as the golfer has a semblance of health. As such, it has become my new passion—the fascination that challenges and complements me in my senior years. Even though I awake some mornings and my body tells me, "There's no way I'll make it through eighteen holes," I manage to get up and play a decent round of golf. I witness men in their seventies and eighties shoot their age! I hope soon to join that club!

I have heard all the remarks and rhetorical questions: "Golf is the dumbest sport around." "Why do people chase a little white ball?" I agree to some extent with those comments, but look at any course on the weekend and see how many people "chase that ball." Mark Twain once said, "Golf is a good walk spoiled." The game, although one of the most challenging, by its very nature is also one of the most scenic. There are many who play the game for the walk and beauty of the courses. I'm not one of them; I'm too competitive. But that's not to say I don't enjoy the natural surroundings.

I played golf for the very first time the summer before my senior year in college. I can still visualize one shot that flew over 250-yards, high and straight. The ball gleamed and sparkled in the sunlight. Beauty and challenge—a combination to inspire John Leara. The sight of it against a backdrop of green trees and blue sky sparked my fascination. Here was a life-long sport with many facets. I could endlessly play it, study it, practice it and refine it. Strength, dexterity, coordination, imagination, and rhythm have contributing roles in this game. I prided myself in possessing those qualities.

I played once a week that summer of 1961 with a football buddy Jerry. He was a really good golfer. I admired his ability to hit the ball so beautifully, so straight so often. I didn't know what I was getting into, for he made it look so easy. I was in awe of the game, watching him play it. The hope of getting par on any one hole intoxicated me. Jerry regularly scored par, shooting 37's, 38's and 39's for nine holes. However, I did not.

In 1961 I just knew that I could teach myself to hit the ball and score well. I had always been self-taught when it came to sports. "I have learned every game by watching and practicing. The same should be true of golf," I thought. "I'm strong. I'll work at it, practice and sharpen my skills just like I did when I learned to play football." Big mistake! It took me 45-years to break 80.

In 1965 at the age of twenty-five, I was bench pressing 225-pounds and was as physically fit as I had ever been. But, I couldn't shoot in the 70's. I thought my strength was an asset. Wrong. At age 71 with three shoulder surgeries behind me and unable to lift 10-pounds over my head, I played the best golf of my life. Obviously, physical strength is not the most important factor in this game. But in my twenties and thirties, my mind-set couldn't see that truth.

Weekend golf was the norm from 1961 until I met Dorci in 1968, and then I put playing the game on hiatus. Around 1983 I returned to the game.

When our son, Matthew, was about twelve, we began playing together. Many a morning during summer vacation, before the heat and humidity of Missouri became too oppressive, we'd play nine holes. We walked around on a "cow-pasture" of a course in rural Missouri, with rough terrain and sparse grass, playing our round in about ninety minutes. During that entire summer, I scored 39 only once; the other rounds were in the 40's. Not a standard I was proud of on such a rinky-dink course, only 2900-yards for nine holes.

Unfortunately for Matt, rather than buying him a set of left-handed clubs, I had him play with my right-handed ones. I'm "cheap," although I prefer to use the word "frugal." He had so much talent. In hindsight I realize that not buying him clubs suitable to his natural swing probably kept him from achieving his best on the course. He might have gotten a better college scholarship to play golf than he did for baseball. But in '83 I thought that since other great golfers played from the "wrong side," he would just have to learn to play from the right. And that he did; shooting a few rounds in the 70's.

In the late 80's with my retirement from teaching on the horizon, and after declining the coaching position for my remaining years at Wright City High School, I resurrected a serious interest in golf. While playing with Matt, my competitive juices began flowing. I wanted to play more. Coaching had its rewards but for me it didn't measure up to actually performing. Golf was my new challenge. During summer months and in good weather during the school year, I headed for one of the many local courses.

"Challenge" is the key word. Why did I jump off a 50-foot bridge? Why did I jump trains? Why did I attempt a giant swing on a horizontal bar? On and on and on. "Challenges" filled my life. Golf lay there waiting to be conquered. (Something no one has ever, actually, done. The pros only attempt to.) My neck problems prohibited strenuous sports like racquetball. "No pain, no gain" had lost its luster at this stage of my life. So, with an ugly slice, a left to right ball flight, my journey began, in little steps at first.

The fascination renewed, my resolve increased. "Wisdom," however, stood behind "stupid" and "cheap" in my brain. I asked myself, "How do golfers shoot in the 70's? How do pros shoot 65?" I actually still believed I could get better *sans* lessons. At age 44, with neck and shoulder pains, I continued to think, "I can figure out how to hit that damned ball where I want it to go!" I bolstered my misconception by telling myself, "Lessons are for sissies." I was being "macho." Seeking help from a professional shows maturity and common sense. Wise people who are anxious to learn have figured that out. Obviously, I didn't fall into that category.

When I retired in the mid-90's, I took a job as a marshal at a golf course thirteen miles west of Wentzville. The semi-private course rolled over gentle hills in a very picturesque, rural Missouri setting. Pay amounted to minimum wage but the perks included use of carts and a couple complementary rounds of golf per week. Now, I could play more golf and improve my game. For the next four years, twice a week I would arrive early in the morning, before scheduled tee times, and play a quick round alone.

Then, early, one fine morning in the fourth year of my job, playing a quick round of golf lead to the demise of my employment. And, luckily, that was all I lost, for things could have ended much worse for me except that skills from my youth returned to serve me well. Having learned how to fall when exiting trains at age six, my body was prepared for the events of that fateful day even though I was close to sixty years old.

On that particular morning, having finished fourteen holes, I stood on the tee box of the fifteenth hole, a par five. A lake lay in front of me with the fairway trailing off into a dogleg left. The sound of perfect contact rang out as my driver hit the ball, and it lifted into the early morning sun making it impossible to track. I felt certain of my accuracy and its flight over the water. I suspected I'd be more than pleased with this drive.

Springing into the cart, I headed out, anxious to take my second shot, wanting to maintain my brisk pace of play. Paramount in my mind was finding my ball to affirm my success. I zipped back and forth in the cart—"...the ball...the ball, where is my ball?" Giving no thought to the slope of the fairway, I jerked the steering wheel to the right. The cart veered right; my body flipped left. My reflexes went into their train-jumping, football running-back mode. I instinctively rolled hard without hurting myself. Standing up, I momentarily relished my physical agility. "Wow, John! You moved like you were back on the football field," I thought, taking pride in my youthful maneuvers.

Then I spied the cart headed straight for a ravine. The glory of my accurate drive and the adrenaline rush from my jumping prowess quickly faded with the realization of my job's fate. I sprinted after the cart. Moving too fast, too quickly, I tore my calf muscle. Even with my calf throbbing, I thought, "Damn, I'll never know how well I hit that ball!" Concern for the golf cart and my torn muscle took their rightful places behind my beautiful drive.

Another worker who saw the incident reported the cart's plight. Shortly thereafter, a tractor pulled it from the creek bed. My train jumping skills had kept my body from serious harm but had not saved the cart. My four years' tenure did not balance favorably against the loss of a $3000 cart. No more job; no more perks. This job would no longer be part of my plan to improve my golf game.

So, in the year 2000, five years after retiring from teaching, I lost my job as a ranger but finally came to the realization that I needed instruction. Yet, even with this realization, I was still too cheap to pay for one. As it happened, my first "golf lesson" was free. Only fifteen minutes long, the lesson was a promotion offered in conjunction with an investment brokerage presentation during a luncheon. I thought I was being so clever. "A free lesson, John. It will knock five strokes off your game."

In the weeks after I made the reservation to that luncheon, I envisioned all sorts of scenarios resulting from this tutorage. I lay in bed, running ideas through my mind. My excitement grew. "Yo, John," I should have told myself, "Wake up! It's only fifteen minutes. It's a freebee. How valuable can it be? They want you to sign up with their investment firm." Instead, my anticipation grew. It was greatly disproportionate to the value of the event. In the actual lesson, which lasted only ten minutes, the pro instructed me to concentrate on making my right hand dominant. It was a valuable tip, but hardly matched the "makeover" I was expecting.

Not until age 65 did I allow "wisdom" to come out from behind "stupid" and "cheap" in my head. I finally paid for a lesson. The "waking up" process had taken 21 years. Being frugal has been a life-long stumbling block for me, and not just when it came to golf lessons. Like my battle with a refrigerator.

In 2002, too cheap to pay movers to transfer our belongings into our new home, I elected to do so with the help of a few friends. We'd save a couple hundred dollars. Dorci reminded me that I was 62; it didn't register. Andy's brother (this is the last house we built in Wentzville with Andy Burt) and I were struggling with the refrigerator as it came off his pickup truck. I tried to muscle it and tore my rotator cuff. I couldn't move my right arm. The tear required surgery, the results of which were never satisfactory. In 2008 I had a second surgery on the same shoulder to relieve the discomfort I suffered since the first operation. I do consider myself lucky to be able to play golf after the injury and surgery. But, if only I'd paid professional movers…

My thoughts always ran to "We'll save dollars. We don't need comfort." Thus I bought a van without air-conditioning when we lived west of Tucson, AZ. I reserved a 36-foot houseboat on Lake Powell for a vacation with our family, my brother and his wife, and my nephew's family who brought their golden retriever. That was ten people and a dog on a three-bedroom boat. I sold Dorci's Ford LTD and we got around in my Volkswagen. One year, with money especially tight, Dorci drove an old car my sister lent us. The convertible top was less than waterproof; mushrooms grew under the floor mat; and from several holes in the floor, Dorci watched the road pass by. I also did not register the vehicle and, unfortunately for my wife, she was stopped one day by a police officer. I think her good looks saved her from a ticket.

Just as I had not done right by Matt with his clubs, so, too, was the case for my wife. In our retirement, I have encouraged her to play the game regularly. However, I did not want to spend much money on clubs. Shortly after moving to Arizona, I decided to spend money on a lesson for her with a pro I admired. She had problems with distance and getting the ball up in the air.

The pro took her to the driving range and told her to swing. As he analyzed her movement, he asked to see her driver. "John, what is Dorci doing with this driver? It's for a man. It has a man's regular shaft!"

"Well, that's a club I didn't want anymore," I said sheepishly, knowing I was in trouble for my hand-me-down.

"For Pete's sake, she needs a ladies' club with a flexible shaft," the pro responded. "She'll get a lot more distance that way." Then he looked closer. "Does this say ten degrees?" the pro asked in disbelief. "No wonder she can't get any loft. She should have at least a fourteen degree driver."

Dorci eyed me. She had never protested when I would say, "This is good enough for you" when it came to clubs or balls. Now someone was finally putting me in my place. I needed to buy her the proper equipment, something I should also have done for my son.

I guess in my old age I've decided to loosen the purse strings. After our move to Prescott, Arizona in 2004, I met the pro at Prescott Country Club. (This is the same man who would reprimand me over Dorci's equipment.) He often shot in the low 60's. I decided it was time for me to pay for a lesson. During his instruction, he didn't try to change my swing but instead analyzed my movements and instilled confidence. I appreciated this. "Rely on your hands, John. They won't let you down." Seeing my weak shoulder turn—rightly so after two surgeries in the previous years—he said, "John, you need to turn your shoulders more."

"Like this?" I said, swinging the club with more shoulder motion.

"Perfect."

Unable to practice all that he had suggested because I still had shoulder discomfort and neck pain, I stored much of it away. I would wait to apply it on the tee with my friends.

And so it was, in the summer of 2006 at age 66, I broke 80 for the first time in my life. I shot 78 on July 18th, and since then I have repeated that feat many times. Unfortunately, my shoulders, neck and other health issues keep me from playing for months at a time. Otherwise, I believe I could boast of many more games below 80.

Bill Wenner, a friend for the past eight years in Prescott, is among the "senior" golfers with whom I played once a week. While my game has improved each year, he has slowly lost his passion for it. We rib each other constantly. I complain about his slow play, sometimes resorting to profanity to get him to putt his ball—all because he talks too much. Bill picks on me, joking about any one of a slew of my idiosyncrasies.

A few years ago he sparked my competitive side by constantly claiming that my handicap would never fall below 10. It hovered around 12 for a couple years. "You're too old and not good enough," and so on he teased. That compelled me to work on my short game. He continued to needle me, all in good fun.

Finally I said, "Bill, I'm going to make you eat crow. I know I can do it!"

"Aahh, you'll never make it."

The debate continued. Occasionally when handicap reports came out, Bill asked, "So, are you there yet?" I'd say no and he'd respond, "You'll never do it." Many of our golfing friends knew about this banter, that Bill had challenged me and I had told him he'd eat crow.

Then, when two other operations interrupted my golf play, I tended to think Bill was correct. In the many months of recuperation when

I couldn't play a round of golf, I still went to the course. For hours I practiced my chipping and putting. I became a regular fixture each day. My golf buddies, seeing me always there, became wary of the day I returned to playing eighteen holes.

Ever looking for variety, I challenged myself with innovative amusements. Before leaving, I'd have to make thirteen 25-foot putts and one 50-footer. I created what I called "horseshoes golf." Two players use two golf balls each in place of horseshoes. They work their way around from hole to hole. As in horseshoes, only one player scores per hole. The ball that stops closest to the cup gets a point. Any putt that goes in is tantamount to a ringer. A few of my golfing friends accepted my invitation to play "horseshoes golf." None ever beat me. In fact, one of the few people who ever really rivaled me was Dorci. She would sink 30-foot putts and intensify the competition. However, she only won once.

On June 13th of 2010, I turned seventy. I celebrated the fact that I had been one year without injury or surgeries. Since moving to Arizona, I seemed to have been plagued by illness and surgery: severe vertigo confined me to bed for five weeks in the fall of 2004, shoulder operation on my left side after falling down half a flight of stairs in 2005, prostate surgery in 2006, kidney removal in 2007, and finally hernia and right shoulder in 2008.

I vividly recall the beautiful weather that June. I shot a 78, 75, and 79 within a two week period. My handicap went to 9.8. I had done it!

Knowing what a good sport Bill would be, Dorci and I invited him, his wife, Sharon, and another golfing couple to dinner. Bill would be served "crow." Dorci made up a cardboard bird with black feathers attached, and we had a lot of laughs with "crow" poetry and stories. And Bill likes to point out, "The taste of crow only lasted a few days which was about the same length of time John kept his single digit handicap."

Such antics and laughs accompany the game with my friends and me, all in our sixties and seventies. We are humorous to observe. In fact, "observe" is the key word here. Remember how I described the first time I played golf? The sight of a 250-yard drive, seeing the beauty of it sailing into the air and down the fairway had inspired me. That vision had aroused my desire. Well, now, when my friends and I hit the ball, the first thing anyone says is, "Can you see it? Where did it go? Does anybody know where it landed?" The ball is visible for about 130-yards and then it's lost to our eyes. Locating it becomes a guessing game. We hope that it continued in the right direction, but none of us can actually see the path with our eyes.

* * *

The word "sailing" has sparked my old brain. Not the "sailing" golf ball but the kind one does in a boat. I can't imagine any person not having some dreams about the future. In my forties I began talking to Dorci about what I'd like to do in our retirement. One possibility was traveling the inter-coastal waterways. We would purchase a nice motorboat, maybe a sailboat, either sell or rent our home, and take off for a year to travel. I envisioned making the circuit that included the Mississippi River to the Gulf, over to Florida and up the East Coast, into the St. Lawrence Seaway to the Great Lakes and back to the Mississippi. Dorci never took to the idea of living on a boat for a year, and my plan never gained any traction.

"Sailing" intrigued me. I had once sailed in a small dinghy the length of Lake St. Louis near our home—all two miles of it! On one of our family summer vacations, when we made a huge circular route to get to California, we traveled through Minnesota. On Lake Bemidji we rented sunfish sailboats for Beth, Matt and Briana to try. We continued our drive through the northern states and spent some time camping in the San Juan Islands near Seattle. Once again we tried sailing. This time Beth, Matt, and I rented a small boat and sailed for several hours in the Puget Sound. It wasn't until afterwards when we had brought the boat back in that someone told us of the sharks that swim there. Had I known ahead of time about sharks in the water, I would not have gotten in that boat. Since seeing the movie Jaws, I had developed fear of waters which could hide them.

Then there was the trip Dorci and I made to the British Virgin Islands. What a grand vacation—glorious weather (with one exception!) and some of the earth's most beautiful scenery. My original scheme included renting a boat that the two of us alone would then sail around the islands. I professed experience, claiming that my several adventures qualified me to skipper a sailboat. Dorci quickly squashed that idea. She scoffed at my proposal, picturing properly stored equipment and neatly wound ropes. Reflecting on my personal habits of throwing socks on the floor, hanging jackets on doorknobs, misplacing car keys, and leaving clothing hither and yon, she assured me that any boat I controlled would be in shambles within an hours' time. And that didn't even take into account my general lack of knowledge or skill in tying any sort of sailors' knots. What was I thinking? What did I know about currents and winds? Did I know the differences between one sail and another? Could I read a nautical map? I thought that having tacked back and forth on Lake St. Louis and in the Puget Sound, I could successfully tend to the tasks of a sloop, or whatever kind of boat we would choose.

So, with Dorci refusing to step foot on a boat without a proper captain, we hired Mel Bolton for the next several days to maneuver us around the islands in the BVI. He had recently arrived there having sailed his own seventy-five foot yacht up from New Zealand. Within forty minutes of leaving the dock, a fierce squall fell upon us. Mel immediately turned the helm over to Dorci, advising her in no uncertain terms to grip the steering wheel with both hands and "hold on tight." And, although the gushing rain made seeing most difficult, she had to "stay the course!" His emphatic tone implied, "Our lives are in your hands." He then started shouting orders at me because the raging wind made hearing almost impossible. Words like "cleat," "shackle," "trim," "jib," "halyard," "port," and "starboard," resounded through the air as we worked furiously to keep afloat. Yes, I said "keep afloat." I quickly learned the danger of "listing" as the gunwale tipped ever closer to the water. Dorci, who for the most part stood in one spot, had difficulty maintaining her post. The captain and I struggled as we rushed about with the boat severely listing and as the squall continuing to bluster. Sails had to be lowered, ropes had to be tended. For thirty minutes we worked furiously.

As quickly as it had struck, the storm blew away. The nightmare was over and time seemed to stop. Or, time seemed to start. We had our lives back. We could actually think and register those thoughts. We sat for a few moments, relishing the calm, stunned and amazed at the fact that we were safe and the boat had survived unscathed.

Mel, the captain, remarked, "That was the worst squall I've ever encountered." Dorci and I looked at each other, shock on our faces. This man who owned and lived on his own seventy-five foot cutter, who had just sailed it up from New Zealand with only one crew member, who had basically sailed around the world one way or another, a man who hired himself out to other people as a captain, this man sat there telling us that we had just survived a storm like no other he had ever seen. Was this a portent of things to come? Fortunately, no; the rest of the week held adventure but no danger—except for Dorci's lone snorkeling far removed from the boat where she was too distant for me to rescue her from any sharks that might attack. My phobia for sharks was always lurking in my mind around salt water.

Of course the most prominent thought that occurred to both Dorci and me was, "And here I had thought that I could cruise in and among these islands." Yes, I sought adventure and physical challenges throughout my life. I had jumped from a fifty foot bridge. What could be more crazy than that? There is that word again: "crazy." My notion that I could man my own sailboat around the British Virgin Islands isn't best described by the word "crazy." It had been so naïve as to be just plain "stupid."

"Stupid" though I may have been in expecting to charter a boat on my own, that trip to the BVI's was one of the best vacations Dorci and I ever took. Any descriptions I would include of the scenery, the ocean, the secluded beaches, the snorkeling, would be poor attempts to convey the beauty and thrills we experienced, all of which overloaded our senses. Instead, I'd like to mention "peanut butter." We were in the BVI's for eight nights. After a couple of nights sleeping aboard the boat, we rented a room at the Leverick Bay Hotel. Although we had been married over thirty years, vacationing in a place akin to paradise inspired us to regard this trip as a real honeymoon. Dorci, caught up in a playful yet amorous mood, was motivated to make the evening memorable. Without going into R-rated descriptions, suffice to say that in the absence of honey or whipped cream, Dorci substituted peanut butter. Needless to say, the evening was most unforgettable, more for its laughter than any erotic events.

* * *

Since I previously wrote about some of my golfing buddies, there is another friend I want to mention in this chapter about the smallest of balls. He would be laughing now at the mention of him and me and the phrase "smallest of balls" because of its anatomical implication—not in reference to golf. An interest in golf is not something we share. In fact, the converse is true. Bill Woodall thinks golf is one of the most boring, silly games ever conceived. He cannot understand how I spend hours playing the game and, even worse, watching it on television. Thus, when discussing golf, we banter back and forth, I on its merits and he on the lack of them.

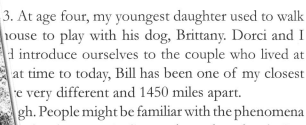

3. At age four, my youngest daughter used to walk ⟨to his⟩ house to play with his dog, Brittany. Dorci and I ⟨would⟩ introduce ourselves to the couple who lived at ⟨that⟩ time to today, Bill has been one of my closest ⟨we are⟩ very different and 1450 miles apart.

⟨laugh.⟩ People might be familiar with the phenomena ⟨where⟩ laughter or giggling makes others laugh. But ⟨from an⟩ adult. But Bill's laugh is so spontaneous and ⟨it⟩ has uplifted me many a time. It is loud and ⟨joy⟩ and appreciation.

⟨first⟩ time I was exposed to this laugh. We were ⟨his first wife) home to dinner. I was talking ⟨boring⟩ him about football, when Briana ⟨came⟩ and excited to show me something. In the ⟨without⟩ losing a beat, I said, "Oh, that's nice, Bri" ⟨returned with⟩ my conversation to Bill. He burst out laughing. The "blip" and nonchalance of my quip to Briana had cracked him up. He had to explain to me what he found so humorous then continued laughing, pulling me into his jovial spirit.

Strange how friendships develop. I think one of the things I like best about Bill is his sense of humor and appreciation for the lighter side of life. Which is not to say he hasn't been through some trying times: loss of his job, divorce, leukemia. He and I have consoled and advised each other many a time. I'm sure our personal difficulties helped cement our connection. I still don't know how our bond formed, for we are very different from each other.

I love sports and follow them avidly, filling many hours of my day reading about teams, watching sporting events on TV, or participating— these days playing golf. Bill, on the other hand, finds football and golf, especially golf, very boring. He, instead, spends hours at his computer, something I can't do because of neck pain.

Because of his savvy with computers and technology, I asked him to edit some film for me. After a long search, I was able to get copies of some of my college football games on VHS tapes. He agreed to try to condense them. I went to his house and pointed out the scenes I wanted to keep, the plays I ran. It took many hours. In fact, we didn't finish in one session. As Bill describes it, "It ended up turning into a marathon, play-by-play, color commentary of an entire season of college football!"

I can't imagine how boring this was for him, watching these poor quality, old black and white movies taken from a stationary single camera—no commentary, no close-ups—just college athletes who look about 2 inches tall scurrying around the turf. We could hardly distinguish player numbers. Add to that the fact that I repeatedly said, "Oh, there I am... I think. Yeah... no...wait a minute... Let's watch that again." Bill probably saw most of each game a couple times. How "lucky" could he be!

Bill was so bored, in typical sarcastic fashion he later told me, "It made me yearn for a discussion about golf." The end result was rather chopped up with random 'John plays.' Bill told me, "I can't believe someone took the time to convert those movies from 35mm film to VHS."

Many more differences than similarities between us exist. He would stare in disbelief when I recounted various cross-country car trips Dorci and I or the family took. Bill, a former flight attendant, chooses to fly often. I have an aversion to flying (not fear) and have traveled by plane fewer than a dozen times in my entire life. Bill is a "techie" and is fascinated with and will buy the latest gadgets and bells and whistles. Me, I feared microwave ovens which appeared for retail sales around 1967 and outsold gas ranges by 1975. I didn't purchase one until 1981. My frugality, in addition to my non-technical nature, lies in direct contrast with him.

Bill sunbathes, drinks Diet Cokes all day long, and never works out. Although I have a tan (a very distinctive line where my sports socks stop, below which my feet look like dead fish), it's from playing the links three times a week. I dislike carbonated drinks and probably consume no more than a dozen in a year's time. I am ever aware of keeping fit and staying limber with stretching exercises and miles on the treadmill when I'm not on the golf course. When it comes to money, I think I've made my position clear in some of my foolishly frugal stories.

Bill helped me immensely late in my teaching career. We talked incessantly on the phone, something uncharacteristic for two men. Supposedly, women do all the gossiping; but Bill and I have proved that to be an old wives' tale. For years we were bosom buddies. He listened well, suffering through my complaints about the state of public education. Conversely, I was ears for him during the bad times he endured.

Recently, as we were reminiscing about some of our fun times, Bill said he enjoys telling people about my antics. "John is the only person I know that in the late 20th century purchased his *first* car with POWER windows and AIR CONDITIONING! Around that time was when John also introduced me to the term *niggardly*. Of course, at first I thought it was a racial slur. Then I discovered it meant *miserly* and was the perfect word to describe him. I use it exclusively when I tell stories about John."

We built our last house in Wentzville on a golf course. Bill and his wife Karen (his second wife) decided to build on the same course. We lived two blocks apart for about a year. I didn't care to play that course and may have walked it only a couple times. Ironically, Bill and Karen walked it almost daily, before and after tee times, with their two dogs. Also ironic, the proximity of our homes at our first meeting and upon our leaving for Arizona.

* * *

Golf currently represents the epitome of my fascination with balls. Its many layers intrigue me. I love the power game off the tee—that perfect "ping" that comes from the ball struck hard and straight with a driver. Chipping requires a different approach. The finesse of irons or hybrid clubs to accurately place the ball with a good stroke takes many hours to perfect. Putting is a game in and of itself. Numerous books are devoted solely to the skills required on the green.

One of the best golfing gifts I received was from my son one Father's Day, a set of three books by Bob Rotella. I devoured them. They have become my golfing bible. I believe they have brought about as much improvement in my game as has all my practicing. In fact, I thought they were so effective that I felt reluctant to share the books with my competitors, thinking they, too, would totally improve—and win my money. However, other players to whom I've lent these books have not taken to heart what Rotella says.

In <u>Golf is Not a Game of Perfect</u> he says, "The correlation between thinking well and making successful shots is not 100%. But the correlation between thinking badly and unsuccessful shots is much higher." He has influenced me to visualize my putt and just go for it. "Good golfers gain control over the ball by feeling that they are giving up control." Previous to reading these books, my mind was destroying my game. So, I'd like to conclude this chapter with a big "Thank you" to Bob Rotella.

CHAPTER 15

MY LOVE OF THE PHYSICAL

The writing of this book has taken many years, mostly because Dorci has devoted "spare time" to its typing and editing. These days, I frequently tell people that every hour of her day is consumed by some activity—no sitting around for her unless she's at the computer working on my memoir. Thus, for a long time my writing has taken second place to her comings and goings.

I started this endeavor, as I previously noted, to leave some record of my life and my love of sports to my children and grandchildren so that they might come to better understand their father and grandfather. But as I wrote, I began to expand my purpose, thinking and hoping that I might publish my story, that it had value for many other readers. If nothing else, I have entertained Dorci, as frequently happens, with my expectations for this manuscript. One day I said, "You know, my book has as much value as some of the other biographies and memoirs I've read. It's as good as any Pulitzer Prize winner." A few days later I told her, "Aw, I don't think anyone will want to read this. It's not very good." And so, my prospects are as varied as the pains in my body and the scores on my golf card and run the gamut from success to failure.

When Dorci told me I needed to write a conclusion, I balked at first. Just as I had balked when she mentioned some two dozen other ideas I'd

216

neglected to include in this book—like our children and her. But, knowing her inherent wisdom possesses validity, I acquiesced to her suggestion. Everything written in this book portrays the truth as closely as humanly possible. How do I know this? I've been told all of my life that I am honest, sometimes bluntly so. I recently watched a TV program that proposed the idea that someday humans can have their memories changed. Scary! I hope I'll be long gone by then.

My seventy-fourth birthday has just passed and my thoughts go negative. By this age I should have learned something valuable to pass on. Instead of thinking positively however, I think more can be learned from the negative. I guess in some ways that makes this story consistent. I am reminded of Ben Franklin who seemed to include the negative in his suggestions for a virtuous life. For example, "Eat not to dullness; drink not to elevation" refers to a man's tendency to overindulge and the need to conquer primal urges.

In my senior years I seem constantly confronted by what turns me off in life. There is everything right about the rule for Christian living: "Love thy neighbor." But, I wish the Lord had included "Accept accountability for your behavior," particularly with regards to bad behavior. I can't tell you how many times in my life I have witnessed people failing to accept responsibility for destructive behavior. Some people live in denial. Do they purposely wipe memories from their minds instead of facing up to the truth? Do they make believe it is not so? Denial, denial, denial. Why is it so hard to say, "I screwed up"? This is certainly a theme in my life. Hopefully I acknowledge my flaws and admit my weaknesses.

I am reminded by my wife of at least one time I didn't. We were visiting Briana who had recently moved to New York City, Brooklyn to be exact. I stayed in the apartment while Dorci and Bri went shopping. When they returned, Bri discovered she had forgotten her key. "No problem," they thought, even though rain had begun falling. I was inside and would let them in.

They rang the bell. Inside, I heard a sound but "doorbell" didn't register. They, too, heard the bell sound coming from inside the apartment. They knocked then pounded. I was oblivious to the idea that someone was at the front door. Their ringing and knocking went on for a good fifteen minutes before I decided to investigate the noise. Now, fifteen minutes doesn't seem that long—that is, unless you are standing in the rain! When

I finally opened the front door, still unaware that they were on the other side, they were both quite wet. Then I exacerbated the situation when I didn't apologize. All I could do was plead innocence, unfamiliarity with the doorbell sound and a lack of audio acuity. Dorci became angry. How could I be so oblivious? Why didn't I say I was sorry, that I screwed up? It wasn't the first nor would it be the last time that I demonstrated such unawareness. Or, should I call it "denial"?

Even though I think more can be learned from the negative, I was well aware of the power I wielded over my students and was mindful of avoiding destructive behavior. During my 25 years of teaching when twenty to thirty students sat in my classes every day, no doubt some did not like me—the arrogant ones. Their attitude or writing told me so. I didn't so much worry about them. My hope was that the shy, lonely students found some confidence and solace from me and the materials we studied.

I, myself, obtained inspiration from reading American classics, like the essays of Emerson and Thoreau from whom I am still able to quote verbatim, so powerful are they. Sayings like the following became cautions or mantras for my life:

"The mass of men live lives of quiet desperation." (From "Walden" by Thoreau)

"There is a time in every man's education when he arrives at the conviction that envy is ignorance; that imitation is suicide; that he must take himself for better, for worse, as his portion; that though the wide universe is full of good, no kernel of nourishing corn can come to him but through his toil bestowed on that plot of ground which is given to him to till." (From "Self-Reliance" by Emerson)

I hoped not to live in quiet desperation; instead, to find fulfillment in and through my love of balls. I accept my limitations, once I realize what they are. New acquaintances have frequently been put off by my frank self-assessment ("I yam what I yam") and my lack of self-importance. Whereas, according to Dorci, those traits ingratiate me to others. I was inspired to make something valuable of my portion through my own toil.

The physical component of constructing homes attracted me even though I had never built anything in my life. Here was activity without the competition found in sports. Dorci and I hammered 16 penny nails into two by fours to raise walls. We both derived pleasure from this aspect of the challenge and also the creating, planning and decision making that occurred throughout all phases of construction. The first home was built in 1974-75 while I traveled on the rode selling dresses. I certainly needed a physical challenge and outlet then, since driving 50,000 miles a year in Missouri and Iowa ran counter to my nature of needing activity.

Emotion and passion have proved to be two-edged swords throughout my life. Throwing myself into competitions, both as a participant and a spectator, exemplifies this double blade. Yes, giving my all and the desire for victory produced gratifying rewards and, in some cases, once-in-a-lifetime memories. Dorci says that freely demonstrating my emotions endears me to others. But, expending all my energy and adopting a must-win attitude also set me up for disappointment, disappointment which could be manifested by my cursing the TV or suffering physical ailments.

Because I have placed so much importance on being active, adjusting to a body that daily grows older has been difficult for me. I truly miss the agility and strength of my youth. Well into my "golden years," I continued to fantasize in my nocturnal musings of carrying a football and running into on-coming opponents. Occasionally, I kicked a fantasy ball which, in reality, turned out to be Dorci's back. The night I fancied I was punting the ball and jammed my foot into the wall, I was lucky not to have broken a toe. Or, even more dangerous, in one dream I threw myself into the end zone, landing on the nightstand at two in the morning. The back of my head hit the wood before I ended up on the floor. I feared the worst. After days of dealing with the trauma, applications of ice and heat, I began to feel the pain in my neck subside to its normal state of constant, burning ache. Maybe because of the distress from that dream, it was the last of my nighttime reveries about playing football.

Although my dwindling physical strength and chronic pain have sometimes depressed me, I have found comfort in my golf game. Golf—the friend to seniors. Without the virility of youth, I am able to play better golf than I did twenty, thirty or forty years ago. My current goal is to eventually shoot my age. Since I've already scored a 75, I just have to maintain my game for one more year, no small feat for this crumbling body.

With that goal in mind, and remembering whatever successes I was able to attain, some of which were preceded by years of hopes and dreams,

I conclude that all of those feats pale in comparison to my life's most important triumph, being a husband and father. Here is another of life's ironies, that as much as balls and physical activity fascinated me, consumed my dreams and powered my motivation, something presumably so normal and ordinary as marriage and parenthood surpassed all my expectations for happiness and self-realization. My marrying Dorci and fathering three children fulfilled me in ways I never knew. The inherent love, intimacy and pride that evolved and grew from having a wife and children supersede any other accomplishments I realized. Even though I had expected to be married and have a family, I had no concept of the gratification and joy that awaited me. My fascination with balls, my love of physical activity and challenges never fulfilled me as totally as my relationship with Dorci and my roles as father and grandfather.

APPENDIX 1

CAPE GIRARDEAU SOUTHEAST MISSOURIAN
TUESDAY EVENING, OCTOBER 3, 1961.

John Leara, Rodney Miller Top SEMO Back, Lineman

John Leara and Rodney Miller were the two outstanding players for State College when the Indians downed St. Benedict's College in Atchison, Kan., Saturday, 14-0.

Leara, a halfback, gained top back of the game honors for the second time in the young season. Although he f a i l e d to score against the Ravens, Leara was way out in front among Indian ground gainers and almost personally set up the second touchdown with several key yardage pickups.

The hard - driving halfback gained 121 yards in 18 carries for an average of 6.7 yards. He has been the best ground-gaining back for State College in all three games played so far.

Leara is a 179-pound senior from St. Louis, playing his prep ball at Roosevelt High School.

Rodney M i l l e r, 188 - pound guard, was in on many tackles, several of the bone-rattling variety, and his blocking commendable. He also saved the Indians from being scored open as he gathered in a Raven pass in the last quarter to halt a serious threat by St. Benedict's.

Miller is from Jackson and a senior.

Leara.   Miller.

Collins Stopped.

The Indians had threatened in the first quarter but Collins was stopped on the one-foot line when he attempted to sneak over on fourth down. St. Benedict's, taking to the air, threatened seriously twice. Right before the half the Ravens moved to the SEMO-8 before time ran out and in the last quarter marched to the 20 but Rodney Miller intercepted a pass to halt the threat.

Glenn Hornug, sophomore quarterback, was the chief offensive show for the Ravens. He completed 9 of 17 passes to account for all of the losers' 149 yards gained the aerial way. His chief target was end Dave Herne who caught four good for 54 yards.

Kurre was the Indians top pass receiver. He caught four, picking up a total of 64 yards.

St. Benedict's h i g h l y touted backs were almost stopped cold by the fired-up State College line. Ron Lewis, speedy halfback picked up only 28 yards in nine carries for a little better than a three yard average. Rugged fullback John McGlinn g a i n e d a

THE ARIZONA DAILY STAR

Coach's Hysterics Cause Baboquivari To Forfeit

SELLS — Benson High School was awarded a forfeit victory over Baboquivari Friday night in a B-East football game which is believed to be the first forfeiture during a game in Arizona high school history.

Benson was leading 15-0 in the fourth quarter when referee William Rauh Jr. of Tucson awarded the Bobcats the game.

Rauh called the forfeiture after calling a penalty against a Warrior for hitting a Benson player and Warrior coach John Leara went on the field in protest, kicked an official's hat twice, cursed at the officials and then picked up the hat and threw it at Rauh. Leara was unavailable for comment.

"This is the first time I've ever had this happen in the 15 years I've been working as an official," said Rauh.

The game score is officially listed as a 15-0 victory for Benson.

In the third quarter, an offensive holding penalty was called against Baboquivari and assistant Baboquivari coach Gary Tom went out on the field in protest.

Tom was expelled from the game and 45 yards in penalties was stepped off against the Warriors — 15 for holding, 15 for unsportsmanlike conduct because Tom shoved Rauh, and 15 yards for a coach going onto the field.

Rauh requested a police escort after the forfeiture and was provided one for 10 miles.

Benson took a 6-0 lead in the second quarter as Ronald Ellsworth dashed 21 yards for the end zone. Fred Trujillo followed with a 12 yard jaunt and Dan Baerra's extra point kick gave Benson a 13-0 halftime lead.

A safety in the third quarter put the Bobcats ahead 15-0.

APPENDIX 3

Baboquivari Win Opens Grid Race

By BILL BETTERTON
Star Staff Writer

The B-East High School football conference race opened Friday with a surprise.

Baboquivari, the conference doormat in the past, won its first conference game ever by clipping Thatcher 14-6 in Sells.

The Warriors are 3-0 overall, which means Baboquivari will have its best season ever this year. "We've won every game so far by the skin of our teeth," said Baboquivari Coach John Leara.

"The defense was superb," he added. "We hoped to score four touchdowns. One TD was called back, so I guess you could say we scored three."

Paul Hendricks was credited with 17 tackles and gained 28 yards on four carries. Tim Si-quieros was the leading ground gainer with 51 yards on 11 carries.

In another B-East contest, Sahuarita got back on the winning track by destroying Tombstone 66-0. Javier Blanco, passed for two touchdowns and ran for two others.

Despite 123 yards of penalties, Benson opened its B-East season with a 21-0 win over Duncan. Ron Kirby scored on a six-yard run and then returned a pass interception 50 yards for the final score in the fourth quarter.

Hayden won its 14th straight game by dropping Payson 32-0 in a B-Central opener. Nick Blancarte led the defending state champions by scoring two touchdowns and throwing a TD pass to Ernest Busta-monte

APPENDIX 4

THE ARIZONA DAILY STAR

TUCSON, THURSDAY, OCTOBER 11, 1973

Warriors Find Key To Success

By BILL BETTERTON
Star Staff Writer

Someone looking through the high school football standings would be surprised to see Baboquivari among the leaders in the Class B-East.

The warriors have never been there before nor won more than one game in a season until this year. After four games this year, the Warriors are undefeated.

Two of the victories were in conference play. They had never won a conference game before.

"Everyone's in shape, plus we have some juniors and seniors starting on the team," explained coach John Leara. "We have had good fortune, some good kids and good conditioning.

"When we run wind sprints at the end of practice, all 24 boys are running hard," said Leara. "My assistant coach Pat Franks has really got them in shape."

The Warriors dropped Duncan 20-6 last Friday for their second B-East win and largest margin of victory. The 20 points was also the most points Baboquivari has scored for one game in two years.

"It was the first game we've won this year that we knew we were going to win before the game was over. The other three have gone to the wire," said Leara.

With an offensive line that averages slightly over 155 pounds, the Warriors are in no position to overpower teams. And with the fastest runner clocking an 11.5 100-yard dash, Baboquivari can't run around too many teams.

Baboquivari nipped Gila Bend, 7-6, in the opening game, clipped St. John's, 6-0, and then knocked off Thatcher, 14-6, for its first conference win ever.

Earl Francisco (5-11, 190) is the biggest player on the line. "He has done nothing but work. He's developed into a great young man," said Leara.

Guards Morris Antone (5-4, 140) and Phil Lewis (5-4, 140) couldn't win any heavyweight fights, but are getting the job done along with tackles Angelo Listo (5-9, 188) and Dave Miguel (5-7, 155).

Flanker Mickey Widener (5-6, 140) has been the one of the primary targets of quarterback Neal Miquel (5-4, 130), who took over from the injured Ken Antone, but against Duncan, Gary Twotwo (5-11, 144) caught the first touchdown pass. Gary's brother Gilbert (5-10, 130) plays the other end.

The Warriors gained 214 yards rushing against Duncan with tailback Paul Hendricks (5-10, 155) leading the all-Indian squad with 78 yards Tim Siquieros (5-9, 145) who also plays tailback, injured his hip in the first half and didn't play the rest of the game. Fullback Alan Antone (6-1, 165) added 53 yards on seven carries.

But while the offense has struggled to score, the defense has kept the Warriors in all four games.

Alan Antone, Listo and Francisco play on the defensive line with Richard Antone (5-6, 160) at nose guard and Mark Puella (5-7, 145) at defensive end.

Hendricks and Siquieros are also starting linebackers, but Mike Miguel (5-8, 170) and Oliver Antone (5-4, 140) have seen duty there.

Widener and Gilbert Twotwo play in the defensive secondary, along with Ron Escalante (5-10, 150).

D-8 The Arizona Republic   Phoenix, Sunday, Oct. 14, 1973

Baboquivari stays unbeaten with 21-8 win over Clifton

Baboquivari, a team that just three weeks ago won its first conference game ever, stretched its league mark to 3-0 and its season record to 5-0 by pounding Clifton, 21-8, Friday.

Baboquivari scored in each of the first two periods, then matched a fourth quarter Clifton tally to notch the win.

The Warriors get their sternest test to date next week when they play co-leader Benson.

Benson, the state's fourth ranked team, topped No. 5 Florence, 7-6, with a fourth period touchdown and Rick Kirby's extra point. Florence faces a B Central showdown next week with Hayden, a 50-6 winner over Camp Verde Friday. Thirty-six first half points turned the Hayden game into a rout early.

Johnny Meyers scored three touchdowns to power the third B East co-leader Sahuarita past Duncan, 50-0, and John Heckathorne ran for one score and passed for three to lead second-ranked Blue Ridge in a 57-0 decision over Valley.

Defense played a big part in many of the other Class B games also. Antelope blanked Bagdad, 20-0, as Rick Correa scored twice.

William Bennett passed for two touchdowns and ran back an interception for another as William buried St. Johns, 45-6, and Ron Lee scored four times as Phoenix Christian erupted from a scoreless first period and clobbered. Billy Shepherd scored twice and Mohave crushed Gila Bend, 41-0.

Tom Nosie returned an interception for a score and Lu-

pino Lupe ran for another score as Alchesay held on for a 13-6 defeat of Payson.

CLASS A — Two undefeated teams bit the dust in key league clashes Friday night.

Morenci scored twice in the first half on short runs by Tony Lazzaraga and held off Willcox, 15-6, in an A South showdown.

Marana spotted defending South and state champion Miami a 10 point halftime lead, then came on to record a 15-10 triumph. Jose Knagge hit Rick Heismer with a pair of second half touchdown passes for the Marana scores.

Superior opened its A South season by blanking Ray, 20-0.

Gilbert ran its record to and opened the A Centr season with a 21-7 win ov previously unbeaten Gerar The Gilbert defense, whi surrendered its first score the game, provided the wi ner on Juan Marmalejo fumble recovery run in t fourth period.

Ken Maddox scored nii points for Eloy in a 15-0 blan ing of Buckeye. The win se up the showdown betwee Gilbert and Eloy next week.

Two A West powers, Lal Havasu and Bourgad romped to easy wins whi darkhorse candidate Dysa squeaked out a close 20-1 win over Mingus.

Kevin Campbell and Ro

APPENDIX 6

D-4 The Arizona Republic
Phoenix, Wed., Oct. 17, 1973

TIME OUT!

Patsy Baboquivari pushover no more

By DAVE CASSADY

If there was one Class B team in the state that was regarded as a patsy in the past fews years, it had to be Baboquivari.

The tiny Indian school at Sells had won just twice in the last four years. And those were victories over an independent Southwest Indian team in 1971 and a Ft. Grant team that later dropped inter-scholastic competition last year.

But nobody had better take the Warriors lightly this year. After opening with a 7-6 squeaker over Gila Bend, they topped St. John's Indian, 12-7, then recorded their first league win in the school's eight year history, beating Thatcher, 14-6.

The following week, it was a 21-6 win over Duncan and last week, the Sells team grabbed its fifth straight win of the season and a share of the B East lead by beating Clifton, 21-8.

This week, the Warriors face the state's fourth-ranked B team Benson, which is 2-0 in the league and half a game behind Baboquivari and Sahuarita.

Coach John Leara, in his second year, has been one of the reasons for the big turnaround, but he gives much of the credit to first-year assistant Pat Frink and the players themselves.

"The kids have worked for this," says Leara. "Last season, even when we yere losing, the kids didn't get down. They seemed to know that they'd have their chance this year.

"This is basically a junior-senior ballclub and we start 18 players. That plus great conditioning is one of the big reasons we're winning."

Leara gives Frink credit for the conditioning. "Pat is a former professional basket-

ball player (Cincinnati Royals) and he works with the kids in their conditioning. He gets out there and runs the sprints with them."

While Baboquivari hasn't really overpowered anybody, the defense has yet to allow more than once score in a game, and in the last two games, the offense has produced three touchdowns per game.

Paul Hendricks, a player who was ineligible last year, is one of the main reasons for the Warriors' success. The 160-pound senior is the No. 1 a ballcarrier and top defensive player at middle linebacker.

Leara is proud of his passing attack featuring 128 - pound quarterback Neal Miguel (nine for 17 vs. Clifton) and the receivers, Gilbert and Gary Twotwo, a brother combination at end, and flanker Mike Widener. Gilbert Twotwo with five and Widener (4) are also the heart of the pass defense that has picked up of 14 interceptions in five games.

Leara doesn't know how his team will fare against Benson. He doesn't scout opponents. ("It's demeaning to the assistants to work all week with a team, then have to spend game nights someplace else. Most of them really hate it.")

But he's not worried. He's already won more games this year than in the school's entire history and he's assured the team of its a first non-losing season ever. That and the fact that more than half of the school's 100 boys are out for football bodes well for future Baboquivari teams.

The Arizona Daily Star

TUCSON, SATURDAY, OCTOBER 20, 1973

Benson Takes Showdown

BENSON — Rod Dressler scored the game's only touchdown on a 2-yard run with 9:20 remaining Friday night as the Benson Bobcats won a B-East showdown with the Baboquivari Warriors, 7-0.

The touchdown was set up by a Warrior fumble at their own 20 recovered by Benson. Three plays later Dressler carried it in and Ron Kirby added the extra point.

The victory gives Benson a 3-0 conference record and a 5-1 mark overall. The loss was Baboquivari's first after five victories and dropped the Warriors to a 3-1 conference record.

Baboquivari threatened on several occasions, getting to the one-yard line four times, the last time coming in the closing seconds of the game when they reached the half-yard line as time ran out.

Benson frittered away a number of scoring opportunities also, losing twice on fumbles and once on an interception deep in Baboquivari territory.

Baboquivari	0	0	0	0	— 0
Benson	0	0	0	7	— 7

APPENDIX 8

The Arizona Republic, Phoenix

Eight coaches cited

The Arizona Republic, Phoenix

Republic names nominees for prep grid award

By DAVE CASSADY

Eight of the state's prep football coaches have been nominated for the Republic's prep football coach of the year award.

The winner will be announced at the all-state banquet Dec. 10.

Three AAA coaches, one each from the AA and A ranks and three from Class B teams make up the list of nominees.

The listing of nominees is a change in format from past years. The selection committee felt that more coaches should receive recognition for their fine efforts during the season than the one named coach of the year and it was decided to announce those coaches considered by the committee.

From the AAA ranks are a pair of veterans and a relative newcomer, Van Howe of Palo Verde, Jess Parker of Camelback and Ron Cosner of Marcos de Niza.

Howe coached Palo Verde to its first playoff spot in the schools 11-year history and the Titans are c u r r e n t l y the state's lone remaining unbeaten AAA team. A win in this week's state title game would make them the winningest team in Tucson history (13-0). PV was 2-8 last year.

Parker has directed Camel-back to an 11-1 season and the other state final berth. His teams have beaten the top two ranked AAA teams, Central and Marcos de Niza, in the playoffs so far. Both teams were unbeaten prior to the playoffs.

Cosner took the second-year Padres to an 11-1 season after a 2-8 finish last year. It is the first year that MDN has had a graduating class and only the second year of varsity competition for the Padres.

Bill Epperson of Coconino directed a team with just eight seniors to the state AA championship and an 8-2-1 record. His only losses were to Flagstaff in the season opener and Winslow on a last-second scoring play in the league opener.

Dan Dunn of Gilbert directed the only undefeated team in the state besides Palo Verde. Another coach who opened the season with a junior ball club, his club was smaller than most of the teams it faced, but recorded an amazing seven shutouts while going 11-0.

Fred Skoglund was forced to rebuild his team after graduating most of his line from last year's B West runnerups. He did the job as his Thunderbirds lost only to A power Lake Havasu and Needles, Calif., in winning the state B title. The semifinal win was over unbeaten and No. 1-ranked Blue Ridge.

Blue Ridge's Joe Girardi is the second Class B coach nominated. He took a school that had won six games in eight years and directed them to an 11-1 season in 1972. Graduation decimated h i s team, but he responded with another unbeaten regular season before losing in the state semifinals.

John Leara almost worked a miracle at Baboquivari, long the laughing stock of the state football ranks. Leara took a team that won just once last year and directed it to an 8-2 season.

The team had never won a league game before this year, but under second-year coach Leara, it almost won the league title, losing only in a showdown to champion Benson, 7-0, and runnerup Sahuarita.

APPENDIX 9

Just on a lark, I thought it would be fun to try to list all the sports, physical activities and challenges or games in which I have participated. "Participated" means I didn't just attempt it once but actually tried to master it, or at least performed it several times. The list is in no particular time order. I was curious as to what I could remember—I'm not sure that it is complete.

archery
badminton
ball and jacks
baseball
basketball
billiards
bocce ball
body surfing
bottle caps
bridge jumping (50')
calisthenics
camping
canoeing
card tossing
catch
chipping
cork ball
corn hole
croquet
darts
diving
Evil Knievel jumping
fishing
float trips
football college
football high school
gymnastics
handball

handstands
high jump
hiking
horseback riding
horseshoe golf
house building
hula hoop
hunting
hurdles
ice skating
Indian ball
jet skis
juggling
marbles
marching
motor cycle jumping
motor cycle riding
pinball
ping pong
pole vault
punting
putting
racquet ball
rock climbing
rock jumping (40')
roller skating
rope swinging
rowing

running
sailing
scuba diving
sharp shooting
shuffleboard
skipping rocks
sledding
snorkeling
snow skiing
soccer
softball
squash
step ball
surf boarding
swimming
target practice
tennis
touch football
train hopping
trampoline
tree climbing (40')
tumbling
volleyball
walking for miles
water skiing
weight lifting
yo-yo

14198194R00152

Made in the USA
San Bernardino, CA
20 August 2014